The Principles of
Deleuzian Philosophy

Plateaus – New Directions in Deleuze Studies

'It's not a matter of bringing all sorts of things together under a single concept but rather of relating each concept to variables that explain its mutations.'
Gilles Deleuze, *Negotiations*

Series Editors

Ian Buchanan, University of Wollongong
Claire Colebrook, Penn State University

Editorial Advisory Board

Keith Ansell Pearson, Ronald Bogue, Constantin V. Boundas, Rosi Braidotti, Eugene Holland, Gregg Lambert, Dorothea Olkowski, Paul Patton, Daniel Smith, James Williams

Titles available in the series

Christian Kerslake, *Immanence and the Vertigo of Philosophy: From Kant to Deleuze*
Jean-Clet Martin, *Variations: The Philosophy of Gilles Deleuze*, translated by Constantin V. Boundas and Susan Dyrkton
Simone Bignall, *Postcolonial Agency: Critique and Constructivism*
Miguel de Beistegui, *Immanence – Deleuze and Philosophy*
Jean-Jacques Lecercle, *Badiou and Deleuze Read Literature*
Ronald Bogue, *Deleuzian Fabulation and the Scars of History*
Sean Bowden, *The Priority of Events: Deleuze's Logic of Sense*
Craig Lundy, *History and Becoming: Deleuze's Philosophy of Creativity*
Aidan Tynan, *Deleuze's Literary Clinic: Criticism and the Politics of Symptoms*
Thomas Nail, *Returning to Revolution: Deleuze, Guattari and Zapatismo*
François Zourabichvili, *Deleuze: A Philosophy of the Event* with *The Vocabulary of Deleuze* edited by Gregg Lambert and Daniel W. Smith, translated by Kieran Aarons
Frida Beckman, *Between Desire and Pleasure: A Deleuzian Theory of Sexuality*
Nadine Boljkovac, *Untimely Affects: Gilles Deleuze and an Ethics of Cinema*
Daniela Voss, *Conditions of Thought: Deleuze and Transcendental Ideas*
Daniel Barber, *Deleuze and the Naming of God: Post-Secularism and the Future of Immanence*
F. LeRon Shults, *Iconoclastic Theology: Gilles Deleuze and the Secretion of Atheism*
Janae Sholtz, *The Invention of a People: Heidegger and Deleuze on Art and the Political*
Marco Altamirano, *Time, Technology and Environment: An Essay on the Philosophy of Nature*
Sean McQueen, *Deleuze and Baudrillard: From Cyberpunk to Biopunk*
Ridvan Askin, *Narrative and Becoming*
Marc Rölli, *Gilles Deleuze's Transcendental Empiricism: From Tradition to Difference*, translated by Peter Hertz-Ohmes
Guillaume Collett, *The Psychoanalysis of Sense: Deleuze and the Lacanian School*
Ryan J. Johnson, *The Deleuze-Lucretius Encounter*
Allan James Thomas, *Deleuze, Cinema and the Thought of the World*
Cheri Lynne Carr, *Deleuze's Kantian Ethos: Critique as a Way of Life*
Alex Tissandier, *Affirming Divergence: Deleuze's Reading of Leibniz*
Barbara Glowczewski, *Indigenising Anthropology with Guattari and Deleuze*
Koichiro Kokubun, *The Principles of Deleuzian Philosophy*, translated by Wren Nishina
Felice Cimatti, *Unbecoming Human: Philosophy of Animality After Deleuze*, translated by Fabio Gironi
Ryan J. Johnson, *Deleuze, A Stoic*

Forthcoming volumes

Justin Litaker, *Deleuze and Guattari's Political Economy*
Nir Kedem, *A Deleuzian Critique of Queer Thought: Overcoming Sexuality*
Jane Newland, *Deleuze in Children's Literature*
Sean Bowden, *Expression, Action and Agency in Deleuze: Willing Events*
Andrew Jampol-Petzinger, *Deleuze, Kierkegaard and the Ethics of Selfhood*

Visit the Plateaus website at edinburghuniversitypress.com/series/plat

THE PRINCIPLES OF DELEUZIAN PHILOSOPHY

Koichiro Kokubun

Translated by Wren Nishina

EDINBURGH
University Press

Edinburgh University Press is one of the leading university presses in the UK. We publish academic books and journals in our selected subject areas across the humanities and social sciences, combining cutting-edge scholarship with high editorial and production values to produce academic works of lasting importance. For more information visit our website: edinburghuniversitypress.com

DURUZU NO TETSUGAKU GENRI
By Koichiro Kokubun
© 2013 by Koichiro Kokubun
Originally published in 2013 by Iwanami Shoten, Publishers, Tokyo
This English edition published 2020
By Edinburgh University Press, Edinburgh
By arrangement with Iwanami Shoten, Publishers, Tokyo

English Translation © Wren Nishina, 2020, 2021

Edinburgh University Press Ltd
The Tun – Holyrood Road
12(2f) Jackson's Entry
Edinburgh EH8 8PJ

First published in hardback by Edinburgh University Press 2020

Typeset in 11/13 Sabon LT Std by
Servis Filmsetting Ltd, Stockport, Cheshire

A CIP record for this book is available from the British Library

ISBN 978 1 4744 4898 7 (hardback)
ISBN 978 1 4744 4899 4 (paperback)
ISBN 978 1 4744 4900 7 (webready PDF)
ISBN 978 1 4744 4901 4 (epub)

The right of Koichiro Kokubun to be identified as the author of this work has been asserted in accordance with the Copyright, Designs and Patents Act 1988, and the Copyright and Related Rights Regulations 2003 (SI No. 2498).

Contents

Acknowledgements for the English Edition vi
List of Abbreviations vii
Translator's Preface x

Prologue 1

1 Method: How to See Things in Free Indirect Discourse 9
  Research Note I: On Naturalism 26

2 Principle: Transcendental Empiricism 28
  Research Note II: The Synthetic Method 68

3 Practice: Thinking and Subjectivity 70
  Research Note III: Law/Institution/Contract 98

4 Transition: From Structure to the Machine 100
  Research Note IV: The Individual Soul and the Collective Soul 141

5 Politics: Desire and Power 143
  Research Note V: The State and Archaeology 187

Afterword 189

Bibliography 194
Index 199

Acknowledgements for the English Edition

Those individuals who made the original Japanese publication of this book possible I have already named in the 'Afterword' to this volume. Here I should like to add to that list the names of those whose assistance was indispensable in the preparation of this English edition, the first of its kind for my work. In no particular order: Ian Buchanan and Claire Colebrook, whose tireless work with the Deleuze Studies series at EUP has given me the platform from which to release this work; Carol Macdonald and Kirsty Woods, who have had to put up with missed deadlines, unanswered emails, the whole lot; Joff Bradley, who offered invaluable suggestions for improving the manuscript; Tim Clark, for his meticulous work with the final typescript; and lastly my translator Wren Nishina. And of course you the reader, who alone can fulfil the solitary voyage that is the life of the book.

K. K.

List of Abbreviations

Gilles Deleuze

B: *Bergsonism*, trans. Hugh Tomlinson and Barbara Habberjam, New York: Zone Books, 1991; *Le bergsonisme*, Paris: PUF, 1966.

CC: *Essays Critical and Clinical*, trans. Daniel W. Smith and Michael A. Greco, Minneapolis: University of Minnesota Press, 1997; *Critique et clinique*, Paris: Minuit, 1993.

D: *Dialogues II* (with Claire Parnet), trans. Hugh Tomlinson and Barbara Habberjam, London: Continuum, 2002; *Dialogues*, Paris: Flammarion, 1977; new edition, 1996.

DI: *Desert Islands and Other Texts 1953–1974*, ed. David Lapoujade, trans. Michael Taormina, New York: Semiotext(e), 2004; *L'île déserte et autres textes: textes et entretiens 1953–1974*, Paris: Minuit, 2002.

DR: *Difference and Repetition*, trans. Paul Patton, London: Continuum, 2004; *Différence et répétition*, Paris: PUF, 1968.

ES: *Empiricism and Subjectivity: An Essay on Hume's Theory of Human Nature*, trans. Constantin V. Boundas, New York: Columbia University Press, 1991; *Empirisme et subjectivité: essai sur la nature selon Hume*, Paris: PUF, 1953.

F: *Foucault*, trans. Seán Hand, London: Continuum, 2006; *Foucault*, Paris: Minuit, 1986.

FLB: *The Fold: Leibniz and the Baroque*, trans. Tom Conley, London: Bloomsbury, 2013; *Le pli: Leibniz et le baroque*, Paris: Minuit, 1988.

KCP: *Kant's Critical Philosophy: The Doctrine of the Faculties*, trans. Hugh Tomlinson and Barbara Habberjam, Minneapolis: University of Minnesota Press, 1990; *Philosophie critique de Kant*, Paris: PUF, 1963.

LS: *The Logic of Sense*, trans. Mark Lester with Charles Stivale, ed. Constantin V. Boundas, London: Continuum, 2004; *Logique du sens*, Paris: Minuit, 1969.

LIST OF ABBREVIATIONS

MCC: *Masochism: An Interpretation of Coldness and Cruelty*, trans. Jean McNeil, New York: George Brazillier, 1971; *Présentation de Sacher-Masoch: le froid et le cruel*, Paris: Minuit, 1967.

MI: *Cinema 1: The Movement-Image*, trans. Hugh Tomlinson, Minneapolis: University of Minnesota Press, 1986; *Cinéma 1: l'image-mouvement*, Paris: Minuit, 1983.

N: *Negotiations 1972–1990*, trans. Martin Joughin, New York: Columbia University Press, 1995; *Pourparlers 1972–1990*, Paris: Minuit, 1990.

NPh: *Nietzsche and Philosophy*, trans. Hugh Tomlinson, London: Continuum, 1986; *Nietzsche et la philosophie*, Paris: PUF, 1962.

PS: *Proust and Signs*, trans. Richard Howard, Minneapolis: University of Minnesota Press, 2000; *Proust et les signes*, Paris: PUF, 1964.

SPP: *Spinoza: Practical Philosophy*, trans. Robert Hurley, San Francisco: City Lights Books, 1988; *Spinoza: philosophie pratique*, Paris: Minuit, 1981.

TI: *Cinema 2: The Time-Image*, trans. Hugh Tomlinson and Robert Galeta, Minneapolis: University of Minnesota Press, 1989; *Cinéma 2: l'image-temps*, Paris: Minuit, 1985.

TRM: *Two Regimes of Madness: Texts and Interviews 1975–1995*, ed. David Lapoujade, trans. Ames Hodges and Mike Taormina, New York: Semiotext(e), 2007; *Deux régimes de fous: textes et entretiens 1975–1995*, Paris: Minuit, 2003.

Félix Guattari

AOP: *Anti-Oedipus Papers*, ed. Stéphane Nadaud, trans. Kélina Gotman, New York: Semiotext(e), 2006; *Ecrits pour l'anti-Œdipe*, Fécamp: Lignes manifeste, 2004.

MS: 'Machine and Structure', in *Molecular Revolution: Psychiatry and Politics*, trans. Rosemary Sheed, Harmondsworth: Penguin, 1984; 'Machine et structure', in *Psychanalyse et transversalité: essais d'analyse institutionnelle*, Paris: F. Maspero, 1972; La découverte, 2003.

List of Abbreviations

Gilles Deleuze and Félix Guattari

AO: *Anti-Oedipus*, trans. Robert Hurley, Mark Seem and Helen R. Lane, London: Continuum, 2004; *L'anti-Œdipe*, Paris: Minuit, 1972.

TP: *A Thousand Plateaus*, trans. Brian Massumi, Minneapolis: University of Minnesota Press, 1987; *Mille plateaux*, Paris: Minuit, 1980.

WPh: *What is Philosophy?*, trans. Hugh Tomlinson and Graham Burchill, London: Verso, 1994; *Qu'est-ce que la philosophie?*, Paris: Minuit, 1991.

N.B. citations will give first the page number of the English translation followed by the page number of the text in the original French, e.g. (DR, 26/35).

Translator's Preface

Translator's prefaces, as we all know, are written to be ignored – a sad but inevitable fate. All the more so for a preface to a text such as the present volume, whose exposition, structure and argument are veritable models of clarity and distinction, those twin standards of philosophy that Descartes famously upheld as the golden metric for philosophic concepts. Elsewhere Professor Kokubun has mused that he feels more like a Cartesian than a Spinozist in disposition (scandalous for a Deleuzian!); it is for you, the reader, to judge the accuracy of this self-assessment.

This, however, puts the translator in an awkward position. For any lack of clarity and distinction that has dared to creep into the ensuing pages will necessarily be of my own doing (rather like the housekeeper who will with every justification be held responsible for a theft while he or she is cleaning the house). In particular I must insert a short obituary for my favourite word in the English language, 'verily', which appeared approximately 500 times in the first draft of the translation. These were erased (to my utmost chagrin) *in toto* after both our long-suffering editors and two anonymous reviewers raised more eyebrows than I can count. In retrospect, for the best: Kokubun's emphases are always merited and immaculately limelighted, and the locusts of 'verily' (swarming straight out of the Old Testament) would only have occluded it.

Now it is one thing to be in possession of great philosophic acuity and originality, quite another to have a sense for philosophical pedagogy (one might be forgiven for assuming these were in inverse proportion, if not for occasional exceptions like Kokubun). The latter, at the very least, requires a very precise identification of what is difficult to latch onto in one's own thinking, a skill precious as diamond. This must be one reason why Kokubun's explication of Deleuzian practical philosophy as pedagogy and apprenticeship (in Chapter 3 of the present volume) is, as you will soon see, so successful.

Translator's Preface

> We learn nothing from those who say: 'Do as I do.' Our only teachers are those who tell us to 'do with me', and are able to emit signs to be developed in heterogeneity rather than propose gestures for us to reproduce. (DR, 26/35)

As he quotes Deleuze. It is perhaps debatable how successfully Deleuze put into practice what he preached, his remarkable lectures (many of which are unfortunately still pending in English translation) notwithstanding; Kokubun, for his part, has clearly taken these words to heart.

This pedagogic fervour comes to the fore in the 'Research Notes' interluding each chapter, which is a surprising stylistic innovation of this work (although there is a clear forerunner in Giorgio Agamben's *scholia*). In these we are privy to Kokubun's thoughts in the very process of their crystallising. The tone of the research notes is somewhere in between the intensely private scribbles one carves into the margins of books, and the philosophical lecture, assertorical but at the same time spontaneous. In other words, they are embodiments of Kokubun's great generosity: what another philosopher might hide under lock and key Kokubun offers ungrudgingly to the world. And this so that we can, quite literally, 'do with him', apprentice ourselves to the way he reads, thinks, writes. Behind each note we can almost hear the man whispering in our ear: 'do as I do'.

A final word on the text. It would perhaps be more accurate to call what you have before you an English *edition* rather than an English translation. Working closely with Kokubun and always with his seal of approval, I have expanded certain passages while cutting some others, mostly endnotes which would serve no interest for the English reader. In other news, the 'Addendum on Kant' in Chapter 2 was written from scratch following the suggestion of our anonymous readers, as a brief intervention into one of the more expressly philosophic of the Anglo-American debates on Deleuze.

* * *

Translation, as I now know, is arduous business, and in truth there were many around me who propped me up during the process, without whom I may never have finished what I started (happens a lot to me). Acknowledgement is due to my family, who tolerated the pile of Deleuze's books which had taken up permanent residence on the dining room table; Nii-san, who knew how to distract me just before I descended into insanity (next time, please a little earlier each time . . .); my dear friends, who promised to buy a copy of the book

TRANSLATOR'S PREFACE

once it was out, thereby forcing me to keep typing (I'm following you guys up on that!); Mr. Misao Murase, without whose help I would still be camping out in libraries hunting for citations; and last but not least Professor Kokubun himself, who not only decided to entrust his work into the hands of a veritable nobody, but has since shared with me the great fount of his erudition and experience, philosophical and beyond. Indeed he has become something of a mentor to me, for which no amount of gratitude could possibly be adequate.

もろ指を
染にしが、いつか
しとなりて
やがて『原理』は
プリンシプルズに

I dedicate this translation to my grandmother, who is partially to blame for what I have become. For what I will become, I have only myself to blame.

W. N.

Prologue

Gilles Deleuze, one of the twentieth century's greatest philosophers, was born in the 17th arrondissement of the French capital in 1925. Little Gilles was your average Parisian child, with a fondness for collecting stamps in his spare time, as Deleuze was to recall later in life. The Second World War began when he was fifteen; evacuated to Normandy, it was there that lessons on French literature given by a young professor awakened his intellectual curiosity. The encounter with philosophy was to take place not long after, in his final year of lycée. Recognising in his very first philosophy class his calling for the discipline, he took up a life of research as a matter of course. His thesis at the Sorbonne on the British Empiricist David Hume became his first publication. Following a decade of intermittent 'silence', in the 1960s he produced study after study in close succession, radically reconstituting every field he deigned to intervene in. But it was his 1972 *Anti-Oedipus*, co-authored with psychoanalyst-turned-political-activist Félix Guattari, that secured him lasting fame. Embraced as one of the prime representatives of what came to be known in Anglo-American circles as the postmodernist/poststructuralist movement, his reputation spread far and wide. And yet through all this bustle he himself was largely to stay put in his 17th arrondissement flat. Disliking travel, he spent little time on the likes of lecture tours, concentrating instead on his university teaching and his publications. Indeed, his life remained remarkably constant throughout. Plagued for decades by a respiratory condition, in the last years of his life he was forced to use an oxygen inhalator. This physiological burden may well have proven too much, and on 4 November 1995 he threw himself out of a window at his home. It is a curious irony of history that his death coincided with the assassination of the then Prime Minister of Israel, Yitzhak Rabin, who had ratified the Oslo Accords and reconciled with Yasser Arafat; Deleuze had previously (in 1982) published a text entitled 'The Importance of Being of Yasser Arafat'.

Deleuze's readership continues to grow all over the world, and research on his work is prolific. There exists a dedicated journal, there are international conferences on his work, and every year a vast number of research papers are churned out. Yet none of this proves in any way that Deleuze's works are today being *read*; if anything, we have reason to believe the very opposite. One of the lasting contributions made by twentieth-century philosophy is the recognition of the profound complexity of the act of reading. Nonetheless, this lesson is most prone to be forgotten precisely for those authors who are discussed most frequently. Thus, the present study aims to do just one thing: to *read* the works of Gilles Deleuze. In this way we seek to prepare the minimum conditions which will enable one to read Deleuze. The admittedly grandiose title of this volume is intended to give expression to this undertaking. By 'principles' we mean the fundamental structures at the basis of things; 'The Principles of Deleuzian Philosophy' therefore signifies the fundamental structures at the basis of Deleuze's philosophic thought. We believe that a proper understanding of these will pave the way towards a proper understanding of the concepts and theses which arise from them. If on the other hand the principles are not made sufficiently clear, those concepts and theses will be condemned to fragmentation, becoming nothing more than receptacles for the wishful thinking of each individual practitioner.

Where then should an investigation into the principles of Deleuzian philosophy begin? We will select as our point of departure that aspect of his thought which is at present most enthusiastically contested. For it is where debate is most clamorous that the act of *reading* is maximally problematised.

* * *

The assessment of Deleuze's thinking seems to be polarised around the issue of politics. Those who see the germs of a new politics in Deleuze are pitted against those who maintain that politics is absent in the works of this thinker. The question we must ask is therefore the following: why do different commentators see two incompatible figures of Deleuze, the political and the apolitical? And which is the 'correct' figure of Deleuze?

The popularity of Deleuze's thought has grown explosively in recent years, in particular within Anglo-American academia, but it is noteworthy that much of what has been written in this vein has concerned itself with a 'political Deleuze'. Even restricting ourselves to scholars who deal *explicitly* with political themes, we can cite Nicholas Thoburn (2003), who emphasises the importance of

Prologue

Deleuzian micropolitics; Ian Buchanan (2000), who has continued to publish widely on the relation of Deleuze to politics; Jason Read (2003), who reads Deleuze's work as a renewal of Marxism; several collections of essays, such as *Deleuze and Politics* (Buchanan and Thoburn (eds) 2008) and *Deleuze and Marx* (Jain (ed.) 2009) . . . and this list does not even feign to be exhaustive. There was once a time, back in the late 1990s, when theorists were concerned that Deleuze's thought was read one-dimensionally as a glorified Bergsonian vitalism, or else as an ontology of virtuality,[1] but since 2000 it is undeniably the 'political Deleuze' that has taken centre-stage in the research.

Some may dispute this, but the most substantial effort in this direction has probably been Antonio Negri and Michael Hardt's *Empire*, published in 2000. It is well-known that the new political subject they christened the 'multitude' owes a great deal to Spinoza, but it was during the course of his study of Deleuze that Hardt had caught the shadows of such a vision in the first place. Hardt claims in his *Gilles Deleuze: An Apprenticeship in Philosophy* that the early Deleuze moved back in time from Bergson to Nietzsche and finally to Spinoza, in whom he discovered 'an avenue to enter the field of practice' (Hardt 1993: 117). Based on this framework, he links such Deleuzian concepts as 'multiplicity' and 'assemblage' to a vision of radical democratic society, and develops a political utopia of his own in the process by which the 'multitude' is reformed and renewed. At the basis of *Empire*'s detailed analyses of the international political/economic situation lies a total fidelity to this framework. As for Negri, the importance of Deleuze (especially the commentaries on Spinoza) for his work goes without saying. Negri's *Savage Anomaly*, completed behind bars and published in 1981, has Deleuze's *Expressionism in Philosophy: Spinoza* (1968) as its central point of reference (incidentally, Deleuze himself provided the foreword to the French translation of *The Savage Anomaly*, released in 1982). It requires no leap of the imagination to see that the great international popularity of *Empire* contributed in no small part to the present dominance of the image of the 'political Deleuze'. In any case, the fact is that many seek in Deleuze the vision of a new politics, or claim to have in fact discovered such a politics, and their writings are in turn read by others, establishing an influential paradigm.

At the other extreme, however, are certain theorists who consider the attempt to locate a politics in Deleuze to be severely misguided, instead proposing forcefully the image of the 'apolitical Deleuze'. At the forefront is Slavoj Žižek, who asserts: '[i]t is crucial to note that *not a single one* of Deleuze's own texts is in any way directly political; Deleuze "in himself" is a highly elitist author, indifferent toward politics' (Žižek 2004: 20; original emphasis). One can detect here a sarcasm directed at the facile crossing of Deleuze with the political, which according to Žižek is characteristic of the current, principally Anglo-American reception of Deleuze's work. No mercy is shown towards those theorists whom he thinks are content just to project their own political aspirations onto Deleuze.

Despite this, Žižek's underlying motivation is if anything to sketch out the possibility of a genuine 'political Deleuze'. By unleashing a deliberate provocation, he hopes to incite vocal, 'political' opposition. By contrast, there are certain theorists for whom it goes without saying that Deleuze's thought has no relation to politics, that Deleuze himself had no interest in politics. Alain Badiou is a prominent example: according to him, Deleuze subsumed every event of those 'a-changin' times' – the last years of the colonial wars, Gaullism, May '68, the red years, the revival of Mitterandism, the collapse of socialism . . . – under the monologic ready-made interpretative framework of the 'Virtual' (Badiou 2000). Deleuzian thought, it is argued, can explain away all and any political event using the all-powerful concept of the 'Virtual'; and that which explains everything ultimately explains nothing at all. It is clear that for Badiou there is quite simply no politics in Deleuze. Likewise, René Schérer (1998) relates that in a private conversation Jacques Rancière responded negatively to the question of whether a Deleuzian politics is possible. For Rancière, the question does not even merit a proper academic discussion.

It is worth noting at this point that the 'apolitical Deleuze' is not merely a trope rehearsed by theorists hostile to Deleuze. Peter Hallward, in the conclusion of his study of Deleuze centred around the notion of 'creation', flatly asserts: '[a]lthough no small number of enthusiasts continue to devote much energy and ingenuity to the task, the truth is that Deleuze's work is essentially indifferent to the politics of this world' (Hallward 2006: 162).[2] Hallward's diagnosis is not an arbitrary interjection, as we can sense from his accurate assessment of the situation that 'no small number of enthusiasts' have taken it upon themselves as a 'task' to apply Deleuze's thought to the political. He problematises the hegemonic reception of Deleuze's thought precisely because he too is under its spell. It is too early to tell if Hallward's claim is justified; his unease, however, is justified.

Superficially, Deleuze's writings are decorated by such concepts as 'becoming' and 'becoming-revolutionary', concepts which seem

Prologue

to lead straight to a transformation of the world. However, as we will see in greater detail, Deleuze is also a philosopher who ascribes great importance to passivity, and is consistently suspicious of such notions as the will, or activity. Far from these two tendencies coming into conflict, they entwine to constitute the unified body of his philosophy. To put it schematically, one undergoes becoming when one is affected by forces and powers. We can formulate this in another way: Deleuze thought endlessly about what it means for 'something to change' (intransitively), but he spent precious little time on what it means 'to change *something*' (transitively). The philosophy we can extract from this might well be a Heraclitean one of never-ending flux, but it is not the philosophy of revolutionary intervention hoped for by much of Deleuze's current readership. It must be admitted therefore that the figure of the 'apolitical Deleuze' put forward by Žižek and others has conclusive grounds. It is entirely unclear how Deleuze can answer the suspicion that his philosophy amounts to this: *all things which happen, happen thus because they were meant to happen thus*. It goes without saying that we are here at a maximal distance from the political, howsoever conceived.

Now Žižek provides an important point of reference in taking this question further. According to him, Deleuze's own philosophical method must be sought in the early monographs (*Difference and Repetition*, *The Logic of Sense*, etc.) and the shorter introductory volumes (*Proust and Signs*, *Coldness and Cruelty*, etc.), which must be distinguished from the books Deleuze co-authored with Félix Guattari. The stakes here are sky high, for if Žižek is right then the currently ascendant 'Anglo-American' 'political Deleuze' is none other than a '*Guattarised*' Deleuze. Dismissing *Anti-Oedipus* as Deleuze's 'worst book', Žižek takes every possible measure to dissolve this 'Guattarised' image of Deleuze.

If at times Žižek dabbles in provocation for its own sake, this should not detract from the immense importance of what he has drawn our attention to. And this can only be grasped once we are equipped with a better understanding of the position occupied by Guattari in the present reception of Deleuze. Having graced the world with his successive *magna opera Difference and Repetition* (1968) and *The Logic of Sense* (1969), an encounter with political activist Guattari, at the time working in psychiatric therapy, led to the publication of *Anti-Oedipus* in 1972 under both their names, following a two-and-a-half year period of intense collaboration. The two continued their joint intellectual labour beyond this initial success, giving birth to such works as *Kafka: Toward a Minor Literature* (1975) and *A Thousand Plateaus* (1980). It is crucial to bear in mind that these books do not follow the usual format assumed by co-authorship. Typically, such works begin by individual authors first writing up their respective sections separately, which are then amassed together; in Deleuze and Guattari's case, however, such division is wholly absent. All we have is the single volume, with both of their signatures appended. If such a format was not the first of its kind, as a work of philosophy it is radical. We set aside for the moment the various difficulties which arise from this practice of 'dual writing (*écrire à deux*)'. What must rather be highlighted at the outset is the following: because of this unprecedented format, the fact that the collaborative works such as *Anti-Oedipus* are written by both Deleuze *and* Guattari (henceforth we employ the label 'Deleuze-Guattari' to refer to this unique authorship) is all too often ignored, or at least passed over. As Stéphane Nadaud, editor of the vast reams of text Guattari wrote for *Anti-Oedipus*, has noted, the works of Deleuze-Guattari are referenced by countless academics as if they were the works of Deleuze *tout court*.[3]

We are now in a position to understand more fully the importance of Žižek's assessment that it was Guattari who introduced into Deleuze's apolitical philosophy its allegedly political elements. Hence those theorists who desperately want to politicise Deleuze are offered an attractive possibility: cover over the elitist, apolitical side of Deleuze by treating the works of Deleuze-Guattari as if they were Deleuze's own, so as to exaggerate the political weighting. When something unfavourable crops up in Deleuze, simply pick and choose by masquerading the works of Deleuze-Guattari as the works of Deleuze himself. In other words (though Žižek does not go quite so far), the confusion of Deleuze and Deleuze-Guattari is no more than *the base expression of the desire of those theorists who want to re-engineer Deleuze into the political thinker he never in fact was.*

Indeed we must press our suspicions one step further: was not the figure of the 'political Deleuze' we have been chasing just the mirage of Guattari? Were the aforementioned 'no small number of enthusiasts' not expending an inordinate amount of energy and ingenuity in interpreting the thought of Guattari instead? As a matter of fact, the *Anti-Oedipus Papers* have revealed that the multifarious concepts which appear in the work of Deleuze-Guattari – (de-/re-)territorialisation, (de-)codification, desiring-machines, connection/conjunction/disjunction, collective enunciation, the love between the orchid and the wasp ... – all hail from Guattari.[4] In other words: if we wish to problematise the parallel existence of the political and apolitical figures of Deleuze in the literature, we must begin by determining with precision the relation between Deleuze and Deleuze-Guattari.

If now we decide to distinguish the two authorships of Deleuze and Deleuze-Guattari, we face yet another difficulty. This is, so to speak, the ambiguity inherent in the object of study. With Deleuze-Guattari, we have before us a uniquely original way of developing a philosophical, historical and social theory, based on unprecedented concepts which can only be categorised as 'their thought'. To that extent, any prospective student of Deleuze-Guattari's thought is presented with a clear researchable object. Compare Deleuze himself, and the situation is radically different, for the majority of his works are monographs interpreting other philosophers and authors. In these works, Deleuze undertakes detailed studies of the respective philosophers' concepts, or the authors' themes; in other words, what populates Deleuze's books is the thought of the philosopher or author he is writing about, and not the thought of Deleuze himself. Descartes put forward a philosophy of the Cogito, Kant developed the transcendental method, Hegel embroiled all things in the dialectic, and Bergson strained to see reality differently with duration. Deleuze's works, however, are not written in this way. Deleuze always begins from some determinate object, and relentlessly interprets it; in spite of this, such works are unproblematically read as expressions of 'Deleuze's philosophy'. There can be nothing more obvious than this fact, and yet it is just as much of a fact that far too many scholars of Deleuze are oblivious to it, or else wilfully neglect it. If a piece of research has failed to discharge the prejudices held by the writer, that is, if it includes not purely information gained from the object of research but theories held by the writer prior to his/her study of the object, then such research should be cast aside as imprecise. This principle applies to all and any writer who undertakes scholarly research. Deleuze himself cannot be an exception: if, for example, Deleuze's studies on Spinoza are not liberated from his own prejudices, that is, if they contain theories held by Deleuze prior to his study of Spinoza, then we must simply discard this work as inaccurate. However, the present situation is very different. Take for instance the following remark by Hardt, made in the context of explaining his own approach to reading Deleuze: '[i]f a philosopher presents arguments with which Deleuze might find fault, he does not critique them but simply leaves them out of his discussion' (Hardt 1993: xix). *If* what Hardt says is true, all Deleuze is doing is arbitrarily stitching a patchwork from the relevant texts, based ultimately on his own prejudices. *If such an imprecise and unfaithful procedure is indeed at work in Deleuze, why does Hardt not attack it?* What gives us the right to accord Deleuze's essays this special status of immunity? A scholar who reads philosophy like this is not a scholar but a charlatan. This then is the pressing issue which we must confront in the following pages: is Hardt's account of Deleuze's method really valid? Does Deleuze really mix and match texts at will, to make a philosopher say what he wants them to say?

Unless and until we overcome these difficulties, the process of theorising Gilles Deleuze will remain unanchored. How can one expect to be able to study Deleuze's thought, his philosophy, when one does not even know where to look? We would be no better than those hapless explorers who fantasise about the lost treasures of the ancient world. There is a very real possibility that much of what circulates under the banner of Deleuze is in fact nothing more than such idle daydreaming; all this hype surrounding him was nothing more than transcribed personal prejudice megaphoned under Deleuze's name. Therefore, we must begin from a deceptively basic question: where is it that we must look to find 'Deleuzian thought'?

Notes

1. See for example Akira Asada's remarks in Uno and Asada 1997.
2. Hallward provides a useful overview of the debate surrounding the figure of the 'Anglo-American', 'apolitical Deleuze' in the section referred to here.
3. 'We refrain from listing those studies concerning *Anti-Oedipus* which cite only the name of Gilles Deleuze. How can one not be moved to sorrow at such a treatment, if one cares to understand how the two friends had worked together?' (AOP, 11; this passage has been omitted wholesale from the English edition, hence the translation is our own).
4. We must accord due consideration to Badiou's approach to reading Deleuze. In his *Deleuze: The Clamor of Being* cited earlier, Badiou (2000) restricts his attention to the works Deleuze wrote on his own. Guattari's name is not even mentioned, nor is there any programmatic prohibition against confusing Deleuze and Deleuze-Guattari. Badiou would no doubt say that this is blindingly obvious, since his is a study on Deleuze; in fact, we can go so far as to say that such an attitude is *more* faithful to Deleuze than are those theorists (partial to Deleuze) who have no qualms in equivocating between the two authorships.

1
Method: How to See Things in Free Indirect Discourse

Our investigation began by problematising the possibility of a 'political Deleuze'. This led to the prior question of the relation between Deleuze and Deleuze-Guattari; to ask about this relation in turn, we need to start by asking where Deleuze's philosophy is to be found. What sanctions the extraction of a 'philosophy' from texts whose self-imposed task is the relentless interpretation of something other than, strictly, Deleuze's philosophy? And if this a valid gesture, what makes it so? Any meaningful discussion of Deleuze must take its departure from here.

Free Indirect Discourse

Helpfully, this question is one that has already been formulated by Alain Badiou. It is worth analysing this in detail. Badiou begins with the apparently dismissive claim that Deleuze always and everywhere says the same things. 'Certainly, the starting point required by Deleuze's method is always a concrete case' (Badiou 2000: 14). Deleuze did not care for general theories, instead always opting to start his reflections from a particular. However, according to Badiou this does not imply that Deleuze considered each determinate case to be irreplaceable, unsubstitutable with any other; on the contrary, the endless array of cases (debates in the history of philosophy in *Difference and Repetition*, a canonical philosopher like Spinoza, art forms such as cinema, a great contemporary like Foucault, literary figures of the likes of Proust . . .) are all reduced to mere examples, each displaying 'no significative difference'. This is because '[i]t is always a question of indicating particular *cases of a concept*' (2000: 14; original emphasis). True, Deleuze sets off from the concrete case, but he does this only to inspect how the various concepts he has developed in advance (say, the 'Virtual') are at work in them. And, Badiou continues, these concepts are uniformly '*monotonous*' (2000: 15):

> This also explains something that has often surprised Deleuze's readers: the constant use of the free indirect style, or the deliberate undecidability of 'who is speaking?' If I read, for example: 'force among forces, man does not fold the forces that compose him without the outside folding itself, and creating a Self within man' [F, 14], is this really a statement of Foucault's? Or is it already an interpretation? (2000: 14)

This 'something that has often surprised Deleuze's readers' is the fact that one encounters with great frequency statements in Deleuze's work that seem in no way attributable to the writer in question. Needless to say, the remark from Deleuze's *Foucault* cited above is not a direct quotation from the works of Michel Foucault (1926–1984); but it seems too far-fetched to qualify as an indirect report of his words either. This forces the following question: in this text of Deleuze discussing Foucault, *who is the speaker, the speaking subject?* Is interpreting Foucault a mere excuse for Deleuze to put forward his own thinking? If so, Deleuze's interpretation of Foucault is inaccurate *simpliciter*, for it reflects to an inexcusable extent the interpreter's own prejudices. Badiou, however, pre-empts such an assessment: '[for Deleuze] the case is never an object for thought' (2000: 15). When Deleuze examines a particular case (such as Foucault), he never in fact thinks *about* this case. The case is never an actual 'object' for Deleuze's thinking.

Of course, if Badiou seems for a split second to take up Deleuze's cause, this is not because he respects Deleuze's philosophical method, but because he wants to keep it at (rather more than) arm's length. When all is said and done, Badiou is effectively saying: Deleuze's method is peculiar, let's just leave it at that. Now our unease at this point is entirely justified. For though Badiou's confrontational attitude occludes this, excepting the final evaluation such an assessment is *identical to that upheld by interpreters favourably inclined towards Deleuze*. Namely, that one should police all inaccuracies of interpretation, unless the interpreter happens to be Gilles Deleuze (recall Hardt's remark: '[i]f a philosopher presents arguments with which Deleuze might find fault, he does not critique them but simply leaves them out of his discussion').

Badiou however is sufficiently confrontational at core to distinguish himself from the mere followers of Deleuze, by proposing a subtle perspective which holds the key to stepping beyond this undesirable choice between bad and worse (either tolerate Deleuze's method, or adhere to it). This is the problem of the 'frequent usage of free indirect discourse' in Deleuze.

Method: How to See Things in Free Indirect Discourse

'Free indirect discourse (*discours indirect libre*)' is a mode of speech situated in between direct speech (*discours direct*) and indirect speech (*discours indirect*): words to 'signpost' indirect speech (the conjunctive, typically 'that', *que* in French) and the reporting verb (say/think, for example, *dire/penser* in French) are omitted, allowing what would have been a subordinate clause under ordinary indirect speech to keep its original person, grammar and tense, and become a stand-alone independent clause. Not commonly used outside literature, authors such as Gustav Flaubert (1821–1880) and Jane Austen (1775–1817) were fond of this technique as a way to explore the characters' words, feelings and monologues.

Let us examine each mode of speech in detail. In direct speech, the reported content is transmitted by the speaker without alteration:

He said, 'it's not true'.
Il a dit, 'ce n'est pas vrai'.
dixit, 'non verum est'.

The speaker transmits the content just as it was originally uttered. To signpost this to the reader, one detaches the content from the body of the narrative using quotation marks. Direct speech is the mode of speech for *quotation*.

In indirect speech, by contrast, the speaker incorporates the reported content into his own narrative:

He said (that) it was not true.
Il a dit que ce n'était pas vrai.
negavit verum esse.

Because the content is woven into the fabric of the narrative, reporting verbs and conjunctions are required *in order to distinguish the two*. Indirect speech is the mode of speech for *reporting*.

The two modes of speech can also be explained in the context of the philosophical essay. Here, direct speech corresponds to the citation: X writes as follows, 'A is B'. Indirect speech on the other hand first makes explicit that what follows is not the commentator's own opinion, and then uses his or her own words to report this content: according to X, A is B; X thinks that A is B. For all intents and purposes, the average philosophical essay is made up of a combination of these two modes of speech.

What of free indirect speech, then? It is discourse that incorporates the reported content into the narrative *without* signposting the fact that this incorporation has taken place. Sticking to the examples above, it's not true/ce n'est pas vrai/non verum est will appear within the narrative without any punctuation. To repeat, the judgement of untruth is made not by the speaker, but by 'he/she' whose opinion is presently being transmitted by the speaker; yet, the associated signposts which the speaker ought to employ in reporting this judgement ('he said that', etc.) are nowhere to be found. *It is as if we are being given the speaker's own judgement.*

At this point, it is worth pointing out the difficulty of codifying a paradigmatic example of free indirect speech in the manner of the introductory primer of grammar. This is because each instance of free indirect discourse must incorporate the content 'naturally', in a locally specific way. For example, where a simple 'he said, "it's not true"' or 'he said that it wasn't true' would convey the meaning adequately, if one were instead to write unthinkingly, 'it was not true', shoved into the actual body of the narrative, this would be nothing more than a mistake. To avoid this eventuality, the body of the text has to fulfil certain conditions to receive free indirect speech 'naturally'; however, such conditions cannot be formalised in advance (indeed, to believe in this possibility would be tantamount to believing in the possibility of formalising the conditions of the creation of art itself). Whether our particular example ('it was not true') can pass as genuine free indirect speech depends on the narrative preceding it, and the expressive hand of the writer him or herself. Which is why, whenever the language primer tries to explain free indirect discourse, it has to resort to direct quotations from authors of the literary canon: each instance of free indirect speech is inextricable from the actual body of the text within which it occurs, and hence its composition cannot be generalised. Each case, each instance, requires a unique method, and will only succeed under this unique method. The grammar books tell us how to transform direct speech into indirect speech, and vice versa (no doubt there will be subtle differences of nuance, but neither are strictly speaking grammatically 'incorrect'); they also tell us how to transform *successful* cases of free indirect discourse back into either direct or indirect speech (though of course there is room for interpretation in performing the actual transformation). But what the grammar books do *not* tell us is how to rewrite direct or indirect speech into free indirect discourse; and this they cannot do, of necessity.

We have thus far established that in free indirect discourse, 1) the opinion of the reported reads as if it is the opinion of the reporter, and 2) it is impossible to formalise its conditions of possibility. Let

Method: How to See Things in Free Indirect Discourse

us consider this in relation to the other two modes of speech. Direct speech is based on the rigid separation between the transmitter and the transmitted: the former accords minimal thought and attention to the content of the latter. Which is why the transmitted content appears without any alteration. By contrast, in indirect speech the transmitted content has to be moulded into the speaker's own narrative of transmission (if a novice learner is tested on the transformation of direct into indirect speech, minimally (s)he has to be able to perform the requisite changes in the person of the subject and the tense of the verb), which is why we must place a signpost word (that/*que*, etc.) to demarcate the transmitter and the transmitted. Now free indirect discourse goes one step further: not only is the reported content assimilated into the very body of the narrative/demonstration, but there is nothing to signpost that such an assimilation has taken place. The transmitted content is made to appear as if it belonged to the thoughts and statements of the transmitter him or herself. If this occurs in a novel, a statement in fact uttered by one of the characters appears as if it were a statement by the narrator. Here there is no longer any fool-proof way to distinguish character and narrator. Transmitter and transmitted coincide.

In other words, if such a discourse were to appear in the philosophical essay, it is inevitable that the Badiousian question of the identity of the speaker will arise. Who is it that utters 'force among forces, man does not fold the forces that compose him without the outside folding itself, and creating a Self within man' – is it Foucault, or is it Deleuze? We have already seen Badiou's own take on the situation: Deleuze is not actually thinking about each particular case, the individual case does not matter, all he wants to do is to impose his own ready-made (as Badiou calls them, 'monotonous') concepts onto the various examples, as a stepping stone to deploying his own philosophy. From our analysis of free indirect discourse, however, we are already equipped with the means to respond to this criticism. If, as Badiou himself says, Deleuze always sets off from the concrete case, *and*, likewise as Badiou says, he makes frequent use of free indirect discourse, then *it is impossible for Deleuze to be imposing pre-existing theories/principles/concepts onto the particular case under the auspices of interpretation*. The use of free indirect discourse cannot be formalised methodologically; if, therefore, Deleuze has no interest in the specificity of each individual case, free indirect discourse is destined to failure. Unless one engineers one's narrative/demonstration in such a way that free indirect speech can emerge 'naturally' from among the direct and indirect reports made of the case in question (and we repeat, in each instance there is but a unique way in which this can be achieved), free indirect discourse cannot take place. In other words, any theorist who successfully employs free indirect discourse must have obsessed over each particular case precisely as an 'object for thought'. The more 'naturally' Deleuze manages to incorporate free indirect discourse into his writing, the more profoundly he has thought about the particular case in question. The frequent use of this mode of speech therefore does not suggest that Deleuze has little concern for his particular cases; quite the contrary in fact, it shows how formidably deeply Deleuze has thought about them. Badiou, whose observations on Deleuze's starting point and his preferred mode of discourse are extremely pertinent, nonetheless went astray at the very end. From the very evidence he himself puts forward, one must rather conclude the exact opposite: for Deleuze, the case absolutely *is* an object for thought.

The Task of the History of Philosophy

It would of course be fanciful to believe that with the preceding we have answered Badiou satisfactorily, once and for all. For why did Deleuze choose to write using free indirect discourse? Why did he write in such a way as to make the identity of the speaker ambiguous? What was it that *required* him to write in such a way? The preceding is but a gentle warm-up.

For a start, what did Deleuze deem to be the task of the history of philosophy? We quote:

> Philosophers introduce new concepts, they explain them, but they don't tell us, not completely anyway, the problems to which those concepts are a response. Hume, for example, sets out a novel concept of belief, but he doesn't tell us how and why the problem of knowledge presents itself in such a way that knowledge is seen as a particular kind of belief. The history of philosophy, rather than repeating what a philosopher says, has to say what he must have taken for granted, what he didn't say but is nonetheless present in what he did say. (N, 136/186)

The philosopher proposes a philosophical theory. Hume systematised empiricism with the original concept of 'belief', while Descartes grounded rationalism on the original concept of the Cogito. However, the philosopher does not always tell us what 'problem' their concepts were designed to answer, or at least not completely. No philosopher

Method: How to See Things in Free Indirect Discourse

is able to narrate the totality of their thought. That is not to say that the philosopher is a trickster, always with a card or two up their sleeve; rather, the philosopher is incapable of knowing everything there is to know about their own thought. *Thinking always reaches beyond the confines of the philosopher's consciousness.*

Let us examine this in greater detail. Deleuze's first publication was a study on the empiricist philosopher David Hume (1711–1776), entitled *Empiricism and Subjectivity: An Essay on Hume's Theory of Human Nature* (1953). Deleuze wrote this text under the supervision of Jean Hyppolite (1907–1968) and Georges Canguilhem (1904–1995) at the age of twenty-eight, yet already the scholarly attitude of his mature writings can be clearly discerned therein. For example, Deleuze identifies Hume's problem as the following: 'how does the mind become a subject?' (ES, 23/3). However, it is not the case that in Hume's texts we find him formulating his own problem in these terms; more astoundingly still, in the texts of Hume cited by Deleuze in this book, the word 'subject' appears not once. This then is none other than the 'problem', understood to be that which the philosopher 'didn't say but is nonetheless present in what he did say'.

Let us next discuss a somewhat more intricate example. Deleuze cites Henri Bergson's (1859–1941) famous criticism of Humean associationism. To review the basics of associationism: according to Hume, the mind is initially nothing more than a collection of ideas lacking any determinate relation to each other, and in this state the mind is incapable of any knowledge. For knowledge to become possible, the disparate ideas constituting the mind must first become linked, become 'associated' with each other. Only when the simple collection of ideas comes to form a system (so to speak), will knowledge come to be. More concretely: every morning we see the sun rise. Each of these perceptions forms a separate idea in the mind ('this morning, the sun rose'; 'yesterday, the sun also rose'; 'the day before that, the sun rose as well' . . .). However, at some point these disparate ideas will enter into association with each other, giving rise to the knowledge that 'the sun will rise again tomorrow'. 'I do not have knowledge when I remark: "I have seen the sun rise a thousand times", but I do when I assert: "The sun will rise *tomorrow*"; "*Every time* water is at 100°C, it *necessarily* begins to boil"' (KCP, 11/20; original emphasis). Having said that, there is no guarantee that the sun will indeed rise again tomorrow. I might well have seen the sun rise a thousand times, but this does not mean the same thing will happen again tomorrow. And yet, in spite of this, at some point we come to *believe* that it will happen. Knowledge can be said to have come about when we affirm in this way something we have never seen, something we have never experienced. It is always *something more* than just the experience of the given. The association of disparate ideas gives rise to belief, just as the leap beyond the experience of the given gives rise to knowledge. When a mere bundle of unconnected ideas comes to form a systematic unity, this is precisely the moment when the mind becomes a subject.

This picture, however, did not satisfy Bergson. True, there always seems to be an association of ideas in the act of knowing. But this does not explain why some ideas associate with each other, while others do not. For, even between the most distant of ideas, 'we shall always find, if we go back high enough, a common genus to which they belong, and consequently a resemblance which may serve as a connecting link between them' (ES, 102/114). Which is to say that in theory any idea can be associated with any other idea. But if so, how do we explain why association takes place between these ideas, and not some others? For example, why must the idea 'yesterday the sun rose' be associated with 'the day before yesterday, the sun rose as well'? Why not with some other idea, say the idea of the rooster crowing in the morning, to form the knowledge that 'the sun rises *because* the rooster wails cock-a-doodle-doo'? In other words, associationism does no more than observe the *fact* that ideas are associated; as for *why* this and not that association takes place, the principle behind the selection is left entirely unexplained. This is the crux of Bergson's critique.

Deleuze, however, shields Hume from Bergson's critique by focusing not on his shortcomings, but on his achievements. 'The least that we can say is that Hume thought of it first' (ES, 103/114). It is undeniable that associationism on its own cannot explain why this and not that association takes place. '[W]hy does this perception evoke a specific idea, rather than another, in a particular consciousness at a particular moment?' (ES, 103/115).

> It follows that, from this point of view, we must define relation as '... that particular circumstance, in which, *even upon the arbitrary union of two ideas in the fancy*, we may think proper to compare them'. If it is true that association is necessary in order to make all relations in general possible, each particular relation is not in the least explained by the association. Circumstance gives the relation its sufficient reason.
>
> The notion 'circumstance' appears constantly in Hume's philosophy. It is at the centre of history ... (ES, 103/115)

Method: How to See Things in Free Indirect Discourse

The respective 'circumstance' of each case, says Deleuze, is the principle of selection that Hume had prepared in advance to answer the Bergsonian critique. Yet, as we can see from the line by Hume quoted above by Deleuze, the 'circumstance' can in no way be said to have been posited consciously as a concept by Hume. There, 'circumstance' simply appears as a bog-standard common noun. Although the term appears several times in the Humean texts cited by Deleuze, in no case do we get the sense that Hume is using it to name a determinate concept.[1] Now let us for the sake of argument assume that we can respond adequately to Bergson's criticism with the concept of 'circumstance' (no doubt there are valid grounds to question this, but they do not matter here); what *does* matter to the utmost is that Deleuze takes up a term, not in any way consciously developed into a concept by the philosopher under consideration, and sets it up as a concept. This then, in effect, is Deleuze's point: Hume had, in spite of himself, made 'circumstance' into a concept. Hume's philosophical theory of associationism is thus revealed to be a complex structure constituted by the various elements of perception, idea, experience, belief *and circumstance*, among others. Crucially, there is no reason why the philosopher who constructs this complex structure will have grasped the totality of their own creation. In essence, the theoretical structure is not exhausted by the manifest content of the text, there remain many latent elements waiting to be brought to light.

Now according to this study on Hume, philosophical theory is a 'developed question', no more and no less. The true domain of philosophical theory 'by itself and in itself ... is not the resolution to a problem, but the elaboration, *to the very end*, of the necessary implications of a formulated question' (ES, 106/119; original emphasis). We can see this as an expression of Deleuze's own attitude towards philosophical reading. The philosophical theory is a problem deployed by the philosopher him or herself, but the philosopher is never able to draw out all the im*pli*cations of his or her own problem. The historian of philosophy is then tasked with bursting open the wall (*pli*) contained in the implications, to 'ex-*pli*-cate' the philosopher's problem. To be capable of this task, we must go back in search of that which gave rise to the genesis of the philosophical theory in the first place.

We must not take the preceding as a philosophical method Deleuze arbitrarily picked out because it happened to take his fancy. For this method is none other than Deleuze's considered response to the question of what the history of philosophy *is*, in other words what it is that we are supposed to study when we study philosophy. If the history of philosophy were a mere exercise in retracing the thought of a philosopher, minor reconfiguration or otherwise, *this could be nothing more than restating what the philosopher has already said* (the undeniable value of such textbooks of philosophy notwithstanding). At the other extreme, as already discussed, if the historian takes to narrating their own philosophy under the banner of the canonical name, *this ceases to be a study in the history of philosophy altogether* (this would simply be another set of philosophical views). How then does one go about the task of the history of philosophy? By discovering the hidden problem that compelled the philosopher to think; by sketching out this problem which the philosopher was not conscious of in its entirety; if called for by the problem, by not hesitating to deploy concepts which remain merely latent in the works of the philosopher, while having the audacity to pass over those themes which the exegetic tradition has deemed a requirement in any discussion of the philosopher in question. Such is, in Deleuze's eyes, the task of the historian of philosophy, a task which he himself was to carry out with the utmost rigour. Until we come to recognise this fully, we will inevitably fall back into the assessment proffered by Hardt and by Badiou ('[i]f a philosopher presents arguments with which Deleuze might find fault, he does not critique them but simply leaves them out of his discussion'; 'the case is never an object for thought'). For these interpreters restrict their attention to the explicit statements of the philosopher, in the belief that the totality of a philosopher's thought is under his or her conscious control. But that is not the case: the philosopher's thought extends far over yonder.

This thought that exceeds the philosopher's consciousness, a thought irreducible to the manifest content, extending beyond the words consigned to paper, topologically prior to the body of the narration – for Deleuze this thought constitutes a type of image, an 'image of thought (*image de la pensée*)' (DR, chapter III). Crucially, we must not understand by the term 'image' something vague and undefined; on the contrary, the image of thought is expected to fulfil a distinctly critical function. The term first appears in Deleuze in the context of the problem of how to make a beginning in philosophy: the starting point must have discharged all existing presuppositions, otherwise this would be but another inheritance. However, in reality such purity is unattainable. Even for René Descartes himself (1596–1650): in doubting everything, and extracting the single indubitable truth of the Cogito, did he succeed in bracketing all presuppositions to establish an absolute beginning for philosophy? Of course not. Before 'I think, therefore I am' can stand as the inaugural truth, we have to know what the words 'I', 'thought' and 'being' mean. 'The pure self of "I think" thus appears to be a beginning only because it has referred all its presuppositions back to the empirical self' (DR, 164/169). In this way, the image of thought is a tool to expose the presuppositions a philosopher has repressed in the process of verbalising his or her thought. By going back to the problem which compelled the philosopher to think, one hopes to bring to light certain hidden presuppositions at the level of the image of thought.

We can thus formulate the task Deleuze prescribes to the historian of philosophy: go back to the 'problem' which the philosopher in question faced unconsciously, or else was unable to explicate *in toto*; carefully dissect this problem; and bring to light the image of thought in which this problem is anchored. The frequent recourse to the free indirect style, which has been at the forefront of our investigation thus far, is precisely because this is the proper method to attain the image of thought. For we get no closer to this image if all we ever do is parrot the explicit narrative of the philosopher under consideration. Instead we must situate our own discussion *on the same plane as the philosophy that is being discussed*. This proximity inexorably blurs the distinction between theorist and theorised to the point of undecidability. And it is this undecidability that makes possible the theoretical descent to attain the requisite image of thought.

But we still cannot be content. The moment we formulate Deleuze's philosophical method in this way, the following difficulty arises: what is the relation of Deleuze's method in the history of philosophy with 'Deleuze's philosophy', that which has even now so deftly eluded us? Or equivalently: how can we extract from one who reads the history of philosophy in this way, a determinate 'thinking' of his own?

The Task of Philosophy

Deleuze was to take up the thematic of the image of thought once again at the end of his life in *What is Philosophy?* (1991),[2] where it is given the name 'plane of immanence (*plan d'immanence*)' and further explicated in its relation to the 'concept'. An essential link is posited between the work of philosophy and the concept: 'philosophy is the discipline that involves *creating* concepts' (WPh, 5/10; original emphasis). We will examine the meaning of this proposition in time; for the moment, allow us to skip ahead and examine what the word 'concept' means. Deleuze defines the concept as constituted by several 'components (*composants*)', as the 'consistency (*consistance*)' of these components (WPh, 15, 19/21, 25). Every concept is built up of various component parts. Take the concept of the Cogito, created by Descartes: although we tend to treat the Cogito as a technical term, needless to say the word itself can be parsed as the first person singular present active form of the Latin verb *cogitare*, 'I think'. In other words, just writing 'cogito' on the page signifies no more than a simple 'I think', and *this is not yet a concept*. The Cogito only becomes a concept when it appears alongside the proper name 'Descartes'; the concept *cannot be detached from the signature appended to it by the philosopher who created it*.[3] This particular concept is composed of the elements 'I doubt (*je doute*)', 'I think (*je pense*)' and 'I am (*je suis*)', whose consistency is conferred by the 'I (*je*)' which traverses all three. Three disparate components assembled together by the 'I', such is the conceptual mapping of the concept Cogito (WPh, 24–7/29–31). If even one of these components is lacking, the Cogito topples as a concept.[4] The concept is thus nothing but its components compressed into a point.[5]

Now the concept, which is made up of various components, is in turn located on the 'plane of immanence'. But why the *plane of immanence*? This is because no concept wanders in isolation: a concept is necessarily bridged to other concepts,[6] such as to require a theoretical space in which this network of concepts is to take place. Returning to our model concept of the Cogito, everybody knows that the proposition 'I think, therefore I am' concludes in the proposition 'I am a thinking thing (*res cogitans*)'. But it is not as if there existed a magical short-circuit between these two propositions; such a deduction becomes possible only when it is located within a complex web of concepts. No concept is meaningful until it is thought together with the concepts with which it forms a conceptual network: the site of this relationality Deleuze terms the 'plane of immanence'. But why the plane of *immanence*? This is because concepts on a given plane are determined solely by their relations with each other, and not by any causes outside of this relationality, causes which are *transcendent* with respect to this plane. For example, it is meaningless to try and explain a concept based on external social influences. No doubt, the philosopher who created a given concept will have been under the influence of a great many social forces; however, the concept itself can only be understood as part of the conceptual network located on the philosopher's plane of

Method: How to See Things in Free Indirect Discourse

immanence. The concept is a concept only insofar as it exists within the relationality of the plane of immanence.

Now for the crucial part. Deleuze states, with respect to the plane of immanence, that the concept is *simultaneously relative and absolute* (WPh, 21/26). We have already covered the concept's relativity. The concept *qua* concept is always determined internally by its components, and externally by its related concepts as well as the plane of immanence as a whole.[7] Such relations and constraints are here termed the relativity of the concept. Crucially, however, the concept is at the same time in itself absolute:[8] that is to say, it constitutes an unconstrained totality in itself. Allow us to explain. It was said that the concept is composed of various compositional elements; however, in no sense have these components been made-to-order for the concept in question (trivially, the phrases 'I doubt', 'I think' and 'I am' all possess an independent existence, above and beyond their part in the Cogito). As a result, the components of a concept are like so many incongruent fragments, forcibly compressed where there is no inherent tessellation. 'Philosophical concepts are fragmentary wholes that are not aligned with one another so that they fit together, because their edges do not match up' (WPh, 35/38). How then can such unmatching components stay woven together in a single concept? This is by virtue of the plane of immanence upon which the concept is located, which is to say, *by virtue of the image of thought*. In our old friend the Cogito, we require Descartes' particular image of thought, which sought an absolute foundation for thought through methodological doubt, to transmute the self-sufficient fragments of 'I doubt', 'I think' and 'I am' into determinate components of a concept (when Thomas Hobbes (1588–1679) retorts that the very same reasoning could be applied to produce the delightful *'ambulo ergo sum* (I walk, therefore I am)', it is clear that he is thinking within an image of thought incompatible with that of Descartes). Deleuze also explains this in the following way: '[c]oncepts are the archipelago or skeletal frame, a spinal column rather than a skull, whereas the plane is the breath that suffuses the separate parts' (WPh, 36/39). The concept is an archipelago of disparate and independent islands. Or, if we prefer something more, shall we say, ossified, it is not a container like the skull, rather the spine, which is a collection of bones strung together by forces other than the bone (muscles, nerves . . .). The plane of immanence is then what traverses all this, giving them the breath of (a) life . . .

Therefore, 'all things being equal' is inapplicable to the concept:

if one were to inject even a single additional component, the entire surrounding relationality would be irrevocably altered. Deleuze's favourite example is the criticism Immanuel Kant (1724–1804) made of the Cartesian Cogito.[9] In Descartes, it is the 'I think' that gives rise to the 'I am': the 'I' in the mode of thinking determines the being of this same 'I'. But, Kant retorts, the way in which my existence is determined, and the form in which it comes about as determinate, have not been sufficiently clarified. In what form is it, then, that my being comes to be as determined? Kant replies: in the form of time. Kant thus reintroduces time, which Descartes had previously banished into exile, back among the components of the Cogito.[10] It is in time alone that the thinking 'I' can determine 'my' own being. But at this point a gap arises between the thinking 'I' (active ego) and the being determined by this 'I' (passive ego), since with the reintroduction of temporality the self has been divided into its pre- and post-determination renditions. Consequently, I am determined as a passive ego, while from the perspective of this passive ego the active, thinking 'I' necessarily becomes an Other (hence Deleuze's extraordinary claim that Rimbaud's 'I is an other (*je est un autre*)' is a possible poetic expression of Kant's philosophy[11]). According to Deleuze, it was none other than Kant who discovered the fault line internal to the self. By adding time as a component to the Cartesian Cogito, he ended up giving the concept a complete overhaul. In this way Kant 'sets up a plane and constructs a problem that could not be occupied or completed by the Cartesian cogito' (WPh, 32/35).

It seems that we are steadily attaining a clearer vision of Deleuze's philosophy, or at least of its topography. We have seen how Kant constructed a problem foreclosed to the Cartesian Cogito. In the process, he created the concept of the 'cracked Cogito' (as Deleuze terms it), as well as a new concept of time. And Kant achieved this through a critique not so much of Descartes himself as of the problem which at root had motivated Descartes. It is vital to keep in mind that the critique of the problem is not one method among many for the discovery of a new problem and the creation of a new concept; for Deleuze, this is the *only* viable method in existence.

On this point, Deleuze remained remarkably consistent from his first monograph on Hume to his last programmatic statement, *What is Philosophy?* 'In philosophy the question and the critique of the question are one';[12] '[h]owever, even in philosophy, concepts are only created as a function of problems which are thought to be badly understood or badly posed' (WPh, 16/22). The philosopher must critique the problem to discover the problem, and thence derive his or her concepts. And exactly the same summary assessment must apply to Deleuze's own philosophic thought: he too worked by criticising the problems we have inherited from the history of philosophy, in the process happening upon new problems and generating new concepts. This is precisely the reason why we cannot help but encounter Deleuze's own philosophy in his relentless work of interpretation: approaching the image of thought through free indirect discourse, he extracted the kernel of the problem from within the manifest shell of the philosopher's words. This allows in turn for the problem to be criticised: for the sake of a new problem, entirely new concepts are created. And, as already discussed, the concept is always *signed* by the philosopher who created it. Now insofar as free indirect discourse blurs the distinction between theorist and theorised, it would seem bizarre that concepts signed and therefore belonging to a determinate individual (Deleuze) should come about. But this is precisely how philosophical concepts appended by the philosopher's signature are created. Finally at this point, we see the philosophy *of* Deleuze come about.

We can go one step further, however, because *mutatis mutandis* the above framework can be applied to the whole of the history of philosophy. One non-trivial consequence is that we are given a convincing explanation of how so many divergent and even outright contradictory ways of thinking have managed to exist side by side in the history of philosophy. Take the debate which raged on between rationalists and empiricists; or the present enmity between so-called 'Continental' philosophy and analytic philosophy. For Deleuze, such oppositions are sustained because each side is situated in an entirely different (and incompatible) problematic genealogy. If the problem is one and the same as the critique of the problem, this forms a historically isolable genealogy, which is then saturated by numerous concepts. Otherwise, we would have the history of philosophy making steady progress towards a single universal 'Truth'; we have 2,000 years of textual evidence to suggest that that is not the case. Is this not because 'Truth' is but a secondary concern for the history of philosophy? It is not 'Truth', but rather the 'problem' and the 'concept' which have always motivated the adventures of philosophy.

Over the course of this chapter we have tried to triangulate the location of Deleuze's philosophical thought. The investigation has yielded the realisation that we must first make clear the problematic genealogy in which Deleuze positioned himself, otherwise it is impossible even to speak of 'Deleuzian' philosophy in a robust sense. We can phrase this differently: the many concepts that Deleuze created only become meaningful when they are correctly situated within this problematic genealogy. This then is the next question we must confront: within what genealogy of the problem did Deleuze try to situate himself?

Notes

1. For instance, in note 82 of chapter 5, Deleuze quotes a passage of Hume which is supposed to explain the relation between circumstance and belief: '[i]t frequently happens, that when two men have been engag'd in any scene of action, the one shall remember it much better than the other, and shall have all the difficulty in the world to make his companion recollect it. He runs over several *circumstances* in vain; mentions the time, the place, the company, what was said, what was done on all sides; till at last he hits on some lucky *circumstance*, that revises the whole, and gives his friend a perfect memory of every thing' (ES, 150/116; my emphasis). The word 'circumstance' does appear, but it is being used as a common noun, not as the name of a concept.
2. *What is Philosophy?* was published in 1991 under the names of both Deleuze and Guattari; however, François Dosse's extensive biographical study has since revealed that this book was written in its entirety by Deleuze, with Guattari's signature appended later at the latter's request (Dosse 2011: ch. 25). Accordingly, the present essay will treat this book as Deleuze's work, not that of Deleuze-Guattari. The importance of this distinction will become clear soon enough.
3. 'First, concepts are and remain signed' (WPh, 7/13).
4. 'Second, what is distinctive about the concept is that it renders components inseparable *within itself*' (WPh, 19/25; original emphasis).
5. 'Third, each concept will therefore be considered as the point of coincidence, condensation, or accumulation of its own components' (WPh, 20/25).
6. 'First, every concept relates back to other concepts, not only in its history but in its becoming or its present connections' (WPh, 19/24).
7. '[I]t is relative to its own components, to other concepts, to the plane on which it is defined, and to the problems it is supposed to resolve' (WPh, 21/26).
8. '[B]ut it is absolute through the condensation it carries out, the site it occupies on the plane, and the conditions it assigns to the problem' (WPh, 21/26).
9. See DR, 106/116; F, 51–2/67; WPh, 31–2/34.
10. A brief caveat is in order here, for the 'time' that Kant summons back into his court is already a new concept of time, his own creation.

Method: How to See Things in Free Indirect Discourse

    This new concept is no longer the Aristotelian notion of time based on quantifiable motion forwards and backwards. Instead of a time subordinated to movement, Kant has movement subordinated to time; prior to all movement, it is now time which functions as the condition of possibility of any movement.
11. See Deleuze's 'On Four Poetic Formulas Which Might Summarise the Kantian Philosophy', included as the Preface to KCP.
12. 'To put something in question means subordinating and subjecting things to the question, intending, through this constrained and forced subsumption, that they reveal an essence or a nature. To criticise the question means showing under what conditions the question is possible and correctly raised; in other words, how things would not be what they are were the question different from the one formulated. This means that these two operations are one and the same; the question is always about the necessary development of the implications of a problem and about giving sense to philosophy as theory. In philosophy, the question and the critique of the question are one' (ES, 106/119).

Research Note I: On Naturalism

Naturalism is one of the fundamental tenets of Deleuze's philosophical inspiration. He takes up this theme in his text on 'Lucretius and the Simulacrum' (LS, 303–20/307–24), an essay on the Roman philosopher-poet Lucretius (c. 99 BC–55 BC). The central problem of this essay is the role of philosophy: '[t]o the question "What is the use of philosophy?" the answer must be: what other object would have an interest in holding forth the image of a free man, and in denouncing all of the forces which need myth and the troubled spirit in order to establish their power? (LS, 314/322). Philosophy imagines what it would mean for man to be free. And in the process it indicts those who would call upon 'myth' or the 'troubled spirit' to patch up the weak links in the powers-that-be. What does this mean? By the 'troubled spirit' Deleuze means anxiety and fear. Crucially, anxiety and fear are not the same as pain. Rather, they are moods *in anticipation of a pain which might one day befall*. It is when one is forewarned of the possibility of some future pain that one experiences a profound tremulation of the spirit, even though this pain has not yet been seen or felt. Instead, it is precisely because the pain is not yet an actuality that fear and anxiety can proliferate boundlessly. This is precisely the origin of religion and superstition, the shady function of which is then named 'myth'.

As regards this myth which mass-produces the troubled spirit, Deleuze points out that it is based on the 'false infinite'. The false infinite is an infinity simply by virtue of its being *limitless*. And this infinite whispers to us, 'try as you might, there will always be things you will never understand', in order to magnify anxiety and fear. However steadfast one's certainties, when this false infinite is preached, one cannot but shudder in an inexorable anxiety. And one who shudders in this way will seek to flee their fear by crying out to power. In turn, those in power will take advantage of this to exercise their rule, and the ruled will wallow in a false contentment, under the illusion that their soul has come to rest. To that extent, those who incite fear and anxiety are the sidekicks of the powers-that-be.

The mere avoidance of pain is a relatively facile problem. By contrast, wrote Lucretius: '[o]ur pleasures face obstacles stronger than our pains themselves: phantasies, superstitions, terrors, the fear of death, in short whatsoever might trouble the spirit' (Deleuze 1961: 25).[1] The philosopher-poet wanted to know how to liberate people from myth and the troubled spirit that it nourishes. According to Deleuze, for this we need to make use of the idea of 'nature'.

Research Note I: On Naturalism

Nature here is not a vacuous synonym of the totality of phenomena. Rather, it is an idea which teaches distinction. What things belong to nature, and what things do not: it is this distinction that the idea of nature teaches.

To define nature is notoriously difficult, but Deleuze explains it as follows. Nature is not opposed to 'custom', for there exist customs which are natural. Neither is nature to be opposed to 'convention', for however firmly rights seem to be grounded in convention, we can imagine such things as natural rights. And nor does nature oppose itself to 'invention'; after all, is not invention precisely the discovery of nature herself? But what nature does oppose itself to is 'myth'. '[M]an's unhappiness comes not from his customs, conventions, inventions, or industry, but from the side of myth which is mixed with them, and from the false infinite which it introduces into his feelings and his works' (LS, 314/322).

In this way, to paint the image of the free man requires that we have a working idea of nature. And no other mode of enquiry save philosophy is capable of discovering this idea of nature. About this Deleuze has an intransigent conviction: 'The first philosopher is a naturalist: he speaks about nature, rather than speaking about the gods' (LS, 315/323).

Note

1. Translator's note: These words of Lucretius are quoted in one of Deleuze's very earliest essays, 'Lucretius and Naturalism', published in the journal *Les Etudes Philosophiques* in 1961. This was later included as one of the essays comprising the Appendix to *The Logic of Sense* (1968), but only after extensive revisions – so much so that the different versions can and should be read as two separate pieces altogether.

2

Principle: Transcendental Empiricism

In the previous chapter we attempted to clarify the topology of Deleuze's philosophy. Deleuze's work is but a relentless interpretation of other philosophers and writers; yet, we cannot help but read these interpretations as positing an original 'Deleuzian philosophy', and indeed we have seen that this interpretive hunch is fully validated.

This realisation we derived from a careful analysis of Deleuze's preferred mode of speech, the free indirect discourse. In undertaking the history of philosophy, Deleuze aims to sketch out the plane (which he called the 'plane of immanence') upon which the thought of the philosopher under consideration resides, and examine the network of concepts to be found there. For this it is not enough to restate what the philosopher has already said, since the philosopher's thought stretches beyond the level of his or her consciousness. The history of philosophy must rather burrow further, to reach the implicit assumptions of the expressly articulated content, or what Deleuze calls the 'image of thought'. Free indirect discourse, which plays on the undecidability between the theorist and the theorised, was deployed for this purpose.

We remember that Deleuze defined philosophy as the 'creation of concepts'; but no concept is ever created in a vacuum. A new concept is created only when a new problem is discovered, and a new problem is in turn only discovered when an existing problem is criticised. In short, as we have seen, '[i]n philosophy the question and the critique of the question are one' (ES, 106/119). To attain the 'image of thought' is to come face to face with the originary problem which motivated a given philosophy. And when one has successfully critiqued this problem, thereby positing a new problem of one's own, this is when the conditions are ripe for new concepts to be created as a response to this new problem. It is clear that the use of free indirect discourse in this way follows inexorably from Deleuze's philosophical vision.

With preparatory work complete, and armed with an understanding of both the 'where' and 'how' of Deleuzian philosophy, we must

Principle: Transcendental Empiricism

now move on to the question of 'what'. Using free indirect discourse, Deleuze discussed a plethora of philosophers. What problems did he discover in the process, or equivalently, what problems did he criticise in the process? In other words: what concepts did he criticise, and what concepts of his own did he create? What, then, is Deleuzian philosophy?

Transcendental Philosophy, Empiricist Philosophy

We have seen that Deleuze's first monograph was a study on David Hume. How are we to understand this perhaps surprising point of departure?

The textbooks of philosophy tell us that Hume developed a philosophy of 'empiricism'. The name is self-explanatory: empiricism seeks the foundation of human reason and knowledge in empirical experience. Empiricism's self-professed nemesis was Continental rationalism, which placed at the foundation of philosophy a principle alien to experience, like the Cogito. Empiricism rejects such a move, and instead proposes to construct a philosophy rooted in the world of experience. As a result, the general assessment is that empiricism lends itself naturally to conservatism: for we should expect to find, in a philosophy which founds itself in a world of experience, a thinking which affirms the presently existing world. It might even be thought that, in contradistinction, it is therefore rationalism which is capable of accommodating radical, revolutionary thinking. Surely a philosophy which posits a non-experiential first principle would lend itself more readily to a repudiation of the presently existing world of experience?

It is precisely this stale prejudice of 'empiricism as conservatism' that Deleuze wordlessly undoes at the outset of *Empiricism and Subjectivity*. Deleuze formulates the problem at the centre of Hume's thought with acute concision: 'the question which will preoccupy Hume is this: *how does the mind become human nature?*' (ES, 22/2; original emphasis). The implication of this problem is as clear as it is relevant: what we term 'human nature' is but the effect of a prior genetic process, hence in any theory of humankind it is wrong to assume even its existence, let alone proceed as if we know what it consists of. The same problem is also rephrased: 'how does the mind become a subject?' (ES, 23/3). Here the 'mind' is a mere bundle of ideas, and the 'subject' comes about when these ideas are systematised through association. Immediately, the vulgar image of a pre-existing subject on the receiving end of sensations from the outside is cast away. The mind is nothing more than a disparate collection of ideas; it is not even the container for such ideas. There is an 'identity between the mind and the ideas in the mind' (ES, 23/3). A system with 'constancy and uniformity' comes into existence only when these disparate ideas making up the mind are associated with each other according to certain principles. The three principles of association are said to be 'contiguity', 'resemblance' and 'cause and effect'; only when the association of ideas based on these principles passes a critical point do we have a subject, *over and above* the mind as the given state.

What Deleuze finds in Hume is a perspective which does not assume the subject, a perspective which instead questions its *genesis*: 'the psychology of affections[1] becomes the philosophy of the constituted subject. Rationalism has lost this philosophy' (ES, 30/13). Rationalism takes the subject as a given. In stark contrast, empiricism problematises precisely that which rationalism had taken for granted. It understands the subject itself as but the *effect of a prior process of constitution*. To that extent, it is actually rationalism that is conservative, since it decides a zero point beyond which it ceases to exercise any suspicion. The same can be said for the notion of 'human nature': '[t]he mind is not nature, nor does it have a nature' (ES, 22/3). Human nature arises rather as a mere effect of the association of ideas. And, crucially, this means that a different association of ideas will generate a quite *different human nature*.[2] The same can be said once again for reason: 'the mind is not reason; reason is an affection of the mind. In this sense, reason will be called instinct, habit, or nature' (ES, 30/14). Take nothing for granted, whether it be subject, nature or reason; instead pursue to the ends of the earth the question of genesis. Correspondingly, to problematise genesis is to think the possibility of change, the conditions of possibility of change. What Deleuze sees in Hume is a philosophy which inquires into the possibility of changing the concepts which philosophy has always taken for granted.

But why did Deleuze read Humean empiricism from this perspective? And why did he have to set off from Hume in the first place? Deleuze's name is of course usually associated with Spinozism and Bergsonism. Such a doxa however seems utterly incompatible with the reality of Deleuze, austere scholar of Hume. For this reason we wish to dwell on this starting-point of Deleuze's intellectual journey a little longer. Once again, why did Deleuze read Humean empiricism from the perspective of genesis?

Principle: Transcendental Empiricism

In the textbooks, Humean empiricism is typically portrayed as having paved the way for Kant's Transcendental Idealism. It was Hume's philosophy, assuming neither subject nor nature nor reason, taking all causality to be open to doubt, which in Kant's own words awoke him from his mythical 'dogmatic slumber'. But Kant was ultimately led (for reasons different from those of Bergson touched upon in the previous chapter) to reject Humean associationism. According to Kant, unless phenomena 'really' display a regularity which is available to subjectivity, the association of ideas could not take place. More concretely: we say, 'the sun will rise tomorrow'. But trivially, this 'tomorrow' is not-yet, indeed insofar as it is 'tomorrow' it must forever be not-yet. All we are given is the fact that hitherto, right up to this morning, the sun has always risen. In spite of this, we inexorably go beyond the individual ideas ('yesterday, the sun also rose'; 'the day before yesterday, the sun rose as well' . . .) to affirm a positive claim about 'tomorrow'. There is an abyss that must be leapt over here, what Hume would call 'belief'. Knowledge is thus grounded on a *beyond* which cannot be reduced to the givens of experience. '[W]e say *more* than is given to us, we go *beyond* what is given in experience' (KCP, 11/19; original emphases). It is at this point that Kant inserts his criticism: for this belief to arise, it must be grounded in experience. Trivially, if the sun sometimes rose and sometimes took a break on whim, there could be no knowledge of any kind.[3] Hence, it is impossible to base knowledge, let alone the principle of causality, on an act of subjective construction. Or so Kant thought.

Now Deleuze accepts the validity of this critique of Hume.[4] However, he does not subscribe to the over-rehearsed narrative that Kant superseded Hume, instead opting to place the two philosophies alongside each other in a strikingly original move. The relevant section is the fifth chapter of *Empiricism and Subjectivity*, bearing the same title as the monograph itself. In what can be read as an overview of the entire work, Deleuze makes the following declaration, almost out of the blue: '[w]e could say that philosophy in general has always sought a plane[5] of analysis [*plan d'analyse*]' (ES, 87/92). The term 'plane of analysis' was dropped from Deleuze's philosophical lexicon thereafter, its function no doubt passed onto the more familiar 'plane of immanence' (we can reasonably suppose that the figure of the 'plane' was deployed to avoid conceiving of the history of philosophy as a Euclidean straight line). From here, Deleuze emphasises that each philosophy situates itself on a different plane, *depending on the problem it is a response to*.

We are given two examples of such planes in the history of philosophy. If we place ourselves on 'a methodologically reduced plane', the question we are prompted to answer is 'how can there be a given?', or 'how can something be given to a subject?' This is the Kantian plane of analysis. Kant had rejected the traditional metaphysical ideal of a correspondence between subjective and objective poles (*adequatio rei et intellectus*): phenomena, as the appearance of the thing-in-itself (object), are henceforth subordinated to the cognitive capacity of the subject. The subject is then incapable of knowing the thing-in-itself, and knowledge is redefined accordingly as knowledge of appearances, based on the categories inherent to the subject. In other words, Kant's first critique is precisely an answer to the question of the condition of possibility of the given, its givenness to a subject. Deleuze is unequivocal on this point: henceforth, '[w]e embark upon a transcendental critique' (ES, 87/92).

On the other hand, if one places oneself in 'a purely immanent point of view', the question to be resolved becomes: 'how is the subject constituted in the given?' We have now set foot onto the Humean plane. The answer to this problem is none other than the mechanism whereby the subject comes into being through the leap of faith beyond the given, explained above. On this plane, the subject is no longer taken for granted, but becomes yet another element to be constituted. For Deleuze, empiricist philosophy was the first to ask this question, unprecedented in the history of philosophy. From this point on, '[t]he critique is empirical' (ES, 87/92).

Crucially, Deleuze does not think that the 'empirical' critique was superseded by the 'transcendental' critique. By clarifying that they each exist on a different 'plane', he rather shows how the two can be juxtaposed. It is of course undeniable that Kant's critique of Hume led to his discovery of an entirely new problem, and this small step was decisive for the history of philosophy. And yet, nevertheless, *there is a problem that Kant in turn stopped posing*. Needless to say, this is the problem of the genesis of the subject itself. The subject, whose genesis is precisely that which needs to be investigated and discovered, is assumed by Kant as a new 'given'; indeed, the specific problem of the Kantian plane, 'how can something be given to a subject', does not even make sense unless the subject is itself treated as a 'given'.

It is perhaps worth introducing some Kantian terminology at this point. Kant was the first to open up the 'transcendental' as a domain of investigation. Transcendental philosophy is concerned with what is

Principle: Transcendental Empiricism

prior to experience, the condition not of the object of experience, but of experience as such. Transcendental investigation seeks to discover the *conditions of possibility of experience*. Ten years after his study on Hume, in *Kant's Critical Philosophy*, Deleuze was to define this as follows: '"[t]ranscendental" qualifies the principle of necessary subjection of what is given in experience to our *a priori* representations' (KCP, 13/22). The '*a priori* representations' are those which we possess innately, prior to any cognition: concretely, the forms of time and space under which the senses receive the multiplicity of sensation from the external world, and the 'categories', namely the series of concepts employed by the faculty of understanding to generate cognition (though of these two only the latter is a 'representation' in the strict sense). For Kant, it is a 'fact of cognition' that we possess such *a priori* representation. No further demonstration is required beyond observing that when we have knowledge, or pass judgement, we do *in fact* receive the external world under the forms of time and space, and we do *in fact* use a whole array of conceptual categories, such as cause/effect and possible/impossible.

In contrast to such 'questions of fact (*quid facti*)', there is a level which Kant terms the 'question of right (*quid juris*)'. This is the problem of how it is possible to apply such *a priori* figures (the forms of the sensibility and the concepts of the understanding) onto experience, given that they are not derived *from* experience. Moreover, what we are dealing here is a necessity and a universality: the 'facts of cognition' reveal that our experience *necessarily* conforms to these representations. How is this possible, indeed, *how is it possible for such a thing to be possible*? The 'transcendental' is the name of the principle underlying this entire mechanism. In the terms in which we initially introduced the matter, it problematises how something like experience is possible in the first place.

Now Deleuze thinks very highly of Kant's discovery of the transcendental domain. But for precisely this reason, he is compelled to pry open the *lacunae* of Kant's version of transcendental philosophy. Fifteen years after *Empiricism and Subjectivity*, in his masterwork submitted for the *doctorat d'état*, *Difference and Repetition* (1968), Deleuze points out the following: '[f]or Kant as for Descartes, it is the identity of the Self in the "I think" which grounds the harmony of all the faculties and their agreement on the form of a supposed Same object' (DR, 169/174). Ever since *Kant's Critical Philosophy*, Deleuze has read the Kantian philosophical system as a 'system of permutations (*système de permutations*)' between the respective faculties (sensibility, imagination, understanding, reason), which exchange functions with each other depending on the purpose to be achieved.[6] The implicit assumption here is that the faculties will work together in cooperation; what Deleuze takes issue with is the fact that this confidence is founded on the 'self-identity of the "I"'. But this can only be a theoretical sleight of hand: '[i]t is clear that, in this manner, Kant *traces [décalquer]* the so-called transcendental structures from the empirical acts of a psychological consciousness' (DR, 171/176–7; my emphasis). The transcendental domain must ground the empirical; yet Kant, in his portraiture of the transcendental, substitutes a carbon copy of the empirical as if tracing over translucent paper. Which is why the 'I', of which we are experientially aware, is allowed to reappear as a phantom shadow in the transcendental realm. In this way Kant's account of the transcendental remains contaminated by impurities left over from experience. Worse, Kant never pauses to question the genesis of this 'I' (named 'transcendental apperception' in the Kantian system), he merely posits/assumes it as something which must necessarily be thought to exist.

The Logic of Sense, published the following year, takes over where the earlier critique of Kant's introduction of the 'the personal form of an I, or the synthetic unity of apperception' into the transcendental had left off (LS, 120/128). In the same vein, Edmund Husserl (1859–1938), who critically inherited Kant's transcendental project, is taken to task for 'inscrib[ing] in the transcendental field centres of individuation and individual systems, monads, and points of view, and *Selves* in the manner of Leibniz' (LS, 112–13/121) (though Deleuze does appreciate the reference to Leibniz); so too Jean-Paul Sartre (1905–1980), Husserl's critical heir, this time for trying to smuggle in 'consciousness' (LS, 114n5, 118, 120–1/120n5, 124, 128). Husserl, and Sartre after him, were unable to shake off the shackles of Kant's methodological procedure, in effect merely trying out so many different versions of 'transcendental apperception'. Deleuze's critique of Kantian and post-Kantian transcendental investigation is encapsulated in the following formula from *The Logic of Sense*: '[t]he foundation can never resemble what it founds' (LS, 112/120).

To summarise what we have learnt so far: Deleuze had begun his career with a study on Hume. Now this reading of Hume exists in a state of tension with Kantian philosophy. Of course Deleuze understands that Kant's criticism of Hume is decisive (which is why in both his studies, on Hume and on Kant, this criticism is given pride of place); further, Deleuze rates very highly the fact that this criticism

Principle: Transcendental Empiricism

in turn opened up the possibility of a 'transcendental' investigation (which is why he traces the development of Kant's transcendental inheritance minutely, to bring to light its deficiency). But for precisely this reason he was compelled to point out the fatal flaw in post-Kantian transcendental philosophy, namely: the oblivion of genesis. The transcendental is what grounds the empirical; and yet, post-Kantian transcendental philosophy contented itself with 'tracing' the transcendental from the empirical, putting aside the problem of genesis. It is precisely this genetic perspective that Deleuze discovered in Hume: what was lost in the historical progression from Hume to Kant is none other than this problem of genesis. And as we have seen, to ask after genesis is in turn to ask after change, the condition of possibility of change. All of which necessitates the following conclusion: in the last instance it is transcendental philosophy which, in no longer asking the question of genesis, has foreclosed the problem of the possibility of change.

The task Deleuze assigned to philosophy then becomes: be faithful to the possibilities opened up by transcendental philosophy, while compensating for what it has forgotten by using empiricist philosophy. In other words, philosophy must be a 'transcendental empiricism (*L'empirisme transcendental*)': first introduced in *Difference and Repetition*, and revisited in his final text 'Immanence: A Life . . .', the term is a veritable oxymoron, but it is programmatic for this philosophy which radically seeks to synthesise the transcendental and the empirical. And this for the simple reason that what philosophy needs is a transcendentalism that can actually problematise genesis.

From this standpoint, Deleuze's thought displays an astonishing consistency. The project of transcendental empiricism had already existed in nascent form in his 1953 maiden work, *Empiricism and Subjectivity*. By his 1968 work *Difference and Repetition*, this had blossomed into the conviction that transcendental empiricism is the only method proper to transcendental portraiture.[7] *The Logic of Sense*, his other masterwork published the following year, made substantial this conviction through its vigorous critique of Kant: in order to sketch a transcendental realm discharged of such impurities as 'I (*moi*)', 'individual (*individu*)' and 'person (*personne*)', Deleuze chose to deploy such concepts as 'sense (*sens*)', 'event (*événement*)' and 'singularity (*singularité*)'. And until the end of life, more than two decades later, he was to remain fixated on the relation of the transcendental and the empirical: *What is Philosophy?*, published in 1991, declares that it is only 'a radical empiricism' that is capable of portraying the transcendental.⁸ This thesis, that the transcendental is the exclusive privilege of transcendental empiricism, was to be upheld up to the final text published in his lifetime, 'Immanence: A Life ...'.⁹ The above is therefore overwhelming evidence to assert that the principle of Deleuzian philosophy is none other than transcendental empiricism. At the foundation of Deleuzian philosophy lies a transcendental empiricist inspiration. Hence the question which next impresses itself upon us is: what is this transcendental empiricism?

Addendum on Kant

Kantian philosophy lacks the perspective of genesis; hence Deleuze, although assessing this philosophy highly, had to make good this *lacuna* with a different philosophy. This has been our narrative hitherto. However, this was presented with the express purpose of clarifying what aspects of what philosophy Deleuze criticised, and what concepts he set out to create in this way. If one is to take up Deleuze's interpretation of Kant in itself, matters become more complicated.

For one, there is the very real possibility that Kant himself was aware of the need for a genetic method. Indeed, not only were the critiques of the so-called post-Kantians (Salomon Maimon, Johann Gottlieb Fichte . . .) directed towards the lack of a genetic method in Kant, these critiques were contemporaneous with Kantianism itself. For instance, Kant's *Critique of Judgement* and Maimon's *Essay on Transcendental Philosophy* were published in the same year, 1790. It is not difficult to ascertain from this the reason why Deleuze regarded the philosophies of the post-Kantians Maimon and Fichte so highly.[10]

Now Deleuze sees in the *Critique of Judgement* a Kant wrestling to uncover an opening into genesis. Let us trace just the outlines. In his book on Kant, Deleuze portrays Kant's critical philosophy as a 'system of permutations', where the four faculties of sensibility, understanding, imagination and reason – mainly the latter three 'active faculties' – interchange their respective roles and combinatorial order to perform an entirely different function. In cognition, for example, reason yields to understanding its dominant position, but takes it back in the domain of practice: in this way, each faculty shifts its 'formation' according to its designated function. Indeed, Deleuze's attachment to the system of permutations is quite unshakeable. It is rare for an introduction to Kant's philosophy to devote any explanation to the role of the understanding in reason's practical interest (the faculty of desire). (Take, for example, Ernst Cassirer's *Kant's Life and Thought*, still seen as the standard primer to Kantian philosophy. Cassirer explicates in greater detail than Deleuze each of the *Critiques*, but says nothing about the role of the understanding in Kant's ethics.) Rather it is the categorical imperative, the meaning of the good in Kant, or the feeling of respect for the moral law, that typically populate the pages of such works. But Deleuze barely touches upon such issues (indeed the famous categorical imperative is left without any sort of

Principle: Transcendental Empiricism

explanation at all). And yet the role of the understanding in the faculty of desire is examined in the minutest of detail. It is precisely this which constitutes the peculiarity of *Kant's Critical Philosophy*, otherwise so tightly composed.

Through a focus on the system of permutations, the following problem crouching in the underside of Kantian philosophy is made apparent. For the four faculties differ at the level of essence. Such essentially different faculties, nevertheless, manage to work *in concert* to bring about a unifying function. But does this not mean that Kant smuggles in a pre-established harmony to ensure the accord of the four essentially different faculties? According to Deleuze, this difficulty is not dealt with in the first two *Critiques*. In these, the accord of the faculties is merely *presumed*. It is instead in the *Critique of Judgement* that we are given an account of how the faculties each work independently, without any one of them occupying a dominant position (unlike in cognition, where it is the understanding that leads, or in the faculty of desire, where reason presides), and yet achieve an accord. In fact it is just this that makes possible the harmony of the faculties.

What brings about this harmony is none other than the interest reason displays towards the beauty of nature. 'The accord between imagination as free and understanding as indeterminate is therefore not merely assumed: it is in a sense animated, enlivened, engendered by the interest of the beautiful' (KCP, 55/79). 'We experience a rational interest in the contingent accord of nature's productions with our disinterested pleasure' (KCP, 54/78). Only because of our interest in the beauty of nature can the various faculties attain in their freedom a cooperation, despite the difference in their respective essences. And only thanks to this free accord, in turn, can the faculties act in concert in their speculative and practical interests. How then does interest in the beautiful, or equivalently the contingent coincidence of nature and our faculties, come about? It is impossible, insists Kant, to find the answer on the side of nature. In his rather quirky turn of phrase, 'it is we who receive nature with favour, and not nature that does us a favour' (KCP, 65/93). In the last instance, as Deleuze writes, 'the final relationship between Nature and man is the result of a human practical activity' (KCP, 69/99). What is termed here 'human practical activity' is then alighted in the direction of 'history': a history wherein man, as the moral being he is, realises freedom in nature. By this point, not only has the internal problem of the accord between the faculties been externalised into the problem of their accord with nature, it is interpolated via history into the future. In this way Deleuze's account of Kant's philosophy draws to a close with Kant's philosophy of history. Astonishingly, we find here an expression whose Hegelian resonances are unmistakable: the 'ruse of nature' (KCP, Conclusion).

Though Deleuze was to come back to Kant time and again after the publication of *Kant's Critical Philosophy*, he would not say anything more on the place of history in Kant's thinking. Was Deleuze finally satisfied with this account, which Kant had scripted as the explication of genesis? There is no doubt that the issue is a fascinating one, especially given the extreme scarcity of Deleuze's remarks on the philosophy of history. But we cannot concern ourselves with this problem any longer, nor can we continue to dwell on the relation between Deleuze and post-Kantian philosophy. For ultimately that is not where the interest of this book lies. Yes, Deleuze's philosophy undoubtedly exhibits a strongly post-Kantian dimension, but as we shall see in the next chapter, for our part we wish to investigate why it is that Deleuze chose not to abide with, precisely, such a 'Deleuzian' philosophy. It is only so as to constitute *this* question as a substantial problem in itself, and thereby to draw out its answer, that we have thus far reminded ourselves, with impatient haste, of Deleuze's transcendental empiricism, with its strong post-Kantian inheritance.

Desert Islands

Transcendental empiricism was conceived in order to move beyond the Kantian variation of transcendental philosophy. At root, this was due to a dissatisfaction at the lack of a viable genetic perspective. Kant was criticised for illegitimately assuming what he could not (functions such as the 'I' and 'transcendental apperception'), and in the process letting go of the question of genesis. In re-problematising genesis, then, what comes before these functions Kant took for granted, what lies at their foundation?

A world prior to the self, a world without the self. To theorise this, Deleuze introduces the rather peculiar image of the 'desert island (*île déserte*)'. And from a very early stage in his career, at that. The idea first appears in a manuscript of the same name (DI, 9–14/11–17), completed in the 1950s but not published until decades later. When Deleuze completed this text he had only his book on Hume to his name. It had originally been penned as part of a magazine feature on 'desert islands', but for whatever reason it was finally not included. Interestingly, when in 1989, near the end of his life, Deleuze drew up a bibliography of his complete works, this short piece was placed within the problematic genealogy leading up to *Difference and Repetition*.[11] This little detail demonstrates that Deleuze attached sizeable importance to this text; it would be rash, therefore, to brush it aside as a youthful misadventure. Indeed, this same topic is taken up again near the conclusion to *Difference and Repetition*, and a discussion on the exact same theme is included in the Appendix to *The Logic of Sense* (the importance of this latter piece is beyond doubt).[12] All the circumstantial evidence, coupled with the actual content itself, provides ample grounds to situate this text at the origin of Deleuzian

Principle: Transcendental Empiricism

philosophy, that is, as the veritable preface to the Deleuzian project of transcendental empiricism.

'Desert Islands' is a strange piece of writing. The discussion sets off from the geographical distinction between continental and oceanic islands; a deeply obscure (presumably philosophical) thesis is introduced: 'that an island is deserted must appear *philosophically normal to us*' (DI, 9/11; original emphasis). Deleuze then attempts to grasp the essence of this figure of the desert island in a uniquely imaginative way. Two classics from the genre of 'desert island literature' (if such we may call it) are touched upon: Jean Giraudoux's *Suzanne and the Pacific* (1921) affirmatively, and Daniel Defoe's *Robinson Crusoe* (1719) critically. Following which we are given a sort of critique of myth, and the short essay abruptly comes to a close. It is not possible to sift through the entire text here, since in the space of a mere six pages the theme shifts at the blink of an eye from geography to philosophy to literature to mythology, each highly concentrated. We will restrict ourselves to the task at hand, setting up this piece as the preface to transcendental empiricism. Central for our purposes is the line quoted above, indicating that the present discussion has a 'philosophical' bearing. Several lines later, we are presented with the even more enigmatic paradox that '[a]n island doesn't stop being deserted simply because it is inhabited' (DI, 10/12). And to top it all off: 'every island [is] and remain[s] in theory deserted' (DI, 10/12).

What are we to make of such puzzling formulations? The key is in the word 'desert (*désert*)', from which Deleuze extracts a 'philosophical' meaning. Desertion, trivially, admits of no people; by contrast, when there are people, the island becomes an *object* inhabited by people who are correspondingly *subjects*. Deleuze's point is then the following: even if a lone individual happens to wash up onto a deserted island, it is doubtful whether such a state of 'non-desertion' (that is, a state with 'subjects' dwelling on an 'object') will immediately come into effect. When one translates desertion into 'philosophical' terms, therefore, it is a world with neither subject nor object. And for this state of desertion to break down, it is not enough for people to start living there. Until such time as the categories of subject and object (which define the state of non-desertion) appear, as if by a certain leap, the desert island will remain deserted. In a real sense then, its state of desertion is independent of whether it happens to be populated or not. Which is why Deleuze also says the following: '[s]uch a creature on a desert island would be the deserted island itself, insofar as it imagines and reflects itself in its first movement' (DI, 11/13).

Now unless we have made it onto your prized list of 'desert island' volumes, so to speak, the preceding must have been dense and mysterious. Let us therefore turn our attention to another essay of Deleuze's dealing with the same theme. In 'A Theory of the Other (Michel Tournier)', first published in 1967 in the journal *Critique* and later included in the Appendix to *The Logic of Sense* with the title 'Michel Tournier and the World Without Others', Deleuze explains this paradox of the desert island more theoretically. The immediate context is a piece of literary criticism on Michel Tournier's (1924–2016) novel, *Friday, or, The Other Island* (1967), itself a retelling of Defoe's *Robinson Crusoe* from a quasi-philosophical perspective, after he is shipwrecked on a desert island. Nonetheless, it is clear from Deleuze's decision to construct his reading around the concept of the 'Other' that this later work shares the same basic motivation as 'Desert Islands'. In many ways 'Michel Tournier' is a mature redevelopment of the earlier essay; indeed the 'Other', which previously had remained germinal, has now explicitly come to the fore.

The essay on Tournier predicates Robinson as 'the man without Others on his island' (LS, 344/354). Trivially, you might say with a smirk. But try imagining this for a second. What must it be like, living on an 'island without the Other'? Is this even within the bounds of the imagination? For in our day to day life we inhabit precisely a world with others. Our spontaneous imagination of the desert island, then, is inevitably one merely extrapolated from this world which is full to the brim with other people. Concisely put, it is but a desertion fantasised from the standpoint of a fundamental non-desertion. Given that we inescapably inhabit the latter state, we always-already take the Other for granted; in particular we take a certain 'effect' brought about by the existence of the Other for granted. Unless we have carefully unravelled these effects, then, we will be forever condemned to project non-desertion onto desertion.[13] If we truly seek to 'become' Robinson, that forlorn 'creature on a desert island' we must first clarify this 'effect' brought about by alterity. We must analyse this effect of the Other, presumed in advance by our non-deserted existence, if only to discharge it from our work of imagination.

We can formulate the effect of the Other as follows: every time we perceive an object or think of an idea, it is the Other that organises a world around it. The horizon of what I can see in a single glance is necessarily limited. Looking up at a building from the street, all

Principle: Transcendental Empiricism

I can see is its façade. Why then do we spontaneously believe that an actual building continues beyond this front wall, that there exist rooms and corridors behind it? We can think, believe and assume all these things, because '[t]he part of the object that I do not see I posit as visible to Others' (LS, 344/355). Only because I take the Other for granted can I process the unseen 'rest of the object' as nonetheless *visible to the Other*. This is of course the condition of possibility of space, but that is not all. My vision is beset by numerous blind spots, for instance I cannot see the front and back of an object simultaneously. In order for me to see the back, a certain amount of *time* has to go by during which I move myself physically about the object in question. Only because I take the Other for granted can I process the object as *continuing* to exist through time. The world organised by the Other thus has the function of constituting this movement in time, which Deleuze describes as the 'laws of transition which regulate the passage from one [object] to another' (LS, 344/354). Only because we can assume, following this principle, 'that when I will have walked around to reach this hidden part, I will have joined the Others behind the object, and I will have totalised it in the way that I had already anticipated' (LS, 344–5/355), can we conceive of the whole of an object based on our partial perspective of it. It is but a minuscule piece of the world that comes under our field of vision. Nevertheless we believe the world to exist: this is because we always-already place ourselves within the spatio-temporal effects brought about by the Other.

Based on the above, we are able to formulate a definition of the Other: the Other is that without which perception would collapse, the 'structure of the perceptual field' (LS, 346/357). In other words, it is what guarantees the objectiality of the object, and *not in itself an object within the perceptual field*. We know by now why this is the case: if the Other were not to exist, the perceptual field itself, and hence the very objectiality of the object, would disintegrate. And that is not all. If the Other alone can maintain the objectiality of the object, where there is no Other *it is impossible to posit something like a self*. The Self is not an *a priori* self-sustaining entity: analogically to the object, it is only because consciousness can depend on the Other's memory of how 'I was (*j'étais*)', with which to posit the 'I' as a changing yet persisting object, that the self can arise. In other words, the self is nothing more grand than 'my past objects (*mes objets passés*)'.[14] It is not the self, the subject, which makes possible the rendering-objective of the external world, rather it is the attainment of this objectivising function that retroactively gives rise to the self. As a result, it is not enough to liberate the Other from among the objects of the perceptual field: if the Other is no object, neither is it a subject who perceives me. For the very division into subject/object of perception assumes the prior existence of the Other. Hence the apparent paradox that without the Other there is no self. We can thus say that the most fundamental effect of the Other is 'the distinction of my consciousness and its object'. 'This distinction is in fact the result of the structure-Other' (LS, 349/360). Needless to say, this proposition implies its inverse: '[i]n the Other's absence, consciousness and its object are one' (LS, 350/361).

We are now ready to think the theoretical/philosophical status of the figure of the desert island directly. The desert island admits of no Other. And when the Other is lacking, no one is there to fill the blanks in my perceptual horizon. It becomes impossible to assume that what is invisible to me nonetheless remains visible to someone else. That is, *what I cannot see quite simply does not exist*, or as Deleuze quotes Tournier's Robinson, 'what I do not see of [the island] is . . . a total unknown' (LS, 345/355). And further: since there is no Other, there can be no self either. 'The distinction of my consciousness and its object' slips away. 'Consciousness and its object are one.' This is why the lone creature on a desert island is 'the desert island itself'. 'The island would be only the dream of humans, and humans, the pure consciousness of the island' (DI, 10/13).

'Desert' designates such a mythical situation, without others and hence no self. Recall the paradoxical formulation in 'Desert Islands', that '[a]n island doesn't stop being deserted simply because it is inhabited'. We can now state why this is the case: mere habitation is not enough, because for the desertion of the desert island to give way, we require the Other *qua* structure of the perceptual field. For it is the Other that brings about the division between myself and the objectile world. Lacking the Other, no such division can take place. Instead of there being the self as subject and the island as object, all we have is a 'unity of the deserted island and its inhabitants' (DI, 11/13).[15]

We would be entirely justified in understanding the above as a theory of the genesis of time and space as the intuitive forms of the senses, indeed as a theory of the genesis of the self/subject who receives the world in its multiplicity based on these forms. Recall that Deleuze had criticised Kant for assuming such functions as the self and transcendental apperception. But he did not stop there, for he used this critique as a stepping stone to develop a genuine genetic

Principle: Transcendental Empiricism

theory of self and space-time. What must not escape our attention is that this theorisation had begun from an insight of Humean inspiration. The previous quotation from 'Desert Islands' continues as follows: 'The unity of the deserted island and its inhabitants is thus not actual, only imaginary, like the idea of looking behind the curtain when one is not behind it' (DI, 11/13–14). The metaphor of the curtain here is but a more poetic evocation of the foundation of experience in alterity, which we saw with respect to Tournier: 'the part of the object that I do not see I posit as visible to Others'. We can go one step further however, for to think that the other side of the curtain, invisible to me, is nevertheless visible to the Other is a matter of *belief*. Insofar as Hume explained the transformation of the given (the side of the curtain we can see) through the function of belief, it can be seen that Deleuze's theory of the desert island sets off from a fundamentally Humean inspiration. And yet, over and above this proximity there is a blazing novelty in Deleuze's account: the introduction of the 'Other'. If knowledge is a function of belief, belief in turn is only ever a function of the Other. Thus, in fleshing out the desert island via a critique of Kant, Deleuze simultaneously undertakes a critique of Hume. The leap out of the given through belief, which Hume was content simply to assume as a fact of cognition, has its own genesis problematised in turn through the role of the Other. Indeed, the study on Tournier even states as follows: '[i]n short, the Other assures the margins and transitions in the world. He is the sweetness of contiguities and resemblances' (LS, 345/355). Needless to say, 'contiguity' and 'resemblance' are two of the Humean principles underlying association. It is true that Hume had 'explained' the association of ideas, or the leap beyond the given, through these principles (resemblance: 'the picture leading our thoughts to the original'; contiguity: 'one room in a building leading us to a discourse concerning the others'). But when push comes to shove, these principles are merely posited as facts of cognition, facts we do not really understand, but always seem to stumble across when we analyse knowledge. Deleuze drives the proverbial nail into this lack of intellectual rigour, by establishing the 'Other' as in turn the genetic foundation of these principles. Which ultimately leads him to assert that man can never become one with the movement forming the island; in reality, 'they always encounter [the island] from the outside, and their presence in fact spoils its desertedness' (DI, 11/13). It is only because the desertion of the island has always-already been '(de)spoilt' that the objectiality of the object, the structure of perception, the self and apperception, all these mechanisms seem always-already to be in place. All the concepts Kant took for granted in fact spring from the Other who comes from some place beyond.

Event

The desert island is thus 'pre-history' for the transcendental empiricist. Once the Other has rudely set foot onto this desertion, only then does our familiar world of experience kick into place. The next question we must ask, then, is how the transcendental is to be reconstituted and reinterpreted. By definition, the transcendental is what grounds the empirical. What then, in brief, *is* the transcendental? This is none other than a question concerning the very subject matter of transcendental empiricism.

To begin at the end: for Deleuze, the transcendental is the 'event (*événement*)', or synonymously, 'singularity (*singularité*)'. 'Singularities are the true transcendental events' (LS, 118/125). In his eyes the two become interchangeable, hence the use of the hyphenated hybrid 'singularity-event (*singularité-événement*)'. As it stands, however, this reconfiguration of the transcendental does not even sound plausible. Indeed, much intellectual effort had to be expended before such an unprecedented concept of the event could come about. Let us follow in Deleuze's footsteps without faltering.

The origin of this concept of the event was the philosophy of Gottfried Wilhelm Leibniz (1648–1716),[16] in particular his theory of possible worlds. The possible world is primarily a way of thinking. Leibniz's favourite example is of course Caesar's crossing of the Rubicon. We who reside in this actual world know this as a historical fact. However, at the same time we are capable of conceiving its opposite: that Caesar did not cross the Rubicon does not, *in and of itself*, constitute a contradiction.[17] After all, for all sorts of reasons Caesar might not have crossed the Rubicon. We are able to imagine a world where the river of no return was not transgressed: Leibniz's suggestion is to reformulate this as 'in a possible world, Caesar did not cross the Rubicon'.

Now what does it mean to say that there is no contradiction in and of itself in a Caesar who did not cross the Rubicon? Let us rephrase this question: what would this come into contradiction with? The answer is obvious: with this, our actual world. The collapse of the triumvirate, the immortal utterance '*alea iacta est* (the die is cast)', victory at the Battle of Pharsalus ... – the crossing of the Rubicon is an *event*, inextricably bound to an 'evental' series (*série*) comprising countless other events. A Caesar who turned his back to the Rubicon *cannot* take part in this world, wherein Caesar did not avert his gaze from destiny. Or in the appropriate jargon: a different evental series, foreclosed from this world, subtends from the Caesar who did not cross the Rubicon. Therefore, the Rubicon is one of an infinity of points at which the evental series irrevocably *diverges*. This impossibility of coexistence between divergent series is termed by Leibniz 'incompossibility'. The two worlds expressed by the two Caesars, our actual world and the other a possible world, are incompossible. By definition then, our actual world is made up solely of *compossible* evental series. More generally, a world is nothing but the 'convergence' of a bundle of compossible evental series. And correlatively, this means that all individuals are themselves in a relation of compossibility to the world. Which is why the Caesar who crossed the Rubicon can be said to 'express (*exprimer*)' this actual world.[18]

Leibniz goes on to say that the concept of the predicate is enveloped by that of the subject.[19] Thus, for example, the subject 'Caesar' contains within it the predicate 'crosses the Rubicon'. A word of caution here: this thesis emphatically does not say that the subject pre-exists in advance (like an empty container), to which predicates are subsequently attributed.[20] Allow us to explain. We saw that at each event the evental series undergoes a divergence. And each time the series diverges, this signifies that *a different individual has come into being*. Harking back to our example, at the event of Caesar's crossing of the Rubicon, we get on the one hand a 'Caesar' who contains the predicate (= event) 'crosses the Rubicon', and on the other hand a different 'Caesar' who contains the contradictory of this predicate (= event), 'does not cross the Rubicon' (the equivocation of the terms 'predicate' and 'event' follows Leibniz's own terminology[21]). As such, the subject does not exist in advance of the event. It is rather the event that precedes the subject, as the genetic condition of the subject. 'Individuals are constituted in the vicinity of singularities [events] which they envelop' (LS, 128/135).

Leibniz's achievement must be recognised for what it is: a genuine genetic theory of individual and world, through the concept of event. The worldview offered here is not a sterile determinism where everything is derived from the subject in natural deduction, but a fluid indetermination where the subject (grammatical, logical, metaphysical) is only ever the trace left behind by the verbal function of the event, and where the world must ceaselessly admit the advent of the event, indeed is nothing but the accumulation of these evental advents. It is understandable that Deleuze, who placed so much emphasis on portraying genesis, should have been fascinated by this philosophy. In fact, in *Difference and Repetition* and *The Logic of Sense* Deleuze devotes a copious number of pages to this philosopher of the Baroque, capping this off with a full monograph entitled *The Fold* (1988), published towards the end of his life.

Fascination was nonetheless to prove one step shy of outright veneration, for Deleuze was to diverge from Leibniz on a crucial point. If Leibniz had constructed an appealing philosophical system based on the theory of possible worlds, its potential went to waste because it was placed entirely at the service of validating God's choice of the 'best of all possible worlds'. Yes, reality could have turned out otherwise; but then why has it, in fact, turned out this way? Well, that's because God willed this world as optimal . . . An infinity of possible worlds made up of infinite variation in the convergence and divergence of the evental series: in the last instance the sole *raison d'être* of this infinity of possible worlds is to glorify the actual world, here and now. The entirety of Leibniz's metaphysics converges in order to uphold the *status quo*, thereby denaturing to mere apologetics. In particular, and with uncharacteristic ferocity, Deleuze attacks the fact that Leibniz 'assigns to philosophy the creation of new concepts, provided that they do not overthrow the "established sentiments"'.[22]

But if Deleuze expresses vehement disagreement with Leibniz in the last instance, this is not so as to discard the concepts created by this seventeenth-century philosopher *in toto*, but rather to construct for himself a concept of the event that had slipped through Leibniz's fingers, clasped as they were in pious submission. The task can thus be formulated as follows: emancipate the event as genetic principle from its subordination to the actual world. In other words, one must rediscover the mechanism of genesis that Leibniz had outlined with his theory of possible worlds, only this time *within the actual world itself*. The Logic of Sense declares this task as a shifting of the problem from 'static genesis (*genèse statique*)' to 'dynamic genesis (*genèse dynamique*)' (the former clearly refers to the Leibnizian theory of the event/series). 'It is no longer a question of a static genesis which would lead from the presupposed event to its actualisation in states of affairs and to its expression in propositions. It is a question of a dynamic genesis which leads directly from states of affairs to events' (LS, 214/217). Do not drive in reverse from the present world backwards to posit a past event, only to make a U-turn to ruminate on

Principle: Transcendental Empiricism

how this event could possibly have been actualised in the present world (if Caesar did cross the Rubicon, we can also imagine a possible world in which he did not, etc.); do instead question directly the relation between the advent of the event into actuality and this actuality itself.

Indeed we can reasonably suppose that the concept of 'virtuality (*virtualité*)', which has become something of a catchphrase for Deleuzian philosophy, was in fact created to accomplish just this task. For what it aims at is the deconstruction of the concept of 'possibility (*possibilité*)'. If the possible world (trivially) 'exists' in a state of possibility, Deleuze first situates this in opposition to the state of reality (*réalité*); he then proposes the opposition of virtuality and actuality (*actualité*) to combat the staticity of the former dualism (for this purpose Deleuze enlists Bergson's concept of 'possibility'[23]). Spontaneously, we imagine possibility as something like a set of options which pre-exist an occurrence, 'really' existing choices only one of which is in fact selected. However, this image has things totally the wrong way around: for 'possibilities' are only ever posited retroactively, always after something has actually taken place. Only because Caesar did in fact cross the Rubicon can we imagine a possible world wherein this did not take place. All of which necessitates the following summary assessment: '[s]uch is the defect of the possible: a defect which serves to condemn it as produced after the fact, as retroactively fabricated in the image of what resembles it' (DR, 263–4/273). A 'genesis' derived from the axis of 'possibility-reality' is but a sham. What we need is to establish a different axis, that of 'virtuality-actuality'. We need to re-orientate our conception of reality, from the realisation of possibilities to the actualisation of virtuals. Genesis, which has lost its way walking backwards through the linear maze of history, must be wrenched back by Ariadne's thread to the here and now.

This concept of the virtual is able to revitalise the genetic potential of the 'singularity-event'. Deleuze discovers a level of virtuality composed of bubbling dispersals of the 'singularity-event', prior to their solidification into the evental series. The level of actuality, in turn, comes into effect when global collectivisation takes place. Reality is then portrayed as a relentless actualisation process of the virtual (later in his career, Deleuze was to reformulate this as the becoming-'molar' of the 'molecular'). We shall see in the next section that Deleuze owes a great deal to psychoanalysis in his theorisation of the pre-serialised 'singularity-event', but the root of this inspiration is also in Leibniz; not, however, the Leibniz who fussed over the pristine serialisation of events, but the Leibniz of the 'minute perception (*petite perception*)' (DR, 265–6/274–6).

Drawing a distinction between 'perception' and 'apperception', Leibniz takes up the example of the sound of waves crashing onto the shore. When we hear the murmuring of the sea, each wave must surely transmit its own resonance to our ear individually. Yet, we are unable to distinguish these individual sounds, let alone their respective sources. Each individual wave surely sounds 'distinctly', and our eardrum surely picks up these distinct sounds, yet they all become 'obscure' in our consciousness. Indeed, it is precisely by lumping together these countless minute perceptions that we arrive at a 'clear', but 'confused', apperception of the 'murmuring of the waves' (in the singular). Leibniz understands this work of apperception as none other than the function of consciousness itself; in other words, it is the forcible synthesis of minute perceptions that generates consciousness *qua* apperceptive faculty. Now Deleuze overlays this with the conceptual distinction between the 'differential (*différentiel*)' and 'differenciation (*différenciation*)' that he develops in *Difference and Repetition*. The former names the power of difference to differentiate between one entity and another, while the latter expresses the genetic process of a determinate individual in its differenciation from exteriority. Each minute perception is a 'unit' of singularity, and hence corresponds to the former, as a differential; nonetheless, insofar as it is impossible for each individual unit to be separated out, it has yet to be differenciated in the latter sense. However, when the 'compression' of the minute perceptions (singularity-events) surpasses a certain limit, this time differenciation (with a 'c') takes place. The minute perceptions which had remained virtual are actualised, generating apperception (consciousness). Consciousness is of course clear in one sense, but insofar as it only arose through the forcible apperception of minute perceptions, it is at the same time confused. What this amounts to is that the actualisation of the virtual can be reformulated as the 'differenciation' of the 'differential'. In both cases, the building block is the 'singularity-event' prior to serialisation.

The theory of the evental series had explained genesis by taking for granted the divergence and exclusion of some series and not others. By contrast, the theory of minute perception can become a model to explain genesis without having to presuppose these processes. It is impossible to overstate the immense influence Leibniz had on Deleuze. The philosophy of transcendental empiricism, conceived

Principle: Transcendental Empiricism

through the confrontation of Hume and Kant, has a godfather in this Baroque philosopher.

The Principle of the Transcendental

It is worth at this point briefly going back over the ground covered so far in this chapter. Deleuze, we recall, thought extremely highly of the transcendental programme for philosophy inaugurated by Kant. At the same time, however, he was critical of Kantianism's inability to carry through with its full potential. Kant illegitimately assumes what he cannot. The self as apperception, time and space as forms of perception, the faculties such as reason: these cannot be taken for granted as ready-made givens. They are the end products of long and arduous genetic processes. Such a genetic perspective Deleuze inherited from Hume's empiricism. In this way we have defined transcendental empiricism as a philosophy that pays meticulous attention to genesis, using empiricism to reconstitute transcendental philosophy. Its objective lies foremost in the reformulation of the transcendental domain.

The transcendental is properly speaking that which grounds the empirical. Kant had nevertheless introduced a great many impurities into his portrayal of this stratum. 'The foundation can never resemble what it founds.' It is inconceivable that the transcendental (ground) should resemble the empirical (grounded). And yet, philosophers who have set themselves this task, starting with Kant, have all smuggled such empirical figures as the self and consciousness into the transcendental realm. Or, to use Deleuze's expression, they have sketched the transcendental by 'tracing (*décalquer*)' the empirical. In critiquing this lack of philosophical rigour, Deleuze aims to develop a theory of the transcendental rid of all impurities.

To this effect, Deleuze began with the paradoxical figure of the desert island, where the absence of the Other entails a disintegration of the self. This is the 'primal scene' of the transcendental, purged of all empirical elements. We have set the stage for transcendental empiricism. Onto this empty stage enters the event (singularity-event), which is the truly transcendental principle of genesis. Through a selective and critical appropriation of Leibnizian serial theory, Deleuze concretises the singularity-event as a minute perception, which he grounds using the concept of 'virtuality'. When Deleuze towards the end of his life remarked that '[e]mpiricism knows only events and other people' (WPh, 48/49), we can see that the Other (desert islands) and the singularity-event as principle of genesis had always been the basic components of transcendental empiricism.

So it seems that Deleuze has now collated the requisite tools to undertake transcendental empiricism. His next task was of course to test out his toolbox in a real situation: psychoanalysis. Both *Difference and Repetition* and *The Logic of Sense* devote a vast number of pages to psychoanalysis. And what is especially interesting in the context of this chapter is the fact that Deleuze establishes a philosophical lineage going from Leibniz to psychoanalysis. Having emphasised that Sigmund Freud's (1856–1939) 'unconscious' cannot be adequately understood through an oppositional logic of negation, Deleuze writes: 'if Freud was completely on the side of a Hegelian post-Kantianism – in other words, of an unconscious of opposition – why did he pay so much homage to *the Leibnizian Fechner* and to his "symptomologist's" differential finesse?' (DR, 133/143; my emphasis). He even goes as far as to claim that the proper interpretation of the unconscious had already been pointed to by Leibniz (DR, 133/143). Needless to say, the Leibniz he has in mind here is the Leibniz of minute perception. Moreover, as we have seen, *The Logic of Sense*, having explained away 'static genesis' using Leibnizian serialism, proposes the importance of developing a 'dynamic genesis'. This proposal is taken up from the twenty-seventh series of the book, and as it so happens it is in the same series that we get the first proper treatment of psychoanalysis. It is also in the twenty-seventh series that we find the following assertion: 'psychoanalysis in general is the science of events' (LS, 242/246). The whole of Deleuze's intellectual history, from a concept of the event inspired by Leibnizian philosophy to its application onto psychoanalysis, is here in highly condensed form.

Now we must not think that psychoanalysis was chosen for this task because it just happened to take Deleuze's fancy at the time. For *Difference and Repetition*, in particular its second chapter, explicitly traces a philosophical lineage that goes from the Cartesian Cogito, to its reconstitution by Kant into the transcendental subject, finally to its redeployment from a genetic standpoint by Freud. In other words, Deleuze situates psychoanalysis as the highest modern representative of transcendental philosophy. It is thus a matter of course that transcendental empiricism, having been furnished with its toolbox, should embark in this direction. More concretely, what must be investigated is Freud's theory of the constitution of the subject.

The popular understanding of Freud goes something like this:

Principle: Transcendental Empiricism

Freudian psychoanalysis discovered the Oedipus Complex, according to which the infant is impelled by the incestuous desire for the mother, and the corresponding parricidal desire against the father who will thwart its fulfilment. But these unconscious desires will not see the light of day, and it is their repression that gives rise to the subject. What we have here is an oppositional, even a dialectical explication of the unconscious. Now Deleuze's discussion of Freud is meticulous, but scarcely anything is said in *Difference and Repetition* regarding the Oedipus Complex. Instead, he chooses to focus on Freud's secondary topology, and in particular on the 'pleasure principle' derived from it.

Initially, Freud had modelled the inner life of man using the triad of the conscious-preconscious-unconscious (primary topology). However, at some point he was forced to recognise the limitations of this model, which led him to develop the new triad of id-ego-superego (secondary topology). The 'id' is indeed a fitting label for something which can only be identified as an 'it', the life force in its distilled purity ('*Es*' in the original German, and the Latin word 'id' which we typically use to render it in English, both mean quite simply 'it'). Freud explains that the id follows what he calls the 'pleasure principle'. Avoid pain and seek pleasure: this alone constitutes the id's principle. However, the infant gradually comes to understand that this principle is not totally viable in real life. It learns to put off the automatic fulfilment of the principle to avoid pain and seek pleasure. This postponement of the pleasure principle Freud calls the 'reality principle'. Harking back to our secondary triad, it is the ego that now heralds the arrival of this new principle. Hence the ego is not a faculty pre-ascribed to the subject in advance; rather it is nothing more than a function which splits off from the id in its relentless struggles with reality. Where Kant *assumes* the ego, Freud explains its *genesis*. And the genesis of the ego will shortly be followed by a tertiary function named the superego. The ego is slowly made aware of its utter insignificance within the grand scheme of things. There exist powers that impose themselves from the outside, against which the ego is contemptibly defenceless. The only option is then for the ego to incorporate these powers into itself, which constitutes the superego. The superego is what keeps watch over the ego. Freud even goes so far as to assert that what Kant referred to as 'conscience' is none other than this superego. For Kant, the fact that even the most irredeemably evil men are tormented by a sense of guilt when they commit wrong, shows that all men possess innately a 'conscience'. In contradistinction, Freud's theory of the superego gives a genetic account of this 'conscience' which Kant had simply taken for granted. We thus have a working model of an ego keeping the pure instinctual life of the id in check, while being itself constantly under the superego's watch, and by means of this two-stage compromise seeking the fulfilment of its desires. This is the outline of Freud's vision of human psychic life.

Immediately, we can see the extent to which Freud's core motivation is a genetic one. In the primary topology, the three levels of the conscious-preconscious-unconscious were merely posited to exist in this way, but this was promptly supplanted by the secondary topology which is traversed through and through by a genetic perspective. This alone would be reason enough for Deleuze's great admiration of Freudian psychoanalysis, but that is not all. For the secondary topology displays a close proximity with Leibniz's minute perception, and the theory of the 'singularity-event'. Allow us to explain this in some detail. Deleuze attempts a highly original reformulation of the relation between the id and the ego: '[t]he Id is populated by local egos (*Le Ça se peuple de moi locaux*)' (DR, 120/129). Prior to the formation of a determinate ego, the first tentative steps leading to the subject, fragments not yet synthesised into the ego seethe in a whirlpool inside the id, as 'local egos'. These local egos are each impelled by a 'partial object'. Such partial objects are the primordial objects of desire (breasts, fingers, lips, anus . . .), which have yet to be stitched together into a wholesome human form. According to Deleuze's Freud, when the dispersed local egos, driven by partial objects while residing in the id, are synthesised 'globally', only then do we get an ego separated from the id.[24] Now plainly this mechanism is identical to the Leibniz-infused process of the actualisation of virtual minute perceptions. Deleuze in fact says this explicitly: '[p]artial objects are the elements of minute perceptions. The unconscious is differential, involving minute perceptions, and as such it is different in kind from consciousness' (DR, 133/143). Or we could just as well replace the references to 'minute perception' with the term 'singularity-event'. Deleuze has found in Freud a variation on the minute perception, or equivalently, a theory of the non-serialised 'singularity-event'. Whether in Leibniz or Freud, what interests Deleuze is always the moment in which the self appears as the end result of a genetic process, rather than something taken to exist in advance.

But one's work does not end when one has identified genesis; one must immediately proceed to problematise this very process itself.

Principle: Transcendental Empiricism

The genesis of the global self, according to Freud, is conditioned by the pleasure principle. Previously, we stated that the ego comes about as the apostle of the reality principle, because the id comes to learn that the pleasure principle is fraught with inconveniences. However, this formulation is open to misunderstanding, for it seems to set up the two principles as oppositional to one another. But this is not the case, for as we have seen, the reality principle is nothing more than an extension of the pleasure principle. We might as well say that the reality principle is but a special case of the pleasure principle. Only because the absolute and foundational validity of the pleasure principle, to seek pleasure and avoid pain, is unquestionable, does the reality principle in turn come to have any operational meaning. The reality principle is, in the last instance, but a means of attaining the final ends of the pleasure principle, and their 'opposition', insofar as it is one, is in no way weighted equally on both sides. The reality principle which governs the ego derives from the pleasure principle. But we must press still further: whence does the pleasure principle in its turn derive from?

It is said that the pleasure principle is the final arbiter in all matters psychic. The crucial issue is whether Freud assumes its function, as some kind of essence or nature of the human psyche. As Deleuze emphasises, it is when Freud turns to problematise the origin of the pleasure principle itself that his properly philosophical, properly 'transcendental' investigation begins (MCC, 111/96). Freud took up this problem in *Beyond the Pleasure Principle* (1920), where he proposed the concept of the 'death instinct' to explain the pleasure principle.[25] Now Deleuze rated Freud's 'speculations (*Spekulation*)' (Freud's own word) concerning the death drive extremely highly, and yet at the same time he was to propose a major modification.

But to begin with *Beyond the Pleasure Principle* itself, all too often this work is understood as follows. For a long time Freud was firmly convinced of the absolute hegemony of the pleasure principle, to avoid pain and seek pleasure, in psychic processes. However, at some point he was forced to accept that the scope of this principle is not unlimited, in particular from his case studies of the repetition compulsion. Especially common among those suffering from traumatic neurosis after the experience of war, this incessant repetition of experiences which can only be unpleasant (for example, the reliving of the moment of trauma every night in one's dreams) was simply impossible to subsume under the rubric of the existing grand principle. From there, Freud was led to propose the hypothesis that psychic processes are governed by not one but two opposing principles, the life instinct and the death instinct, where sometimes one is dominant, sometimes the other . . . in other words, there exists a 'beyond' where the pleasure principle ceases to apply.

Against this common picture, Deleuze starts off by asserting that the 'beyond' of the pleasure principle is in no way to be understood as an *exception* to the rule (DR, 120/128). 'In other words there are no exceptions to the principle – though there would indeed seem to be some rather strange complications in the workings of pleasure' (MCC, 111/96). At first sight, however, the deliberate reliving of unpleasant experiences in the repetition compulsion seems to be in maximal tension with the pleasure principle. To understand Deleuze's enigmatic claim, therefore, we must first examine the mechanism of the repetition compulsion in greater detail.

Freud had explained repetition compulsion in patients of traumatic neurosis as follows. The psychic apparatus performs a protective function against shocks from external stimuli. We can visually picture these external shocks as excessive energy gushing into the psychic apparatus. By 'investing (*Besetzung*)' sufficient energy where this influx of energy from the outside will take place, the psychic apparatus tries to 'harness (*Bindung*)'[26] and counterbalance the otherwise dangerous shock. In this way 'anxiety', for example, can be explained as a psychic mechanism of unequal energy distribution in anticipation of an imminent intrusion from the outside. A heightened energy-processing capacity in the high-risk areas is correspondingly compensated for by decreased performance in the rest of the psychic apparatus (in anxiety, for example, we are unable to think of anything else). Anxiety would thus be a textbook case of the psyche's self-defence mechanism. However, there are times when this procedure fails to kick into gear: when the invasive situation is unforeseen/unforeseeable, say in cases of natural disaster or outbreaks of war, the psychic apparatus is forced to weather a sudden and explosive burst of external energy without the requisite preparation. In such cases, the psychic apparatus is unable to 'harness' this influx. And if this excess energy is overwhelming, the self-defence mechanism itself becomes insolvent: this is traumatic neurosis. How then does the psychic apparatus behave once it has become bankrupt? By fabricating the state of anxiety, it will deliberately bring up the moment of trauma in an attempt to simulate a successful harnessing of the influx this time round. By continuously rehearsing the 'healthy' performance of anxiety to offset external energy, it seeks finally to master the original energetic differential (Freud 1920, vol. XVIII: 31–2/31–2). But needless to say it is no mean feat for the psyche to take back the reins, which is why the scene of the trauma has to return again and again in the dreams of the patient. This is, in outline, the mechanism of repetition compulsion.

Now according to Freud, pleasure is a decrease in psychic excitation, pain its increase. We can thus redefine the pleasure principle as the principle according to which the psychic apparatus avoids states of excitation, and seeks to shield itself from fluctuations. It is easy to see that the protocol of anxiety – prepare for an external influx of energy and harness it – fully conforms to this principle. Moreover, the explanation given above makes it clear that the repetition compulsion itself, too, rigorously obeys the pleasure principle, only it differs somewhat from business as usual, because here the pleasure principle is undergoing auto-repair. Which is why it appears to diverge from a simple functional seeking of pleasure/avoidance of pain.[27] This in turn allows for the following theoretical question: is the pleasure principle really a pre-established rule innately coded into the psyche, or is it not rather something in some sense *set up*? This is because what we seem to find in the psychic apparatus is not so much the pleasure principle *per se*, as a general tendency towards consolidating the dominion of the pleasure principle.[28] It is here at last that this work which Freud named 'speculation', and which Deleuze described as 'transcendental', really comes into its own. From here, Freud will attempt to apply the insights into psychic mechanism he gained from his study of traumatic neurosis to human psychic life in general.

For it is not only external stimuli that can give rise to the repetition compulsion. It is rather a phenomenon observed far and wide, from the play of children to neurosis patients undergoing treatment. This invites the following hypothesis: an excitation whose intensity and unpredictability are comparable to an energy influx capable of causing traumatic neurosis is taking place, but internal to the psyche itself. For Freud, the root of this internal excitation is none other than the instinct of the organism, which he explains as follows: 'an instinct [*Trieb*] is an urge inherent [*Drang*] in organic life to restore an earlier state of things' (Freud 1920, vol. XVIII: 36/38; de-emphasised). This is why the organism discharges tension in order to return to a prior state of equilibrium. The crux of the issue is ultimately how we are to understand this 'earlier state'. Freud the 'speculator' is forced to conclude the following: '[i]f we are to take it as a truth that knows no exception that everything living dies for *internal* reasons – becomes inorganic once again – then we shall be compelled to say that *"the aim of all life is death"'* (38/40; original emphases). If it is true that all life exhibits a tendency to release tension and yearn for bygone equilibrium, based on an instinct to return to the primordial state of things, then the ultimate goal of all life must be the reversion into brute matter, or simply, death. Of course, this conclusion motivates a very basic question: if the goal of all life is death, why do all living things display an instinct of self-preservation, the life instinct of Eros? Freud's answer is simple, and almost satisfying in a strange way: the life instinct is but a part of the death instinct. All life seeks its own death, as opposed to a death bestowed upon it from the outside. Hence 'the organism wishes to die only in its own fashion' (39/41). Whatever gets in the way of this must be eliminated at all costs. Life will not tolerate anything which might obstruct its own journey towards death, a death that is *resolutely its own*. In other words, the life instinct is but a partial perspective on the autocracy of the death instinct.[29]

The Genesis of the Transcendental Principle

In the course of his analysis of *Beyond the Pleasure Principle*, Deleuze declares that '[i]t is in the nature of a transcendental inquiry that *we cannot break it off when we please*' (MCC, 114/98; my emphasis). Freud does not conclude by saying that 'the psychic apparatus is always governed by the pleasure principle', nor is he resigned simply to accept that 'the pleasure principle admits of certain exceptions', but instead thinks these to their utmost limit, and reaches the ground of the world of experience governed by the pleasure principle itself, in the death instinct. Deleuze admired this achievement immensely: this is genuine philosophical thinking, a properly transcendental investigation.

And yet, we must pause for a moment lest our thinking stagnates. The essence of transcendental inquiry lies in not stopping where one would like to. Freud pushed through his investigation of the pleasure principle, which governs the realm of experience, far enough to arrive at the transcendental principle which grounds the former, the death instinct. But is that it? Not at all, we cannot just take the death instinct as a given and be done with it. But Freud had sadly laid down his pen by this point. Which is why Deleuze elects himself as the successor to this transcendental project, and exerts himself to reveal the genetic process behind the transcendental principle of the death instinct itself.

Principle: Transcendental Empiricism

In *Difference and Repetition*, Deleuze writes as follows: 'Freud indicated ... that there is no reflux of the libido on to the ego without it becoming *desexualised* and forming a neutral *displaceable* energy, essentially capable of serving Thanatos. Why, however, did Freud thus propose a death instinct existing prior to that desexualised energy, independent of it in principle?' (DR, 136–7/147; original emphases). What is problematised here is the theoretical status of the death instinct as something fundamentally distinct from the (libidinal) psychic mechanism based on this 'neutral energy'. Freud, for his part, just assumes the death instinct.

To understand this remark of Deleuze's more fully, we need to go back to Freud's 'Mourning and Melancholia' (1917), written several years before *Beyond the Pleasure Principle*. There, Freud had explained the mechanism of melancholia in the following way. Melancholia is a psychological condition caused by the loss of a certain object of attachment. In order to overcome this loss, the melancholic tries to reproduce the lost object inside of the ego. In other words, by redirecting the libido, which formerly flowed towards the object, reflexively into reproducing the object within oneself, one tries to compensate for this loss.[30] In the jargon, this procedure is explained as the renunciation of 'object-cathexis (*Objektbesetzung*)' (the libido ceases to be directed to its original object), and the corresponding 'identification (*Identifizierung*)' with the object (by damming the libido back into oneself, the formerly external object is reproduced within)[31] (Freud 1917: 249/435).

Turning the clocks forward this time, in *The Ego and the Id* (1923), written after *Beyond the Pleasure Principle*, Freud discovers that this mechanism of melancholia outlined above should not in fact be restricted to melancholics, but is instead very much applicable to ego-formation in general, playing a significant role in constructing what is commonly known as character (Freud 1923, vol. XIX: 28/256). First of all, object-cathexis is the prerogative of the id, with its innate desire to display sexual intentionality. The ego, watching from the side-lines while this drama unfolds, gradually comes to learn of this cathexis, and schemes to obstruct it in order to usurp the position of the ego's preferred object. As such, the ego seeks identification with this object. As for the id, having seen the ego become one with the object of cathexis, it goes on to abandon the original object, and turns its attention to the ego. (As a point of detail, whereas the order of proceedings in melancholia goes from choice of object → object-cathexis → loss of object → identification, here we go from choice of object by the id → object-cathexis by the id → identification with the object by the ego → renunciation of object-cathexis by the id. But the minor divergences are immaterial here). In this way the ego's little schemes have come to fruition; the id has eyes only for it. But the ego must not get complacent, for the id is a fickle bird, it never stops choosing new objects for itself, and each time the ego must repeat the arduous process to re-usurp the position of the id's favourite. As a result, the ego comes to accumulate within itself all the past objects of cathexis that the id has spurned, with which it has identified. And it is thought that the character of the ego is a culmination of this ever-increasing precipitation.

Now the libido, of which Deleuze says there is a 'reflux on to the ego', is the id's libido which the ego has successfully diverted towards itself through identification with the id's original object. Freud calls this change of vector '[t]he transformation of object-libido into narcissistic libido' (Freud 1923, vol. XIX: 30/258). Insofar as the id, which desires to display its sexual investment, is here letting go of object-cathexis, we can characterise this change as the renunciation of a sexual goal. We have thus a 'desexualisation (*Desexualisierung*)' of the libido, and it is this desexualised energy that Deleuze called a 'neutral displaceable energy'. In Deleuze's reading, Freud understands this energy as something subsequently taken up by the death instinct. Which is to say, the death instinct is conceived as pre-existing, going around appropriating this desexualised energy. But this model, unsurprisingly, does not satisfy Deleuze. For what reason is there for Freud to propose the death instinct as something existing in advance of desexualised energy, as something essentially distinct from this energy? Such considerations lead Deleuze to suggest the following: 'Thanatos is completely indistinguishable from the desexualisation of Eros, with the resultant formation of that neutral and displaceable energy of which Freud speaks. This energy does not serve Thanatos, *it constitutes him*' (DR, 139/149; my emphasis).

Much is at stake in this suggestion of Deleuze's. Allow us to return to Freud to clarify the discussion somewhat. The desire experienced by the id is of a sexual nature, and is thus none other than Eros. As such, the schemes of the ego whereby it tries to deflect the libido to itself through identification are a veritable 'struggle against Eros' (Freud 1923, vol. XIX: 46/275). And everyone knows that Eros is what introduces discord into life. Therefore, obeying the pleasure principle (avoid strife, steer clear of tension), a mechanism to desexualise Eros kicks into gear.[32] 'Towards the two classes of instincts the

Principle: Transcendental Empiricism

ego's attitude is not impartial. Through its work of identification and sublimation it gives the death instincts in the id assistance in gaining control over the libido' (56/287). According to Freud, then, the efforts of the ego to monopolise the id's libidinal investment are done in 'service' to the id's death instinct.

Against this, Deleuze is saying something like the following: if you're going to go that far, you might as well go the extra mile and say that it is the desexualised libido, or neutral energy, which constitutes the death instinct. And this implies that Deleuze is trying to think *the genesis of the Thanatos itself*. And since the Thanatos is the transcendental principle that grounds the experiential domain organised by the pleasure principle, this in turn implies that Deleuze is trying to think *the genesis of the transcendental principle itself*. Moreover, this genesis is thought in inextricable relation to the experiential pleasure principle.

The pleasure principle is what rules over the experiential realm; insofar as Thanatos, the death instinct, is what grounds this rule, it is worthy to be called a transcendental principle. And Deleuze thought that this transcendental principle *arises* according to the requirements of the empirical pleasure principle. True, the empirical principle must be grounded by the transcendental one; yet, crucially, the transcendental principle does not exist apart from the empirical, it does not *transcend* the empirical. That is not to say that the empirical grounds the transcendental; nevertheless, the transcendental principle arises inseparably from, and simultaneously with, the empirical principle. Thus, just because the transcendental is what grounds the empirical, this in no way implies that the former can exist independently of the latter.

We see clearly that Deleuze has stayed true to his word, and carried out his maxim of transcendental investigation ('we cannot break it off when we please') with the utmost rigour. For Deleuze, Freud had touched upon the essence of transcendental inquiry in *Beyond the Pleasure Principle*. But he faltered at the last minute, failing to push through far enough. For Deleuze, a transcendental philosophy worth its name must ultimately explain the genesis of the transcendental principle itself.

* * *

Transcendental empiricism is the completion of transcendental philosophy by passing through empiricist philosophy. Deleuze wants to portray the transcendental realm puritanically. For this purpose, he sketched its primordial state using the theory of the desert island and the Other, and deployed the event as the properly transcendental raw material of genesis, which takes neither self nor apperception nor consciousness as givens. Transcendental investigation cannot stop just because one wants it to. Any transcendental principle that is discovered must thus be theorised until we finally understand its genesis. One is not permitted to *assume* at any turn. In Deleuze's hands, the term 'transcendental' is given its most exact, and exacting, sense.

Next, we must ask what sort of philosophical practice can be derived from this principle of Deleuzian philosophy, transcendental empiricism, to make good our promise all those pages ago in the Prologue. What are the practical ramifications of this philosophy, which prizes genesis above all else?

Notes

1. Translator's note: Deleuze is using 'affection' in a Spinozist sense, to refer to the modifications a body undergoes.
2. The illusion of an originary and pre-determined human nature nonetheless arises ever so 'naturally' in us because the outcomes of each association of ideas, each resulting system of ideas, differ minimally from one individual to another. And this lack of differentiation is in turn explained by 'circumstance', as we saw earlier: social 'circumstance' requires that individuals respond in an essential uniform way, over and again (ES, 21/2).
3. 'This law of reproduction, however, presupposes that the appearances themselves are actually subject to such a rule, and that in the manifold of their representations an accompaniment or succession takes place according to certain rules; for without that our empirical imagination would never get to do anything suitable to its capacity, and would thus remain hidden in the interior of the mind, like a dead and to us unknown faculty. If cinnabar were now red, now black, now light, now heavy, if a human being were now changed into this animal shape, now into that one, if on the longest day the land were covered now with fruits, now with ice and snow, then my empirical imagination would never even get the opportunity to think of heavy cinnabar on the occasion of the representation of the colour red' (Kant 1998: 'On the synthesis of reproduction in the imagination', A100).
4. In *Empiricism and Subjectivity* Deleuze notes, with reference to Kant's text quoted in the previous note, that 'Kant understood the essence of associationism' (ES, 109/123), while in *Kant's Critical Philosophy* he refers to Kant's reformulation of the problem based on his critique of Hume (KCP, 12–13/20–1).

Principle: Transcendental Empiricism

5. Translator's note: the French word *'plan'* can mean both plane (as in geometry) and plan (as in the phrase 'plan of action'). The English translator of *Empiricism and Subjectivity*, Constantin Boundas, has opted for the latter meaning, whereas Kokubun's analysis here emphasises the former.
6. *Kant's Critical Philosophy* performs the astounding feat of reducing Kant's gigantic philosophical edifice, comprising epistemology (*Critique of Pure Reason*), morality (*Critique of Practical Reason*) and judgement (*Critique of Judgement*), to a 'system of permutations' between sensibility, imagination, judgement and reason. Through this reconstitution Deleuze exposes the fragile nodes of this philosophy (the internal coherence of the faculties with each other, and the external coherence of the faculties with nature). For a more detailed treatment, see Kokubun 2008.
7. 'That is why the transcendental is answerable to a superior empiricism which alone is capable of exploring its domain and its regions. Contrary to Kant's belief, it cannot be induced from the ordinary empirical forms in the manner in which these appear under the determination of common sense. Despite the fact that it has become discredited today, the doctrine of the faculties is an entirely necessary component of the system of philosophy. Its discredit may be explained by the misrecognition of this properly transcendental empiricism, for which was substituted in vain a tracing of the transcendental from the empirical ... transcendental empiricism is the only way to avoid tracing the transcendental from the outlines of the empirical' (DR, 180–1/186–7).
8. 'Sartre's presupposition of an impersonal transcendental field restores the rights of immanence. When immanence is no longer immanent to something other than itself it is possible to speak of a plane of immanence. Such a plane is, perhaps, a radical empiricism: it does not present a flux of the lived that is immanent to a subject and individualised in that which belongs to a self. It presents only events, that is, possible worlds as concepts, and other people as expressions of possible worlds or conceptual personae' (WPh, 47–8/49).
9. 'What is a transcendental field? It can be distinguished from experience, to the extent that it does not refer to any object nor belong to any subject (empirical representation). It is thus given as pure a-subjective stream of consciousness, as pre-reflexive impersonal consciousness, or as the qualitative duration of consciousness without a self. One may find it odd that the transcendental be defined by such immediate givens, but transcendental empiricism is the term I will use to distinguish it from everything that makes up the world of subject and object. There is something raw and powerful in such a transcendental empiricism. It is certainly not the element of sensation (simple empiricism), because sensation merely cuts a slice in the continuous stream of absolute con-

sciousness. Rather, it is the passage from one sensation to another, however close two sensations may be, but as becoming, as an increase or decrease in power (virtual quantity). Must the transcendental field then be defined by pure immediate consciousness with neither object nor self, as a movement which neither begins nor ends?' (TRM, 384/359).

10. On this point we refer to Christian Kerslake's *Immanence and the Vertigo of Philosophy*, (2009), which positions Deleuzian philosophy as the making-thorough of the 'Copernican Revolution'. The path blazed by this work, with its acute and wide-ranging account situating Deleuze in the history of philosophy after Kant, is one that must be traversed by future research on Deleuze. At the same time, however, caution must be exercised in boxing Deleuze into the ranks of the post-Kantian philosophers. Here we refer to Daniela Voss's convincing criticisms of Kerslake's reading (Voss 2013: 9–10). Regarding the relationship between Deleuze and post-Kantianism, the collection of essays edited by Lundy and Voss (2015), penned by scholars at the forefront of Deleuze studies, is extremely illuminating. In other news, Deleuze studies has a strong tendency to keep Hegel at several arms' length; yet, if Deleuze shares a common set of problematics with the post-Kantians, it is only right that Deleuze and Hegel should overlap in a certain respect. Henry Somers-Hall's *Hegel, Deleuze, and the Critique of Representation* (2012), which deals with just this proximity, reads with a great force and conviction.

11. David Lapoujade, who edited the collection *Desert Islands*, comprising Deleuze's essays until then unavailable in book form, relates that in 1989 Deleuze had composed a bibliography of his complete works, which he divided into the following eleven categories: I: from Hume to Bergson; II: studies on (classical) philosophy; III: study on Nietzsche; IV: critical and clinical; V: aesthetics; VI: studies on cinema; VII: studies on (modern) philosophy; VIII: Logic of Sense; IX: Anti-Oedipus; X: Difference and Repetition; XI: A Thousand Plateaus. Of these, 'Desert Islands' was included under 'X: Difference and Repetition' (DR, 292n1.1/7n1.1).

12. 'Michel Tournier and the World Without Others' (LS, 341–58/350–72). Incidentally, it was Akira Asada who saw in the study on Tournier a sort of 'principle of Deleuzian philosophy', on account of which he defined this philosopher as a 'solipsist: indeed so extreme a solipsist as no longer to require even the self' (Zaitsu et al. 1996: 23).

13. Translator's note: it is useful to recall here the earlier discussion on Kantian transcendental carbon tracing. Kokubun's analysis reveals the extent to which Kantianism in transcendental portraiture is a highly spontaneous temptation.

14. 'For my part, I am nothing other than my past objects, and my self is

Principle: Transcendental Empiricism

made up of a past world, the passing away of which was brought about precisely by the Other' (LS, 349/360).

15. Phenomenologist Yasuhiko Murakami's important work on autism has not only revealed the phenomenological structures underlying the condition, but has also contributed to the further development of phenomenology itself (Murakami 2008). What strikes us is the fact that the mechanism of the genesis of perception outlined here overlaps almost exactly with Deleuze's desert island analysis. Murakami relates the case study of the autistic child who makes the 'great discovery' that 'the world extends behind the things I can actually see!' (2008: 86). 'The essence of objectiality does not consist in what meets the eye. Rather, it consists in establishing a permanence which transcends explicit "seeing". In other words, objectiality is not a given of sensation, it is a concept' (91). Murakami's project seeks the 'revision' and further 'development' of Husserlian phenomenology. Fundamental to this project is the attempt to overcome the limitations of Husserl's introspective method through an active 'encounter' between Murakami the phenomenologist and the autist, giving rise to the 'intuition of disalignment' (viii–ix). Criticising the Husserlian transcendental ego through his concept of 'affection upon contact', Murakami paints the same situation as the desert island in Deleuze. 'From our perspective, the Husserlian methodological requirement of a transcendental egology is impossible. This is because even at this most primordial stratum, we cannot but assume the function of the "affection upon contact". Experientially, however, as we have already seen, a situation without the work of the "affection upon contact" is a real possibility' (44). In our terms, to be without the affection upon contact is to be without the Other; as a result, things, that is external objects, do not exist either. The division of the world into inside and outside has not taken place, hence there is no sensation that can legitimately be called 'mine' either. 'Insofar as the self's body is not experienced, the division between self and Other, between self and thing, ceases to hold. It is already misleading to say of this situation that self and Other are undifferentiated; more precisely, they quite simply do not exist' (7). This proximity of Murakami and Deleuze is no mere coincidence. As is well-known, phenomenology has always understood itself to be a more rigorous renewal of Kantian transcendental philosophy. Nevertheless, its founder Husserl was inevitably plagued by limitations, for the simple reason that he had to work largely in a vacuum. Murakami, who at one point notes Husserl's own desire for phenomenology to progress through constructive criticism, does just this (by creating the novel concept of 'affection upon contact', for example). Deleuze too, in his own way, wanted to place Kantian transcendental philosophy on a surer footing. We have seen that this work included a critical overcoming of the limits of Husserl. Therefore,

it is perfectly natural that Murakami's new phenomenology (a genetic phenomenology) and Deleuzian philosophy should resonate with each other. For a comparison of the genetic procedures of Husserl and Deleuze, see Hughes 2008.

16. On the importance of Leibnizian philosophy for Deleuze, see Kokubun 2004.
17. Leibniz's theory of possible worlds is founded on his distinction between 'necessary' and 'contingent' truths. Also known as 'eternal' vs. 'factual' truths, or 'truths of thought' and 'truths of fact', this division constitutes one of the pillars of Leibnizian philosophy (Leibniz 1967, '4/14 July 1686': 54–5/115). Necessary truths are those whose contradictory is inconceivable, as typified by the 'truths of logic, number, and geometry'. In contrast, contingent or factual truths are (as the names suggest) simple facts of reality. In other words, for Leibniz, reality is a contingent affair (Leibniz 1714 (1908), §33: 235–6/89).
18. '[E]ach simple substance has relations which express all the others, and, consequently, . . . it is a perpetual living mirror of the universe' (Leibniz 1714 (1908), §56: 248/103–5). It is this 'simple substance' which Leibniz terms the 'monad'. The well-known definition of the monad, that it 'expresses the entire universe', amounts to the same thing.
19. 'Each unique substance expresses the whole universe in its own way, and included in its notion are all the events that happen to it with all their external circumstances, and the whole sequence of external things' (Leibniz 1686 (1908), §9: 47/44). '[A]lways, in every true affirmative proposition, necessary or contingent, universal or particular, the concept of the predicate is in a sense included in that of the subject' (Leibniz 1967, '4/14 July 1686': 63/121).
20. Deleuze explicitly notes the importance of the fact that relations of compossibility hold between predicates prior to their subsumption into the subject. 'It would be arbitrary to give a privileged status to the inherence of predicates [in subjects] in Leibniz's philosophy. The inherence of predicates in the expressive monad presupposes the compossibility of the expressed world' (LS, 128/135). 'Compossibility does not even presuppose the inherence of predicates in an individual subject or monad. It is rather the inverse: inherent predicates are those which correspond to events from the beginning compossible' (LS, 196/200).
21. In *The Fold* (1988), Deleuze focuses on the statement 'predicate *sive* event (*prédicat ou événement*)' that Leibniz had penned in *Discourse on Metaphysics*, to arrive at the following: '[t]hat the predicate is a verb, and that the verb is irreducible to the copula and to the attribute, mark the very basis of the Leibnizian conception of the event' (FLB, 60/71). For example, that which gives rise to the monad of Adam the sinner is the event 'to sin (*pécher*)'; it is not the case that when we go

Principle: Transcendental Empiricism

far enough in our analysis of the monad of Adam, we will eventually reach the attribute (*attribut*) 'to be a sinner (*être pécheur*)'. For Leibniz, the predicate is an event, which can only be expressed by a verb such as 'to sin'. *The Logic of Sense* further states as follows: '"[t]o green [verdoyer]" indicates a singularity-event in the vicinity of which the tree is constituted. "*To sin* [pécher]" indicates a singularity-event in the vicinity of which Adam is constituted. But "*to be green* [être vert]" or "*to be a sinner* [être pécheur]" are now the analytic predicates of constituted subjects – namely, the tree and Adam' (LS, 128/136; original emphases). According to Deleuze, Leibniz always thinks under the scheme of 'subject-verb-complement', which from antiquity has resisted the scheme of 'subject-copula-attribute' (FLB, 60/71).

22. 'This, however, explains why Leibniz, no matter how far he may have progressed in a theory of singular points and the play, did not truly pose the distributive rules of the ideal game and did at best conceive of the pre-individual very much on the basis of constituted individuals, in regions already formed by good sense (see Leibniz's shameful declaration: he assigns to philosophy the creation of concepts, provided that they do not overthrow the "established sentiments")' (LS, 132–3/141).
23. '[I]t is the real which makes itself possible, and not the possible which becomes real' (Bergson 1946: 122/115).
24. 'In short, the virtual is never subject to the global character which affects real objects. It is – not only by its origin but by its own nature – a fragment, a shred or a remainder' (DR, 125/133).
25. A few words on the term 'death instinct': Freud had called the impetus towards death discernible in living things the '*Todestrieb*'. Most often this is translated as the 'death drive' (Lacan is insistent on this point), but in the present work we have opted for the 'death instinct', in keeping with Deleuze's highly original take on the issue. Generally, French translations have rendered the term as '*pulsion de mort*' (see Laplanche and Pontalis 1973). The word '*pulsion*', from the same Latin root of '*pello* (I drive, set in motion)' as the English words 'compel' and 'propel', for example, unmistakably evokes an energetic release culminating in movement. However, the original German term '*Trieb*' can just as well be translated 'instinct', hence to translate the term as '*instinct de mort*' in French would be equally correct, from a purely linguistic standpoint. In the latter case, of course, the sense would be closer to 'principle', or even 'law (of nature)'. Taking all this into account, and having equivocated 'life instinct' with 'Eros' and 'death instinct' with 'Thanatos', Deleuze argues as follows. It is impossible for us to experience pure Eros or pure Thanatos, in and of themselves. What we are given in the experiential world are instead drives of sexuality and destruction, a hopelessly intertwined Eros and Thanatos. The term '*pulsion* (drive)' is therefore apt to name the appearance of

Trieb in experience. By contrast, in order to render the 'stillness of the transcendental level', that is, the transcendental principle that grounds the empirical, one should opt for the word '*instinct* (instinct)' (MCC, [116]/100). Since the present text analyses the *Todestrieb* as a transcendental principle, following Deleuze's suggestion, we will translate the German uniformly as 'death instinct (*instinct de mort*)'. [Translator's note: the existing English translation (*Masochism: An Interpretation of Coldness and Cruelty*) of this text has chosen to omit the passage to which Kokubun is referring in this footnote in its entirety. It can be found on p. 100 of *Présentation de Sacher-Masoch: le froid et le cruel* (1967) in the original French.]

26. Translator's note: the usual English translation of Freud's *Bindung* (*liaison* in French) is the English cognate 'binding'. In discussion with Kokubun, however, a term with greater nuance was felt to be necessary. Throughout this volume we have chosen to render it as 'harnessing'.

27. '[A] function of the mental apparatus [in the dreams of patients suffering from traumatic neurosis], though it does not contradict the pleasure principle, is nevertheless independent of it and seems to be more primitive than the purpose of gaining pleasure and avoiding [dis]pleasure' (Freud 1920, vol. XVIII: 32/32).

28. Jacques Derrida has given a clear account of this in his 'To Speculate – on "Freud"', included in *The Post Card: From Socrates to Freud and Beyond* (Derrida 1987: 352–3/374). The pleasure principle (which Derrida shortens to 'PP') comes to form a pair with the reality principle (similarly, 'PR') as it establishes its dominion; however, even before this hegemony, there is a tendency within the psychic apparatus which resists PP. Having noted this rebellious tendency as 'pp' (small letters this time), he goes on to propose a formula with pp as numerator, and PP+PR as denominator, to condense the process.

29. Deleuze too emphasises this point: the death instinct (Thanatos) and the life instinct (Eros) are not engaged in hostilities; indeed, in no way are they even opposed to each other (DR, 136/147).

30. For this reason, melancholic patients typically display a decrease in self-regarding feelings, often manifesting itself in excessive self-reproach and self-reviling. This is because all the criticisms which were formerly addressed to the beloved object are turned back against a part of the self, which is of course the lost object reproduced inside the self as phantasmagoria.

31. Incidentally, it is not the case that loss of the object necessarily results in melancholia: one of the necessary conditions for melancholia is that the original object of cathexis was elected on narcissistic grounds. It is this underlying narcissism that ensures the facile renunciation of object-cathexis; it is narcissism also that channels the powerful lingering libido towards an identification with the lost object.

32. 'By thus getting hold of the libido from the object-cathexes, setting itself up as sole love-object, and desexualising or sublimating the libido of the id, the ego is working in opposition to the purpose of Eros and placing itself at the service of the opposing instinctual impulses' (Freud 1923, vol. XIX: 46/274–5).

Research Note II: The Synthetic Method

Alongside the philosophic programme which Deleuze inherited as his own, we can also turn our attention to his philosophical preferences, his philosophical tastes. Deleuze's name is frequently discussed alongside that of Spinoza, and it is this seventeenth-century philosopher that expresses Deleuze's preferences with unrivalled clarity. This is because Spinoza is *the* philosopher of the 'synthetic method'.

Generally speaking, the synthetic method constitutes an oppositional pair with the analytic method, whose chief exponent is Descartes. Without going into too much detail, both of these methods are concerned with the way in which a philosophical theory is set forth. The analytic method begins from the facts which are given, that is the *effect*, which it proceeds to analyse in meticulous detail to arrive at the cause. In contradistinction, the synthetic method begins from the first principle whence all things originate, in other words it moves from *cause* to effect. For Descartes it is the analytic method which is the proper pathway to truth. Deleuze, on the other hand sees in Spinoza's *Ethics* the culmination of the synthetic method as the pathway to truth (EPS, 159–60/144–7).

On a first approach, it may seem that the two methods only traverse the same path, just in opposite directions. However, rotational symmetry is broken when we consider that the synthetic method has a difficulty peculiar to it. It wants to have the one principle as its point of departure, but this principle is not something pre-given. How then are we to get there? Precisely by passing through a sort of analytic procedure. And this principle having been attained, the very procedure thereto is subsumed as the preparatory part of the synthetic method itself. In other words, a more exacting definition of the synthetic method would have to be given in terms of the *change of direction* from the 'regress to the principle' to the 'progress from the principle'. It is in this sense that the synthetic method is not a simple mirror image of the analytic. 'The two types of systems [synthetic and analytic] can thus be distinguished structurally, that is to say, more profoundly than just by a simple opposition' ('Gueroult's General Method for Spinoza', in DI, 147/203).

To explicate this aspect of the synthetic method, Deleuze refers to one passage in French historian of philosophy Martial Gueroult's (1891–1976) work, *The Evolution and Structure of Fichte's Doctrine of Sciences* (1930), countless times, even into his final years:

Research Note II: The Synthetic Method

> The weight of the analytic method becomes more and more considerable, in measure as the principle comes to absorb it completely ... At each stage [the *Wissenschaftslehre*] always asserts that, as a principle must depend only on itself, the analytic method should pursue no other goal than its own elimination; thus indeed it understands the constructive method as alone effective. (Gueroult 1930: 174)

Making use of the analytic procedure one first retrogresses to the principle; the moment this principle is attained, the very procedure thereto is discarded. This change of direction can be seen to be at work both in Fichte's *Science of Knowledge* and Spinoza's *Ethics*.

A philosopher whose ratings have suffered somewhat (due in no small part to his ill-fated *Addresses to the German Nation*), Johann Gottlieb Fichte (1762–1814) is assessed highly by Deleuze. Indeed, the very final text published by Deleuze in his lifetime, 'Immanence: A Life . . .', references Fichte's definition of the transcendental domain (TRM, 390/360). Very likely the reason for Deleuze's great interest in Fichte is that, like Spinoza, he was a philosopher who followed the synthetic method consciously and with conviction.

There is one more philosopher whom Deleuze respected greatly as a practitioner of the synthetic method: Carl Gustav Jung (1875–1961). In the lesser-known essay 'From Sacher-Masoch to Masochism' (1961), Deleuze points out the limitations of Freud's 'analytic method', siding with the possibilities of Jung's 'synthetic method'. As if to parallel the low comparative standing of Fichte as against Kant, today Jung's reputation lags behind that of Freud. Nevertheless, in texts such as *A Thousand Plateaus* and *Dialogues II* Deleuze emphasised time and again the importance of Jung (making reference to E. A. Bennet's *What Jung Really Said* (1966)) (D, 80/98; TP, 30, 235/42, 288). Behind this assessment too is Deleuze's basic privileging of the synthetic method.

3
Practice: Thinking and Subjectivity

In the previous chapter, we identified the principle of Deleuzian philosophy as transcendental empiricism. Underlying this vision was the perspective of 'genesis'. For any given thing Deleuze chances to encounter, he will sketch its genesis, he will study it through its genesis. Correspondingly, this means that for all things, their present state of being must be grasped as a *post*-genetic result; in this way all things, depending on the conditions and the process of their genesis, are capable of undergoing *change*. If one's justification for something is along the lines of 'it is impossible to think otherwise', or 'we cannot but assume such a thing', one can count on Deleuze to give voice to his frustrations.

Deleuze thought extremely highly of the transcendental programme inaugurated by Kant. At the same time, he pointed out that there was a problem that Kant and his followers, in carrying through this programme, had imperceptibly left behind. This is of course the problem of genesis. In the hands of Kant, transcendental philosophy had come to *assume a determinate subject* through the concept of 'transcendental apperception', whose function it was to guarantee the unity of the various faculties. Kant never paused to ask about the genesis of this subject, let alone of the faculties themselves.

It was in the philosophy of Hume, preceding that of Kant, that Deleuze discovered this genetic perspective. The textbooks of philosophy never tire of reminding us that Humean philosophy was superseded by the Kantian. For Deleuze, however, such a summary assessment must remain blind to the problematic aspects of the latter and the possibilities latent in the former. There exists in Hume a thorough desire to understand genesis, penetrated as it is through and through by the question: 'how does the mind become a subject?' This is precisely the question that Kantianism has forgotten.

For Deleuze, the essence of transcendental empiricism lies in the imperative not to 'break it off when we please' (MCC, 114/98). And yet, Kant's version of transcendental philosophy falls into arrested development at a certain point, in fear of the God-knows-what that lies beyond. Against this, Deleuze summons the ghosts of empiricism to aid him in completing the transcendental project. From here Deleuze goes back to a primordial state (the desert island) which does not even assume the self (let alone the subject), populated only by transcendental singularities named the 'event', and he even went so far as to portray the genesis of this transcendental principle itself.

Now that we know what Deleuzian (pure) philosophy is, we must begin to inquire what sort of practice can be developed from it. If you recall, the original motivation of the present work was to discover the relation of Deleuzian philosophy to politics, in the realm of philosophical practice. For this purpose, Chapter 1 asked where Deleuze's philosophy is to be found, and Chapter 2 delved headlong into this location to see for ourselves what this philosophy in fact is. But it is now high time we returned to our first question from this 'long-cut', which has equipped us with the requisite armoury to ask the question in a more substantial form: what sort of practice can be extracted from Deleuzian transcendental empiricism, traversed as it is by the vision of genesis?

The Genesis of Thinking

However counterintuitive it might seem, for Deleuze the crux of the problem of practice is fundamentally the problem of thinking. This latter preoccupied him throughout his career, from the earliest publications to the very end of his life. In the work that first made his name in French academia, *Nietzsche and Philosophy* (1962), Deleuze takes off from the fact that for Friedrich Nietzsche (1844–1900), '[l]ife would be the active force of thought, but thought would be the affirmative power of life', to continue: '[t]hinking would then mean *discovering, inventing new possibilities of life*' (NPh, 94/115; original emphasis). For Deleuze, it is the act of thinking that invents/discovers new possibilities for 'life'. In thinking, one changes 'life' itself.

The problem is then to determine what thinking actually is, and how such a thinking in fact becomes possible. Deleuze had pursued this question from numerous different points of departure, which first came to fruition in *Proust and Signs* (1964). Although this work is ostensibly a study on Marcel Proust's (1871–1922) magisterial novel *In Search of Lost Time*, one would be hard-pressed to find anything like typical literary criticism within its pages. In keeping with his general philosophical method, Deleuze tries to penetrate to Proust's image of thought. And there he discovers an image in defiance of the philosophic one, in particular one which fights the core of rationalist philosophy (PS, 94/115): '*truth* is never the product of a *prior disposition* but the result of a *violence* in *thought*' (PS, 16/24; my emphases). What could this veritably 'philosophic' conceptualisation of the resistance to philosophy possibly mean?

Everyone knows the opening of *In Search of Lost Time*: the taste of the madeleine dipped in tea sets off a whirlwind of involuntary memories for 'I', the protagonist (Book I *Swann's Way*, Part I 'Combray I', end of chapter I). The extraordinary imagery has sealed the fate of subsequent interpretations of the novel as a tale of past memory, but Deleuze insists that such a reading misses what is fundamental. For this novel looks forward, not backward. 'The Search is orientated to the future, not the past' (PS, 4/10).[1] It is a story of how 'I' live through countless tales to come to accept 'my' literary vocation.[2] And the process leading up to this, according to Deleuze, is an endless 'apprenticeship (*apprendre/apprentissage*)', an apprenticeship in the reading of the 'sign (*signe*)'. The taste of the madeleine is a sign which brings back the past, at which point 'I' experience a strange 'delight'; but at first 'I' do not understand what this sensation is. Only after a long apprenticeship do 'I' come to learn to read the sign, and understand the secret of this 'joy'.[3] 'I' do not simply reminisce about the past aimlessly, for 'I' am slowly learning how to interpret the sign, and ultimately attain the 'revelation' of a form of truth.[4] For Deleuze, it is the encounter with the sign and the apprenticeship of its reading that pervades the whole of Proust's work, and not an unhealthy fixation with the past (incidentally, the word 'sign' appears with great frequency in Book VII of *In Search of Lost Time: Finding Time Again*).

The experience portrayed in Proust's work was significant for Deleuze because it proposed a novel vision of what thinking is/could be. The sign, whose reading must be learnt, can only ever be encountered through chance. The sign is 'that which falls', irrespective of whether you want it to or not. But the moment it appears, it will impress itself upon you with a great force. The madeleine compels from 'me' a recollection, independently of my will and my consciousness. There is something 'violent', even 'demanding' about this encounter. And yet it is none other than this violence, this demand, that makes man 'think', that wrenches him towards truth by the hair.[5] This is what Deleuze means when he says that truth is 'the result of a violence in thought': man will never reach truth by his own will power. Truth is rather always the result of having been forced to

Practice: Thinking and Subjectivity

think.[6] Man does not think, he is *made* to think. Thought only ever begins under compulsion, and the sign (bearer of this compulsion) is always the object of a contingent encounter.[7]

In other words, what is being enquired about here is the *genesis* of thinking itself. How does it come about that we engage in thought at all? Deleuze explains this as a form of 'violence', a 'compulsion', that can only be a 'chance encounter'. No one thinks because they want to, one can only think because one has to. This train of thought is developed extensively in *Difference and Repetition*, which in many ways is a consummation of Deleuze's work throughout the 1960s. The devaluation of active will, which *Proust and Signs* had pursued in the realm of art (there is no such thing as art created by an 'effort of will'[8]), is generalised to the thinking activity itself. The following recognition serves as Deleuze's point of departure:

> It cannot be regarded as a *fact* that thinking is the natural exercise of a faculty, and that this faculty is possessed of a good nature and a good will. 'Everybody' knows very well that in fact men think rarely, and more often under the impulse of a shock than in the excitement of a taste for thinking. (DR, 168/173; original emphasis)

Man rarely thinks. There is no such thing as an innate will to think in man. Just from time to time something comes up which shakes him seismically, and he has to start thinking unwillingly. Now Deleuze continues with the discussion as if this were simply a 'fact (*fait*)', self-evident. As it happens there is little by way of explanation to be found in the chapter from which the above quotation is taken (DR, chapter III); but turn back to chapter II ('Repetition for Itself'), and we can see that the recognition of this 'fact' is grounded on the notion of 'habit (*habitude*)', as empiricism would call it. The analysis of habit appears in the course of a theory of time built around the 'three syntheses'. As Takao Egawa has clarified (2003: 189), this theory is not so much designed to be a direct response to the question 'what is time?', as one developed in tandem with the question of our mode of Being, our mode of survival. Hence the connection to our 'fact' of thinking.

The concept of 'habit' is central for empiricism. Already in *Empiricism and Subjectivity*, Deleuze had proposed a certain troubling paradox with regards to habit. In a vague and uncritical manner, we tend to assume that habit is constituted by the routines that we perform day in day out. But Deleuze problematises this, with reference to Hume: habit does always *follow* experience, but it does not *depend on* experience (ES, 116/132). For what is repeated each time is something entirely different from what came before. Never will one and the same action be done again, never will one and the same situation arise again. In this sense each instance of repetition is uniquely irreplaceable.⁹ For these uniquely irreplaceable instances to constitute a habit, then, '[h]abit *decants* something new out from repetition – namely difference' (DR, 94/101; original emphasis). Habit reified in this manner is then capable of structuring human conduct. For this reason Deleuze locates the stratum of habit as that of 'generality': generality implies that each instance is entirely interchangeable.¹⁰ All too often repetition is misunderstood as generality; however, '[r]epetition is not generality. Repetition and generality must be distinguished in several ways' (DR, 1/7).

The 'fact' referred to earlier, then, points to this generality of habit, always coming after experience, but never dependent on it. Man can only live by 'decanting difference' from repetition. For each repetition is new, imbued with a difference. But man cannot survive if he has to face up to this novelty inherent in each and every instance. We need to be able to 'feel' that life is fundamentally a continuity of the Same, if we are to live at all.¹¹ Hence the need for a principle of habit. Deleuze, who describes the formation of habit as a 'passive synthesis', goes so far as to assert the existence of a '*beatitude* associated with passive synthesis [béatitude *de la synthèse passive*]' (DR, 95/102; my emphasis). Man wishes only to let himself dwell comfortably in this beatitude. How then can he possess anything like a spontaneous and active will to think? Philosophy has for too long blinded itself to this basic 'fact'. Already in *Proust and Signs*, Deleuze criticises this myopia in no uncertain terms: '[t]he mistake of philosophy is to presuppose within us a benevolence of thought, a natural love of truth' (PS, 16/24).

In other words, if man does nonetheless engage in thinking, this can only be because he has been forced to do so, as a last resort, after he has run out of all other options. Which is why Deleuze conceives of thought as external to will (even something *un*-willed, insofar as thought is always the result of a compulsion), and even calls this something that disturbs the 'beatitude of passive synthesis' a 'trespasser', a 'violence', an 'enemy'. That 'philosophy is the love (*philo-*) of wisdom (*sophia*)' is a lovely etymological bedtime story we tell our children, and Deleuze is having none of it: at the origin of thought is not love, but essential hatred of wisdom.¹²

Now it is to Martin Heidegger's (1889–1976) vision of thinking

Practice: Thinking and Subjectivity

that Deleuze feels a great proximity (DR, 181–2/188). In 'What Is Called Thinking?' (1954), this philosopher of Being writes as follows: '*[m]ost thought-provoking is that we are still not thinking*'; hence '[e]verything thought-provoking *gives* us to think [*alles Bedekliche gibt* zu *denken*]' (Heidegger 1968: 4/S. 2; original emphases). Man does not think, he is *made* to think. And that which forces us to think, adds Heidegger, is precisely the fact that after all this time, we are still not thinking in a genuine sense. Deleuze was to return to this same remark of Heidegger's years later, in his book on cinema (TI, 162/218); the affinity he felt must have been powerful indeed.

And yet, *Difference and Repetition* parts company with Heidegger at a crucial juncture. For Heidegger assumes a resemblance, even a correlation, between thinking and that which makes us think, amounting to a 'primacy of the Same (*primat du Même*)' (DR, 210n11/188n1). He does not conceive this 'something' that compels thought in terms of trespass or violence, but as a 'gift'.[13] This metaphor is revealing for Deleuze, because it shows that in Heidegger there exist remnant 'subjective presuppositions' that 'deep down man in fact desires and wills to think, man in fact loves the truth'.[14] This hope, this 'subjective presupposition', is what warps Heidegger's vision of thinking in the final instance. Man is all too happy living inside the blessed bubble of passive synthesis. This is the most natural state for man, who merely 'possesses the possibility' to think (to borrow Heidegger's own words). And so long as man is only given 'gifts' which readily harmonise with this natural state, he is not going to accord even a fraction of his time to thinking. In his assumption of resemblance and correlation between thinking and that which makes us think, in his uncritical dependence on the 'primacy of the Same', Heidegger has ended up averting his eyes from the real site of the genesis of thinking.

By contrast, Deleuze christened that which compels thought the 'sign'. The sign is not something gifted, but something *encountered*. And trivially, what we chance upon belongs neither to the given, nor to something which harmonises with the given; '[i]t is not the given but that by which the given is given' (DR, 176/182). In other words, the sign is what trespasses upon the givenness of passive synthesis, violates this givenness, and finally alters it unrecognisably; and only as such is it capable of extracting thought. Which amounts to the following: man starts to think only when a change of the *status quo* is thrust upon him. In this way thinking is inseparable from change.

The Apprenticeship and Method of Thinking

As we saw in the previous chapter, transcendental empiricism takes the event as its fundamental unit, and does not assume the subject. Rather, it is the genesis of the subject itself that needs to be problematised. As such, it is inevitable that this philosophy should accord to will the lowest possible value, and instead locate at the origin of thinking an evental encounter with something which compels thought. For if one cannot take the subject for granted, the same must apply to the will. Moreover, it is easy to see that this theory of thinking harks back to Deleuze's philosophical method. Deleuze had asserted that the problem and its critique are one and the same, and that the creation of new concepts is only possible through this critique of the problem. In other words, if one is to create new concepts, one must first encounter existing problems which induce unease and questioning. Is there not something wrong with how this problem is posed? ... it is such discomfort that lies at the origin of the setting up of a new problem, the creation of new concepts. The crucial point here is that these encounters are always evental, and never the result of a conscious exercise of the will. For man inhabits the 'beatitude of passive synthesis' spontaneously, and the last thing he wants to do is to think about anything. Nevertheless, from time to time he comes across a certain 'something' which forces him to think. Now one might judge such a vision of thinking as much too laissez-faire, even uninterested in the world and its vicissitudes. But from Deleuze's perspective, it is precisely from this fact (that we would prefer to do anything else than have to think) that philosophy should set off. One is tempted to go so far as to suggest that philosophy hitherto took such functions as subjectivity and consciousness for granted, for the very reason that it wanted to shield itself from this horrifying fact. But Deleuze's transcendental empiricism has cast to the flames such human, all too human sensibilities. This is the necessary consequence of elevating the event to the sole resident of the transcendental domain.

Moreover, it is important to keep in mind that Deleuze, though taking his cue from this fact of the will not-to-think, does not therefore conclude *que sera sera* in resignation. At times stressing the role of the contingent encounter, elsewhere he also says: '[t]o encounter is to find, to capture, to steal, but *there is no method for finding other than a long preparation*' (D, 7/13; my emphasis). It is true that one can never start to think of one's own accord, and even if such a thing were possible, it wouldn't be worth a penny. For thinking only comes into its own when it encounters a sign which compels it. However, this is not equivalent to saying that *all you need to do is lounge around, and this miraculous sign will visit you once in a blue moon*. For the sign needs to be read, and this reading is something that needs to be learnt.[15] As a result, the theory of thinking as compulsion by contingency has a necessary counterpart in a theory of apprenticeship in letting the encounter take place, or a theory of education.[16] We recall that *Proust and Signs*, in the self-same breath as it emphasised the contingent encounter and the force of compulsion as Proust's basic thematic concerns, also declared that *In Search of Lost Time* is a tale of learning for the protagonist. So too *Difference and Repetition*, which, in parallel with developing a theory of thinking, offers us a theory of learning.

Regarding apprenticeship, Deleuze writes that it requires not the mindless regurgitation of the Same, but a response to the sign, an encounter with the Other.[17] Man only learns something in order to adapt to an exteriority that cannot be subsumed into himself. And this response is not a mere rehearsal of the Same. We can thus see that Deleuze's criticism of Heidegger's use of the metaphor of 'gift' in conceptualising thinking, to the effect that this betrays a 'primacy of the Same', is only apparently abstract and speculative, for it opens onto an issue of great practical import. The encounter with the Other in apprenticeship is explicated in the following way, using the example of swimming: 'the movement of the response does not "resemble" that of the sign. The movement of the swimmer does not resemble that of the wave' (DR, 25/35). In fact, Heidegger, in 'What Is Called Thinking?', employs the same aquatic example: '[w]e shall never learn what "is called" swimming, for example, or what it "calls for", by reading a treatise on swimming. Only the leap into the river tells us what is called swimming' (Heidegger 1968: 21/S. 22). In effect, what Heidegger intends in this analogy is that one cannot know what it is to think until one has in fact thought for oneself ('what thinking is, we can fathom only when we are capable of thinking'). Once again, Deleuze's position is extremely close to Heidegger's: he too bids us to picture the absurd image of a student imitating the swimming instructor's moves on shore, and the utter futility of this exercise in the face of real incoming waves.

Nevertheless, and once again, Deleuze's theory ends up diverging in a 'minimal difference' from Heidegger's, concerning what it means to 'teach/be taught': 'We learn nothing from those who say: "Do as

I do". Our only teachers are those who tell us to "do with me", and are able to emit signs to be developed in heterogeneity rather than propose gestures for us to reproduce' (DR, 26/35).[18] It is true that we cannot learn to swim by reading essays on the subject, nor by flapping our arms around on land. But, is the alternative really to hurl the neophyte headlong into the water? Exactly the same can be said of thinking. It is true that thought requires the prior encounter with the sign which compels it, but this sign must itself be read. And the reading of the sign is something that has to be learnt. Now evidently this reading cannot be taught through the endless rehearsal of the Same ('do it like me'); for each sign is radically new, radically different. Hence one must learn to repeat the reading of the 'Other', that which contains a difference. The teacher who says 'do it with me' involves the student in an actual case, and demonstrates the proper response to a sign in its specificity. Through this process, the student will gradually come to develop his or her own 'space of encounter with signs [*espace de la rencontre avec des signes*]'[19] (DR, 26/35). Of course, if apprenticeship is the creation of the student's own 'space of encounter', it necessarily implies that the way each individual learns cannot be dictated in advance.[20] Which is why it is counterproductive to distribute a generally applicable model ('the Same') irrespective of difference. The true teacher is one who can say to his or her student: 'do it with me'.

The swimming metaphor is a fertile one, but alas we have come to the end of its shelf life in explicating the apprenticeship to thinking. For thinking obviously entails its own singularity. While developing the learning process as a systematisation of the encounter, Deleuze also considers something like a 'manual for thinking', a sort of 'method' for the activity of thought.[21] The relevant passage occurs in the context of a discussion of the Bergsonian method of 'intuition'.[22] Here it is pointed out that there are three rules to follow for a successful exercise of the method of intuition;[23] of these, the latter two are merely required by the specific mechanics of Bergsonian philosophy, hence we can focus on the first. This first rule states that the assessment of true/false be applied not to the answer to a question, but to the question itself. That is to say, it is eminently possible that the question itself is in error, and it is against such 'false problems (*faux problèmes*)' that one must be on the alert. It is a 'puerile' prejudice to presume that the categories of true and false apply only to the solutions to problems; and the immediate source of this prejudice is the school education system, Deleuze hastens to add. Within this scheme, the problem is something set by the schoolmaster, and the pupil's task is to find the answer, no more no less. A relation of subordination is thus established and reinforced: whereas '[t]rue freedom lies in a power to decide, to constitute problems themselves' (B, 15/4).

What then is a 'false problem'? According to Bergson, false problems can be divided into two types: the 'non-existent problem', and the 'badly posed problem'.

As examples of the former, we are given the 'problem of non-being' (why is there something rather than nothing?); the 'problem of disorder' (why is there order rather than disorder?); and last but not least, the old 'problem of the possible' (why this and not that, when both were equally possible?). The common denominator of all these is a confusion for which a specific psychological motivation can be pinpointed. First, in the problem of non-existence, man imagines nothingness. But in fact this nothingness is a fantasy, for we can only perceive and think plenitude. When one thing disappears, all that happens is that something else comes to take its place: elimination is more properly termed replacement. Hence when we say to ourselves 'there is nothing left', this reveals an indifference towards what does exist in the here and now. When man pictures an absolute nothingness, man is in fact banishing all substantial things, and refusing to see what has come to take their place. A similar analysis can be made of the problem of disorder: disorder is but an order which we are loath to admit as one. For there is organisation even where telos or will are lacking. But when man comes across an order that is contrary to his expectations, he declares that this is veritable 'disorder', thereby substituting his own feeling of displeasure for objective judgement. The problem of the possible, finally, is probably the most well-known of the false problems. In common parlance we say things like 'not this, but that was possible too'. But this is only because we are treating a concrete state of affairs as if it were abstraction. For instance, language permits us to say that it was possible for somebody before Shakespeare to have written *Hamlet*. But we can say this only if we have not bothered to look at the play itself in detail, for as we follow up on each of these details, we will come to see that this predecessor to Shakespeare must have thought everything the playwright thought, have felt everything the poet felt, and have known everything the dramatist knew. In which case, this hypothetical being must have occupied the exact same spatio-temporal coordinates as Shakespeare, coinciding with him in body and soul. In short, he must quite simply have been William Shakespeare himself. When we assert the existence of alternative possibilities in the past, therefore, all we are doing is *abstracting* from concrete reality, and from there working backwards in retrospect. It is all too easy to discern here yet another manifestation of the misanthrope's discontent with the existing state of affairs (Bergson 1946: 106–15/105–13).

Moving on to the second type of false problem, those which are badly posed, these arise because the question contains impurities that have not been satisfactorily analysed away. The problem in this case is an arbitrary hodgepodge of elements which in reality differ in kind from each other. The example we are given is the problem: 'is pleasure reducible to happiness'. Now both 'happiness' and 'pleasure' are consummate composite nouns. Thus, at bottom all this problem is asking for is definitions of complex terms, for which the most we can get will be an exhaustive and tiresome list of their usage in 'ordinary language'. '[I]n examining the states grouped under the name of pleasure they are found to have nothing in common except that they are states which man is seeking' (Bergson 1946: 58–9/52–3). In this way we are condemned to circle around the 'very nature of things': the problem is one without an answer, it is a false problem.

We notice here that the first type of problem also fell into falsity because the object under consideration (nothingness, disorder, the possible) had not been properly analysed. Hence, as Deleuze himself points out, type 1 errors in the last instance depend on type 2 errors (B, 20/9). Effectively, the false problem is one which has been posed badly. The problem itself is false; hence, we toil in vain if we try to furnish an answer to it. And yet, philosophy has never ceased to impose upon itself the resolution of these problems as its great Sisyphean labour, or so Bergson thought. The only reason why we cannot find an adequate solution is because the problem has been badly posed. And Bergson subscribed to the obverse as well: *so long as a problem has been well posed, it will resolve itself of its own accord* (B, 15/4).[24] Therefore, the crucial task, more so even than the actual answering of problems, is the discovery and proper formulation of the problem. Without this, we will somersault into the false problem and circulate around its irresolvability. For Deleuze, Bergson here displays a profound proximity to Karl Marx, the Marx who in *A Contribution to the Critique of Political Economy* (1859) wrote the famous words: 'humanity only sets itself problems that it is capable of solving'.

> In neither example [Marx or Bergson] is it a case of saying that problems are like the shadow of pre-existing solutions . . . Nor is it a case of saying

Practice: Thinking and Subjectivity

that only the problems count. On the contrary, it is the solution that counts, but the problem always has the solution it deserves, in terms of the way in which it is stated (i.e., the conditions under which it is determined as problem), and of the means and terms at our disposal for stating it. In this sense, the history of man, from the theoretical as much as from the practical point of view is that of the construction of problems. (B, 16/4–5)

Whether in literature or philosophy, life or society, there will come a time when man comes into contact with the sign that has the potential to force out thinking. If the encounter is serendipitous, and the individual has learnt the reading of the sign, they will begin to think. But the rest is not smooth sailing, for even if they manage to read the sign properly, if they then proceed to pose the problem inadequately, they will be able to do no more than orbit the false problem in labyrinthine circularity. For instance, to ask the question 'freedom or regulation?' is to have one foot already mired in the false problem, for neither 'freedom' nor 'regulation' have been sufficiently analysed to allow any realistic resolution to the problem. The fate in store for those who insist on asking such problems is that of the electron, spinning round and round. And while they are enjoying getting seasick from all this rotation, in the 'real' world everything is rigorously determined by relations of power. So for a change of air let us pose a true problem: *who* benefits from the posing of false problems? Inevitably, it is those who already hold power in their grip, those with the power to decide. The posing of false problems is an instrument to maintain their dominance, which they hand out like flyers to rob people of the freedom to think. This is why it is imperative to learn how to call out false problems, and pose true ones in their stead: this is in one and the same stroke a genuine social and critical practice. It was therefore no whim of the moment that led Deleuze to extend Bergson's problematic to that of Marx.

The Bergsonian critique of the false problem is thus an extremely powerful one, and one which Deleuze feels a great admiration for. Yet, once again, Deleuze was not fully satisfied with this, and could not stop here; in *Difference and Repetition* he adds another level to this problem of the 'problem' (so to speak). What then was Deleuze unhappy with in all this? Getting ahead of ourselves somewhat, we can say that Bergson, in his zeal to combat the false problem, had in turn overemphasised the dimension of the resolution of problems. True, in society as in the history of philosophy, there is a veritable excess of false problems. This drove Bergson to insist that any problem, as long as it is well-posed, will be answered in no time. But does this not feel, somehow, *too* prim? While recognising that solving problems is of the utmost importance, Deleuze at the same time turns his attention to a dimension beyond this almost naive confidence in the resolution of all well-posed problems.

For this purpose, in *Difference and Repetition* Deleuze introduces a distinction between the 'problem' and the 'question' (note that these were used interchangeably with respect to Bergson, but henceforth they must be distinguished). Schematically, the problem is that from which a question is posed. Thinking, in this sense, moves from the problem to the question.[25] Deleuze also refers to the problem, with reference to Kant, as the 'Idea (*Idée*)' (DR, 214/219). For Kant, the Ideas are those special concepts of reason (not the Intellect), foreclosed as an object of knowledge for man, yet whose investigation we cannot help but undertake. Kant restricts these to the triad of the freedom of the self, the world, and God; Deleuze expands the list in a liberal application of Kant's usage. The 'Idea' in Kant is a problem 'to which there is no solution'; what Kant really means here, says Deleuze, is that the true problem is none other than the 'Idea' itself.

What matters here is not whether this act of interpretative transformation by Deleuze is valid. Either way, what is clear is that the Kantian 'Idea' held a place of importance for Deleuze as an *image*. And this is because the 'Idea' is what confronts us with a question, demanding that it be answered, yet at the same time 'these Ideas do *not disappear with "their" solutions*' (DR, 215/219; my emphasis). True, the problem poses – or better, 'commands'[26] – a question, to which we must discover the answer. Yet this in no way implies that the original problem disappears when the question has found an answer. Quite the contrary in fact – we must always caution against a facile throwing out of the 'spent' problem. The real danger is that we come to believe problems vanquished once and for all and become satiated.[27]

For a problem can only be resolved when certain conditions are fulfilled. Deleuze insists upon the importance of determining these conditions. In this he finds an ally in the modern mathematical theory of problems and solutions, as expounded in chapter IV of *Difference and Repetition*. For Niels Abel (1802–1829) – whom Deleuze extols to the heavens as having performed 'a more considerable revolution than the Copernican' – in thinking the solution 'we must determine the conditions of the problem which progressively specify the fields of solvability in such a way that "the statement contains the seeds of

Practice: Thinking and Subjectivity

the solution"' (DR, 227/233). The aforementioned words of Marx are invoked once again. And again, the point here is that the ways in which solutions to social problems are arrived at depend on the economic conditions underlying these very problems (DR, 235/241).

Having equated the problem with the 'Idea', Deleuze goes on to say that the problem is also a 'multiplicity' (DR, 230/236). Although the precise mathematical sense of the term is at play here, for our purposes it suffices to keep in mind that the manifold is composed of virtualities (indeed, the same section also states that, for example, 'irony itself is a multiplicity – or rather, the art of multiplicities' (DR, 230/236); Deleuze's concept of the 'multiplicity' is not reducible to its mathematical usage). For the actualisation of virtualities, various conditions have to be met. That is, given the problem is an 'Idea', and the 'Idea' in turn a manifold, it follows that the solution to any problem will change depending on these problematic conditions. The true danger, then, is to restrain this virtuality and silence the problem with a triumphant declaration that its unique solution has been discovered.[28] 'A problem does not exist, apart from its solutions. Far from disappearing in this overlay, however, it insists and persists in these solutions. *A problem is determined at the same time as it is solved, but its determination is not the same as its solution*' (DR, 203/212; my emphasis).

Moreover, this theory of the 'problem' is carried over into the discussion of education/apprenticeship. 'Learning is the appropriate name for the subjective acts carried out when one is confronted with the objectivity of a problem (Idea), whereas knowledge designates only the generality of concepts or the calm possession of a rule enabling solutions' (DR, 204/213–14). To come face to face with the problem as an 'Idea' composed of virtualities, and to attempt to make sense of this intrusion in one's own way – this is precisely what 'learning' is. How much less exciting is 'knowing' then, the mere acquisition of a step-by-step set of rules for solving the question posed by the problem! Therefore, if one is to learn, genuinely learn, one must study in one's own way how the problem as 'Idea' is constituted.[29] Which validates Deleuze's last word on the matter: '[i]t is from "learning", not from knowledge, that the transcendental conditions of thought must be drawn' (DR, 206/216).

Deleuze's vision for thinking cannot be separated from his theory of learning. And if it is thinking that can create new potentialities for life, then learning/apprenticeship, teaching/being taught, are immediately relevant for the realm of practice. Such a potentiality is crouched behind Deleuzian philosophy and its theory of thinking, its theory of education.

Subjectivity Added to Matter

We began this chapter by asserting that in Deleuze's eyes the problem of philosophical practice is fully reducible to the problem of thinking. Indeed, we hope to have communicated just how much effort was expended by Deleuze in constructing this model of thinking. And the end result was a theory of great potentiality and fertility. Thinking of course begins as an act of individual practice; but its scope cannot be restricted to the individual, for as we have seen with the theory of the 'problem', inherent in this practice is the potential for a powerful social critique. And finally, if thinking is capable of opening new potentialities for life, we must go so far as to say that the theory of thinking will *eventually* even feed into political practice.

From a different perspective, however, it would seem almost self-contradictory to claim to have demonstrated the practical/political aspects of Deleuzian philosophy based on his theory of thinking. Must we not also have inquired after a dimension outside of thought, what is commonly known as the dimension of 'action'? Recall Slavoj Žižek's summary assessment that Deleuze's philosophy is elitist, with no inherent relation to politics (see Chapter 1 of this volume); if all Deleuze can offer by way of philosophical practice is a perfected model of thinking, we would surely be forced to submit to this judgement.

In fact, towards the end of his life Deleuze did problematise the dimension of 'action' explicitly, albeit in an extremely roundabout fashion, resulting in a redefinition of 'subjectivity'. Crucially, the same inspiration that drove his theory of thinking can also be found here. In other words, we would be justified in reading this discussion as the culmination or an extension of Deleuze's theory of thinking to the realm of action proper. The relevant passage occurs in *Cinema 2: The Time-Image* (1985).

In the preceding volume, *Cinema 1: The Movement-Image* (1983), Deleuze had developed his ideas on what he called the 'movement-image', which he saw as hegemonic in classical film. The movement-image is defined by the sequence of perception and action. A character perceives a certain situation; this perception in turn prompts an action in response from the character. Or, in Deleuze's own words, the situation directly 'extends' to action. Take for example Charlie

Practice: Thinking and Subjectivity

Chaplin's *City Lights* (1931). The Tramp, played by Chaplin himself, meets a Flower Girl at a street corner. Everything about this little girl invites us to feel pity for her; as such, she appears as a figure to-be-helped. The perception of the sense of the 'to-be-helped' extends into Chaplin's subsequent actions (make money boxing, and so on). In other words, the movement-image always comes with a pre-interpreted meaning attached to it, which the character will perceive and then act accordingly. Here, circumstance and action form a unified gestalt. One could call this an image whose 'appropriate response' is evident at a glance. To formulate this smooth and unific transition from sensation to movement, Deleuze also uses such terms as the 'sensory-motor situation' and the 'sensory-motor image'.

However, in the history of cinema the movement-image was to undergo a certain crisis. The crisis beckoned a new type of image, the 'time-image', which is the subject of the second volume. Deleuze sees the transformation from movement-image to time-image as coinciding with the end of the Second World War; the war effected an insurmountable crisis for the movement-image, from whose ashes arose the time-image (MI, 214–16/284–5). From the general direction of our discussions it should be clear that the time-image is an image whose 'appropriate response' is not evident. No longer will perception extend unproblematically into action. The character, unable to respond to the circumstance (s)he faces, is condemned to wander aimlessly about this circumstance. According to Deleuze, the first to experiment with this new type of image was the school of Italian neorealism. Vittorio De Sica's *Bicycle Thieves* (1948) is a paradigmatic example. The protagonist has been unemployed for the last two years, but it had seemed that this hardship was finally coming to an end. His family rejoices; however, his bicycle, without which he cannot do his newfound job, is stolen. Father and son look for the bicycle as if their life depends on it (it does). But not so much as a single pedal is found, and only wasted time accumulates pitilessly. Through all this the son can only observe his father.[30] And in the final scene of the film, seeing his father forced to become a bicycle thief himself, the son's tears will well without end.

In the time-image, there is an abyss that separates the characters' actions and the emptiness of the relentless passage of time. What we have here, in other words, is an image that presents a *mechanically flowing time* indifferent to what happens to take place in it.[31] In the sense that this is a pure image stripped of sense, it is also called the 'optical-sound image'. In films of the movement-image, the characters responded to the circumstances in order to act accordingly, which allowed for a certain identification on the part of the viewer; come the time-image, it is as if the characters themselves have been demoted to the position of viewer, helpless spectators of the circumstances they have been thrown into. '[T]he character has become a kind of viewer' (TI, 3/9).

It is in the context of this distinction between the two cinematic images, and the historical progression that runs between them, that *Cinema 2* effects a redefinition of 'subjectivity'. The key film here is *Europe '51* (1952) by Roberto Rossellini (a well-known representative of Italian neorealism along with the aforementioned De Sica), which Deleuze reads using Bergson's theory of recognition.

Bergson makes a distinction between two types of recognition, the automatic/habitual and the attentive (TI, 42/62). The cow recognises grass and eats it; on the way to the office the accountant reaches the appropriate corner, recognises it, and takes a left; the labourer enters the factory, recognises it as his workplace, and so begins yet another day. This is automatic recognition: perception extends without delay into habitual movement. On the other hand, attentive recognition occurs when someone struggles to recognise the object they have encountered. That is to say, their perception fails to extend into a response of any sort. They will return again and again to the object, and desperately try to extract certain 'features' from it. 'What in the name is that? Was it perhaps this ... no, impossible, perhaps it was that instead?' In this way they will try one identification based on the extracted features, then another, over and over again.

Deleuze, having explained this distinction, attempts to overlay it with the earlier distinction between the two types of image in film history. Automatic recognition effects an extension from perception to movement: it thus corresponds to the sensory-motor image, the movement-image defined by the sequence of perception and action. Let us now compare this image, the offspring of automatic recognition, with the image arising from attentive recognition. At first sight, it might seem that the image resulting from the former process is richer than that of the latter. For whereas attentive recognition just pulls out some indeterminate features of the object, only to discard them in the next instant, automatic recognition would seem to furnish us with a wholesome image of the object itself.

But as is immediately clear, this richness is merely apparent (TI, 43/64), for in fact all automatic recognition does is to reduce the object to the set of properties that would interest us, properties which

Practice: Thinking and Subjectivity

can be extended into responsory activity. What the cow recognises is not each blade of grass, but the abstraction of some grass 'in general'. There is after all no need to recognise each individual blade in its singularity for the purposes of assuaging hunger. And that is not all, for automatic recognition also subtly alters the perception of the object the better to conform to its purposes of extension into action. The street corner I go past five (or more, poor thing) days a week must necessarily look different each time; yet any potentially disruptive elements which could impose themselves between me and my left turn (a different angle of the sun, a new mark on the wall . . .) are simply left out of the picture in advance, for the sake of yet another functional day at the office.

By contrast, all attentive recognition can offer us is a set of 'features', it is true. However, by the same token this recognition, which forces upon us the seemingly fruitless exercise of endlessly extracting and then discarding features of an object, *will each time make us confront the object in itself*. We thus come face to face with the singularity of the object. Even if the features one can gain from each confrontation are limited in number, nonetheless the retroactive consequence of this procedure will be the purely optical and phonetic time-image, which for Deleuze is the 'really rich' image (TI, 43/64).

How does all this relate to *Europe '51*? Irene, a bourgeois woman played by Ingrid Bergman, is too busy hosting parties to spend time with her little boy. In a desperate bid for her attention, the son hurls himself down the stairs. For a while it seems that he has managed to survive the fall; however, after a brief conversation with his mother, who has reconsidered her former attitude, he dies of complications from the trauma to his head. Irene descends into a state of shock. Following the incident, she is enlisted by her cousin Andrea, a committed communist, to participate in giving aid to the poor of the slums.

The relevant scene for Deleuze is when Irene goes to work in a factory to cover for one such poor woman she has befriended. Overwhelmed by the great throngs of people making their way to the factory, the explosive noise of the machinery, and the colossal edifice of metal, she is close to fainting. For her, the perception of the factory is incapable of being extended into the dutiful performance of labour. Automatic perception is obstructed. Trying nonetheless to comprehend what the factory is, she turns to face this object over and over again. In Deleuze's words, 'the same object (the factory) . . . passes through different circuits' (TI, 44/65). That night, Irene returns home a shattered woman, and the next morning she recounts to Andrea her experiences at the factory. 'I thought I saw convicts' (TI, 44/65), she says, a line which Deleuze quotes over and over again (as if he himself were trying to recognise its singularity). To which Andrea responds with a fervent, *automatic* monologue dreaming of communist revolution. But Irene cannot subscribe to this vision. She wants to intervene at a more emotional, spiritual level. Her charity work comes to earn her the accolade of being a 'saint'. And her eyes are no longer that of a shattered woman; she is able to interact with those society has trampled upon with fortitude and conviction.

Deleuze identifies in Irene's transformation a new meaning of subjectivity. Let us follow his reasoning in detail. In the movement-image brought on by automatic recognition, we have subjectivity 'so-called', a subject of sequential extension from perception to action. Something is perceived, and this perception then extends into a response: it is this extension from one to the other that has traditionally been given the name of 'subject'. According to Deleuze's explanation, as soon as a gap arises between perception and action, this form of subjectivity will come about (TI, 45/66). In effect, the subject is that which is tasked with occupying this gap. It is nevertheless crucial that we understand the extension entailed by this form of subjectivity to be pre-determined in all possible ways. In automatic recognition, the action that will follow the perception has been decided in advance. This subjectivity, whose extension is a *fait accompli* (Deleuze calls this the 'first subjectivity' (TI, 45/66)), never results in the new.

Attentive recognition, by contrast, comes about through the work of recollection (the 'recollection-image'). 'What in the name is that? Was it perhaps this . . . no, impossible, perhaps it was that instead?' Recollection too tries to close the aforementioned gap; and if ultimately this work is successful, it will re-establish the sensory-motor sequence of automatic recognition. 'Ah I see, this is a factory . . . this is where I will spend the day working . . .'. However, at exceptional moments it can happen that attentive recognition does not conclude in mere recollection, but, 'lead[ing] us back individually to perception' (TI, 45/67), actualises something virtual. The heroine of *Europe '51* is an exemplary instance of this. The same factory passes through numerous different circuits to beget the perception that 'the factory is a prison'. We have here a *new* subjectivity.

From which we must conclude as follows: 'attentive recognition informs us to a much greater degree *when it fails than when it suc-*

Practice: Thinking and Subjectivity

ceeds' (TI, 52/75; my emphasis). If attentive perception succeeds, all we have is a delayed recognition, a short detour after which we will revert to the sensory-motor fluency of automatic recognition. However, it is possible that recollection will be abortive, and sensory-motor extension will then stumble and stammer; in such cases, attentive recognition is unable to extend to its rightful action, instead linking up with some virtual element. Just like when Irene achieved a new subjectivity through her encounter with the factory. It is impossible to assimilate this to the omnipresent subjectivity of the first type, which proliferates to fill the gap between perception and action. 'Subjectivity, then, takes on a new sense' (TI, 46/67). What emerges here is the second form of subjectivity: Deleuze calls this a subjectivity that 'is added to matter' (*s'ajoute à la matière*)' (TI, 46/67).

For example, the subjectivity that we can discern in Andrea is resolutely of the first kind. He is steadfast in his communist beliefs, and accordingly perceives the poor through the lens of a communistic subjectivity. The sense of this perception is thus pre-determined, extending unproblematically to the activity of aid work. There is here a clear line of demarcation between subject and object; the subject cannot undergo any modulations. Not so with our heroine Irene, however. For crucially, the immediate occasion for her new subjectivity was neither the death of her son, nor the encounter with poverty. Initially, her work with the poor was no more than just tagging along with Andrea. Her (exquisitely respectable) reaction upon seeing their great hardship was to remark what lovely people they are. Instead, what gives rise to her new subjectivity is the perception of the factory: the sound, the size, that sheer mass of people.[32] The perception of the factory is forced to pass through a myriad different variations. She is confounded, she fails to recognise. And the result is the perception, literal and not metaphorical, that the factory workers are 'convicts'. The dawn of her new subjectivity must be sought in this final perception and nowhere else.

Why then is such a subjectivity described as being 'added to matter'? Most likely because this second type of subjectivity lacks the schema of subject-object that is at work for example in Andrea's subjectivity. The subject no longer demonstrates its subjectivity towards an object it has identified for itself; this new subjectivity will arise in accordance with the requirement, the necessity even, demanded by the matter of the world. Hence the formulation 'added to matter', not added to an object.

It should be clear from the foregoing explanation that the theory of subjectivity 'added to matter' fits neatly with Deleuze's vision for thinking. Indeed, insofar as the genesis of this subject follows upon the activity of thought, one can justifiably call it an extension of his theory of thinking. A subjectivity enacted through a pre-defined object(ive) (subjectivity of the first type) can only recognise things in keeping with an existing perceptual stricture: here there is nothing new under the sun. In contradistinction, only the encounter with a perception that destroys one's existing perceptual stricture can give rise to a subjectivity 'added to matter' (subjectivity of the second type). Moreover, *Cinema 2* explicitly indicates that this new subjectivity is connected with the theme of apprenticeship/education: '[h]er glances ... pass through every state of an internal vision, affliction, compassion, love, happiness, acceptance ... she sees, she has learnt to see [*elle voit, elle a appris à voir*]' (TI, 2/9). The second type of subjectivity, just like thinking, is not going to pay you a visit if all you do is lounge around; it can only be chanced upon after a process of learning. Following the death of her son, Irene had first to undergo a lengthy period of learning before she could read the perception of the factory as a sign.

In this case we have seen how Deleuze, who thought so hard about thought itself, tried to apply, even extend, this line of thinking to the domain of action and subjectivity (albeit in the context of a critique of film).[33] To that extent, the relevant sections of *Cinema 2* constitute a rare instance in which Deleuze actively intervened in the realm of practice.

Having said that, however, we cannot help but conclude with the following assessment. It is difficult to avoid the feeling that this account of subjectivity exhibits quite palpably the limitations of Deleuze's philosophical practice. For recall that subjectivity 'added to matter' comes about as a result of the *failure* of attentive perception. Yes, proactive exercise of the will to action too can beget subjectivity, but this is doomed to lapse into the first type of subjectivity, lacking so much as an inkling of novelty. This is why the subjectivity of the new, the second type of subjectivity, is required. *But it is impossible to aim to fail*. For the moment one elevates a certain failure as one's objective, it can no longer be a failure to attain it. And no doubt, this difficulty will immediately be cast back onto Deleuze's theory of thinking. Thought is only born of an encounter with something which compels it. As such, *it is impossible to aim to think*. For one cannot seek to encounter, one can only encounter when one's

Practice: Thinking and Subjectivity

expectations have all fallen into despair. If one encounters something which happens to fulfil one's expectations, this fact on its own disqualifies it from being a genuine encounter. As a matter of fact, *Proust and Signs* rates 'disappointment (*déception*)' highly as the basic condition of apprenticeship.[34]

There is little doubt that Deleuze's theory of learning, and the vision for thinking which arises from it, constitute a powerful theory with immediate practical valence. It is a theory that can educate us in many ways (and we do not say this frivolously). Nevertheless, as soon as this theory is extended to a programmatic discussion of action and subjectivity, it proves difficult to assent to. For what it effectively demands of us is that we *wait for failure*.

This feature of Deleuzian philosophy has been remarked upon by other theorists. François Zourabichvili (1965–2006), for example, showed in his essay 'Deleuze et le possible (de l'involontarisme en politique)' (1998) that Deleuzian philosophy could be summed up under the label of 'involuntarism'. For Zourabichvili, Deleuze had constructed the most involuntary philosophy conceivable. The conclusion of this philosophy, then, is something like the following: '[t]o attain the becoming beyond the possible, such was the direction of Deleuze. To arrive at the identity of the possible and the necessary, a place where the will will be nothing but a false problem' (Zourabichvili 1998: 356). And we must concede that this assessment is spot on: Deleuze has indeed created the most involuntary philosophy conceivable. But is there nothing wrong with this? And was Deleuze himself not in the least troubled by these implications of his own philosophy?

* * *

Thus far we have attempted to provide as comprehensive as possible an overview of Deleuzian philosophy's 'method' (Chapter 1), 'principle' (Chapter 2) and 'practice' (this chapter). The end product has been a vision of Deleuzian philosophy that is after all both realistic (there is no such thing as an active will to think in man) and practical (having recognised the lack of such an active will, it proceeds to emphasise the importance of learning). This philosophy is an extremely enticing one. Yet, at the same time, it is impossible not to feel here a definitive limitation. And is it not this same limitation that theorists who claim that Deleuzian philosophy lacks a politics of any sort have also intuited in their own ways? However astute Deleuze himself was in his political sensibility, however actively he himself participated in politics as an intellectual, this suspicion will always persist.

At this point we are forced to introduce an axial turn in relation to the foregoing line of discussion, for which purpose we would like to propose the following hypothesis: Deleuze did indeed sense that his philosophy had reached some sort of stumbling block; and it was for precisely this reason, in order to break through this blockage, that he plunged himself into an experiment, practically a wager. This wager, needless to say, was the collaboration with Félix Guattari begun in 1969. What if Deleuze tried to re-invent his own style of philosophy by clashing pens with Guattari, a writer of an entirely different disposition? The result? Well, we have it before our very eyes. The collaboration was a success, and several books were composed by this strange Escherian pair of hands, Deleuze-Guattari . . .

As we stated at the outset, we must not confuse the works of Deleuze with those of Deleuze-Guattari, at least without positing requisite theoretical grounds for doing so. For the fact is that there are many differences to be discerned between these two bodies of work. In the next chapter, we will set off from the above hypothesis to penetrate ever deeper into the matter.

Notes

1. And further: 'Proust's work is not orientated to the past and the discoveries of memory, but to the future and the progress of an apprenticeship' (PS, 26/36).
2. 'What is involved is not an exposition of involuntary memory, but the narrative of an apprenticeship: more precisely, *the apprenticeship of a man of letters*' (PS, 3/10; my emphasis).
3. What was it, then, that the protagonist did not know at the beginning? In Book III of the work, *The Guermantes Way*, Proust writes: '[b]ut she [Françoise] was the first person to prove to me by her example (*which I was not to understand until long afterwards*, when it was given me afresh and more painfully, *as will be seen in the later volumes of this work*, by a person who was dearer to me) that the truth has no need to be uttered to be made apparent, and that one may perhaps gather it with more certainty, without waiting for words and without even taking any account of them, from countless outward signs, even from certain invisible phenomena, analogous in the sphere of human character to what atmospheric changes are in the physical world' (Proust 2001, vol. 2: 354–5; my emphases). (Incidentally, according to the Japanese translator of *In Search of Lost Time*, Suzuki Michihiko, by 'later volumes of

this work' Proust means the chapters towards the end of Book V to the beginning of Book VI.) Truth need not be told in words. Rather one must learn how to read the sign, a reading which is unique to oneself. And to achieve this one must be prepared to use up all the time in the world. One can discern here affinities with Bergsonian intuition, and the Spinozist vision of truth.

4. '[A]lready at Combray I used to fix before my mind for its attention some image which had compelled me to look at it, a cloud, a triangle, a church spire, a flower, a stone, because I had the feeling that perhaps beneath these signs there lay something of a quite different kind which I must try to discover, some thought which they translated after the fashion of those hieroglyphic characters which at first one might suppose to represent only material objects. No doubt the process of decipherment was difficult, but only by accomplishing it could one arrive at whatever truth there was to read. For the truths which the intellect apprehends directly in the world of full and unimpeded light have something less profound, less necessary than those which life communicates to us against our will in an impression which is material because it enters us through the senses but yet has a spiritual meaning which it is possible for us to extract. In fact, both in the one case and in the other, whether I was concerned with impressions like the one which I had received from the sight of the steeples of Martinville or with reminiscences like that of the unevenness of the two steps or the taste of the madeleine, the task was to interpret the given sensations as signs of so many laws and ideas, by trying to think – that is to say, to draw forth from the shadow – what I had merely felt, by trying to convert it into its spiritual equivalent' (Proust 2001, vol. 4: 446–7).

5. 'There is always the violence of a sign that forces us into the search, that robs us of peace. The truth is not to be found by affinity, nor by goodwill, but is *betrayed* [*se trahit*] by involuntary signs' (PS, 15/24; original emphasis). In due course we shall be redefining the 'peace' spoken of here as the 'beatitude associated with passive synthesis'.

6. 'What is it that the man who says "I want the truth" wants? He wants the truth only when it is constrained and forced. He wants it only under the rule of an encounter, in relation to such and such a sign' (PS, 16–17/25).

7. 'The accident of encounters and the pressure of constraints are Proust's two fundamental themes. Precisely, it is the sign that constitutes the object of an encounter and works this violence upon us. It is the accident of the encounter that guarantees the necessity of what is thought' (PS, 16/25).

8. 'A work undertaken by the effort of the will is nothing; in literature, it can take us only to those truths of the intelligence that lack the mark of necessity' (PS, 21/30).

9. 'Repetition as a conduct and as a point of view concerns non-exchangeable and non-substitutable singularities' (DR, 1/7).
10. '[G]enerality expresses a point of view according to which one term may be exchanged or substituted for another' (DR, 1/7).
11. 'But contraction also refers to the fusion of successive tick-tocks in a contemplative soul. Passive synthesis is of [this] kind: it constitutes our *habit of living*, our *expectation that "it" will continue* [notre attente que "cela" continue], that one of the two elements will appear after the other, thereby assuring the perpetuation of our *case*' (DR, 94–5/101; first and second emphases mine, third original).
12. '[T]here is only involuntary thought, aroused but constrained within thought, and all the more absolutely necessary for being born, illegitimately, of fortuitousness in the world. Thought is primarily trespass and violence, the enemy, and nothing presupposes philosophy: everything begins from misosophy' (DR, 175–6/181–2).
13. '[A thought-provoking thing] always gives that gift just so far as the thought-provoking matter already *is* intrinsically what must be thought about' (Heidegger 1968: 4/S. 2; original emphasis).
14. 'It is true that Heidegger retains the theme of a desire or a *philia*, of an analogy – or rather, a homology – between thought and that which is to be thought. The point is rather that he retains the primacy of the Same, even if this is supposed to include and comprehend difference as such – whence the metaphors of gift which are substituted for those of violence. In all these senses, Heidegger does not abandon what we called above the subjective presuppositions' (DR, 210–11n11/188n1).
15. We mention in passing the admirable book by Sébastien Charbonnier, *Deleuze Pedagogue* (2009), which sets off from the importance of this theme of 'apprenticeship' in Deleuze to construct what may very well be called a Deleuzian philosophy of education. Traversed as it is by the problem of how to let thinking descend upon the student (p. 25), this is a work which goes beyond the confines of Deleuze scholarship to provide useful insight into pedagogy in general.
16. '[I]t is from "learning", not from knowledge, that the transcendental conditions of thought must be drawn' (DR, 206/216).
17. 'Learning takes place not in the relation between a representation and an action (reproduction of the Same) but in the relation between a sign and a response (encounter with the Other)' (DR, 25/35).
18. In *Proust and Signs*, Deleuze writes as follows: '[w]ho knows how a schoolboy suddenly becomes "good at Latin", which signs (if need be, those of love or even inadmissible ones) have served in his apprenticeship? We never learn from the dictionaries our teachers or our parents lend us. The sign implies in itself a heterogeneity of relation. We never learn by doing *like* someone, but by doing *with* someone, who bears no resemblance to what we are learning' (PS, 22/31–2; original emphasis).

19. When one directs one's attention to the theme of 'learning' in Deleuze, it quickly becomes apparent that the late study on Francis Bacon's paintings (*Logic of Sensation*, 1981) and the two volumes on film (*Cinema 1 & 2*, 1983 and 1985) go beyond mere expositions of 'Deleuzian aesthetics'; they are rather works which confront head-on the task of practice. For each book, in its own way, concerns itself with the proper interpretation of the image; at the same time, they are motivated by the problem of how not to fall into the reproduction of existing forms and formulae. Must these then not be read as practical manuals, on how the sign ought to be interpreted?
20. 'We never know in advance how someone will learn: by means of what loves someone becomes good at Latin, what encounters make them a philosopher, or in what dictionaries they learn to think' (DR, 205/215).
21. It is true that the word 'thinking' sounds like something that can be done empty-handed. Moreover Deleuze, in *Proust and Signs*, does write the following: '[i]n opposition to the philosophical idea of "method," Proust sets the double idea of "constraint" and of "chance"' (PS, 16/25). If the word 'method' cannot but evoke the reproduction of the 'Same', we hope to show in what follows that Deleuze's insights on the problem and the question do constitute a sort of 'method', whose force refuses to be reduced to such Sameness, and which for this reason is practically valuable. Incidentally, as can be seen from the line '[t]o encounter is to find, to capture, to steal, but there is no method for finding other than a long preparation', cited above, it is not as if Deleuze expressed a consistent distaste for the word 'method (*méthode*)'.
22. It is true that there is something 'off' about calling intuition a 'method', for whereas the latter generally implies multiple steps to be followed ordinally, intuition is simple, instant. Indeed Bergson himself wrote that '[t]he use of the word intuition, however, caused me some degree of hesitation' (quoted in B, 13/1). 'The fact is', nevertheless, 'that Bergson relied on the intuitive method to establish philosophy as an absolutely "precise" discipline' (B, 14/2).
23. 'First rule: Apply the test of true and false to problems themselves. Condemn false problems and reconcile truth and creation at the level of problems'; 'Second rule: Struggle against illusion, rediscover the true differences in kind or articulations of the real'; 'Third rule: State problems and solve them in terms of time rather than of space' (B, 15, 21, 31/3, 11, 22; emphases removed).
24. 'I believe that the great metaphysical problems are in general badly stated, that they frequently resolve themselves of their own accord when correctly stated' (Bergson 1946: 111/104).
25. '[T]he movement [of thought] goes not from the hypothetical to the apodictic but from the problematical to the question' (DR, 247/255).
26. 'Questions are imperatives' (DR, 247/255).

27. One of the cases taken up by Deleuze in his discussion of the problem and the solution is the 'solution of the Jewish Problem' (DR, 235/241). Needless to say this 'solution' unleashed unspeakable terror. The Deleuzian theory of the problem and the solution thus cannot be limited to the fields of philosophy or mathematics; it is posed as a problem concerning our very 'image of thought' itself.
28. Bergson himself after all asserted that the problems he wished to eliminate were only those 'which bewilder us because they confront us with a vacuum' (Bergson 1946: 302n7/68n1). Deleuze cites this remark not once but twice, on the latter occasion as 'a very important note' (B, 120n12/10n1). Already in Bergson, the point is not an indiscriminate resolution of all the problems in the universe. If Deleuze could nonetheless not be fully satisfied with the Bergsonian formulation, this was because he required a theory which, rooting itself in the problematic of the 'false problem', defines the 'problem' itself in greater detail.
29. 'To learn is to enter into the universal of the relations which constitute the Idea, and into their corresponding singularities' (DR, 204/214). It is extremely interesting for our purposes that swimming too is explicated from the theory of the problem as Idea thus: '[t]o learn to swim is to conjugate the distinctive points of our bodies with the singular points of the objective Idea in order to form a problematic field' (DR, 205/214).
30. Deleuze points out that in neorealism the child plays an important role. 'The role of the child in neo-realism has been pointed out, notably in De Sica (and later in France with Truffaut); this is because, in the adult world, the child is affected by a certain motor helplessness, but one which makes him *all the more capable of seeing and hearing*' (TI, 3/10; my emphasis).
31. Deleuze draws a parallel between the transition from the movement-image to the time-image in cinema and the transition in the history of philosophy from the Aristotelian to the Kantian conceptions of time. In the movement-image, time is merely referred to in an indirect way: there is first the movement from action A to B to C, and time is secondarily implied as that which inheres in this movement. Deleuze explains this as a 'time subordinate to movement', which corresponds to Aristotle's concept of time, defined as the 'measure of movement, interval or number'. By contrast, in the time-image the pure empty form of time is presented directly: here we have a 'movement subordinate to time'. This latter corresponds to Kant's definition of time as a pure form of the intuition.
32. It is noteworthy that Deleuze only discusses Irene in terms of her sight of the spectacle of the factory, whereas the actual event in *Europe '51* is portrayed such that it is rather the cacophonous noise of the factory which causes Irene to faint. But Deleuze does not so much as touch upon sound in relation to this scene. The primacy accorded to vision

Practice: Thinking and Subjectivity

in Deleuze would be a fruitful avenue for critical research. How often Deleuze-Guattari discuss music in stark contrast!

33. In explicating Deleuze's vision for thinking, we focused on the 'beatitude associated with passive synthesis', a core notion in the theory of time in *Difference and Repetition*, to demonstrate Deleuze's critique of the philosophical tradition which has since time immemorial tried to establish the existence of an active will to think in man. This theory of time is a tripartite one, divided into 1) the time of habit (lived present), 2) the time of memory (pure past), and 3) the empty and pure form of time (future), which corresponds to the three types of recognition: 1) automatic, 2) successful attentive, and 3) failed attentive. From this too we can see the extent to which this construction of subjectivity and the theory of thinking derive from a common inspiration.

34. 'Disappointment is a fundamental moment of the search or of apprenticeship: in each realm of signs, we are disappointed when the object does not give us the secret we are expecting. And disappointment itself is pluralist, variable according to each line. There are few things that are not disappointing the first time they are seen. For the first time is the time of inexperience; we are not yet capable of distinguishing the sign from the object, and the object interposes and confuses the signs' (PS, 34/46).

Research Note III: Law/Institution/Contract

If one were to locate in Deleuze a political philosophy in the classical sense of the term, this would be his theory of the institution, which he inherited from Hume.

The major currents of political thought, among which the most well-known is the tradition of the social contract, have always defined society in terms of law. According to this theory, in the stage prior to the formation of societies, men lived as self-sufficient units possessing natural rights. From which it follows that for the formation of societies it was necessary for men to abandon this innate right and to submit themselves to the rule of law. In this case, 'law' signifies the prescription of a *prohibition* upon natural right, where 'one may do as one pleases'. According to social contract theory, in other words, at the origin of societies lies the law as prohibition.

It is this idea that Hume critiques. To place law at the origin of societies presumes a determination of men as unrepentant egoists. The prohibition of law is necessary to keep in check this fundamental egoism. However, to see egoism as the essence of man is possible only when we have enclosed him inside an abstract 'state of nature' which exists nowhere in reality. In contradistinction, real men and women, as they are studied natural-historically, have always formed bonds with each other, grouped themselves into families; they have always lived enveloping each other within a natural 'affection'. '[T]here are few', says Hume, 'that do not bestow the largest part of their fortunes on the pleasures of their wives, and the education of their children, reserving the smallest portion for their own proper use or entertainment' (quoted in ES, 38/25). The difficulty rather is that this affection is splayed with partiality (ES, 38/24). To undo the undesirable consequences of egoism, all it takes is to keep it suppressed. But the 'partiality of affection' cannot be done away with like this, rather it must somehow be integrated. To that extent, we can say that theories of the social contract have overly simplified the true challenges of the formation of societies.

When one looks at society from such a standpoint, one discovers the institution. By 'institution' we mean here a means to attain some satisfaction, a model for action. For instance, the institution of property exists to satisfy man's greed, the institution of marriage to end the nightly need to search for a partner. And society is nothing but the sum of all of these inventions and adaptations ('Instincts and Institutions', in DI, 19/24–5). Where social contract theories situate a *negative element* (prohibition) at the foundation of societies, the theory

Research Note III: Law/Institution/Contract

of institutions counters with a *positive element* (the model of action). From the latter perspective, law is something which arises *post hoc* (to give a concrete example, only after the institution of marriage had been devised did polygamy become forbidden). Furthermore, once grounded in the theory of institutions, the concept of right is forced to undergo a profound realignment. To wit, it is no longer possible to posit any rights which pre-exist the formation of societies (that is, any rights conceived as 'natural'). It is because man possesses no rights of any kind in advance that he proceeds to form societies in the first place. It is not the case that rights possessed prior to the formation of societies are subsequently suppressed.

Still further, the concept of the institution offers a perspective from which the critique of society can be waged. For it is possible, given any institution, to ask: 'to whom is this institution useful?' (DI, 20/26). For example, while the institution of marriage saves us the trouble of scouring for partners, any number of other institutions can be imagined that would achieve the same end. Undoubtedly all institutions perform a certain function, but beyond that it is necessary to investigate whether an institution does not privilege certain social groups or classes.

In *Coldness and Cruelty*, Deleuze was to add to this opposition of law and institution the third element of contract, to construct an even more complex schema (MCC, 91–2/79–80). By rights the contract requires a bilateral accord of intentions, a due date, and reservations on non-transferable clauses. In stark opposition, the law exercises power on third parties, has no due date, and allows for no reservations of any kind.

It is likely that Deleuze, in theorising the contract, had in mind the history of Galicia, Masoch's place of birth. A long-suffering victim of international politics, this region was subjected to countless annexations and redistributions. Masoch's writings cannot be read apart from this tragic history, and the notion of the contract plays a significant role in his body of work. There are regions which successfully establish laws and institutions, achieving a sufficiency and independence befitting a nation. There are also regions, however, for which such independence is geopolitically quite forlorn. There exist of course paths other than independence through which a region can survive.

4

Transition: From Structure to the Machine

In the previous chapter we inquired into the 'practice' envisioned by Deleuzian philosophy. For Deleuze, philosophical practice is made up of several components, whose consistency comes from the central activity of 'thinking'.

Now Deleuze does not conceive of thinking as impelled by an act of will. Thought can only arise through an 'encounter' with a 'sign' that compels its exercise. Except, in order to receive this sign as a sign, one must first train oneself in its reading, one must undergo an 'apprenticeship'. From here, Deleuzian practice opens up to the dimension of 'education' which prepares this apprenticeship. To that effect, *Difference and Repetition*, in the process of developing a theory of the 'problem', had carefully constructed what we could call a Deleuzian pedagogy.

It is undeniable that the practice conceived in Deleuzian philosophy is both realistic and enticing. Nonetheless, we could not but observe here a major blind spot. Towards the end of his life, Deleuze had shown, in the context of an analysis of cinema, how this vision of thinking as practice could be extended to the domain of activity proper, so to speak. With a nod to Bergson's theory of recognition, Deleuze proposed that it was the *failed* 'attentive recognition' which could actualise virtualities and give birth to the new; it is here that we can see the contours of a 'second type of subjectivity', what he called a subjectivity 'added to matter', irreducible to 'subjectivity' so-called (subjectivity of the first type).

It is inevitable that a philosophy which sees thinking as something externally enforced should result in such an account of practice. Nonetheless, it is impossible for us to pass over the fact that the new account of subjectivity is defined in terms of 'failure'. For it is impossible to seek to fail. Here we see Gilles Deleuze the philosopher treading a treacherous precipice, between the need to eliminate all spontaneity and activity as ultimately whirling around in the sterility of extant schematisms, and the equally pressing desire not to submit to post-desperation apathy. True too is the fact that Deleuze

Transition: From Structure to the Machine

in no way elevated 'failure' into the exclusive object of a forlorn and unfounded hope, instead emphasising the importance of preparation through education with characteristically supple theorising. And yet, through it all we cannot help but feel a certain unease if we are to halt our inquiry here and rest contented.

As a matter of fact, there is evidence to suggest that Deleuze himself failed to be satisfied by the framework of his own philosophy. Would this not be the simplest explanation for why Deleuze, having completed *Difference and Repetition* and *The Logic of Sense*, embarked on the experiment of collaboration with Guattari? We shall see in due course that this work was undertaken in an entirely different way from what we typically associate with collaborative research. As noted at the start of this book, all too often the works of Deleuze are not properly distinguished from those written by Deleuze and Guattari. If it is true that Deleuze experimented with this unprecedented method of authorship in order to overcome some as yet unclarified difficulty inherent in his thought, we must conclude that such undifferentiated interpretation is indeed erroneous.

The collaborative efforts of Deleuze and Guattari bestowed upon the world three major works.[1] The aim of this chapter is to see in what sense the novel terrain opened up by these texts constituted a theoretical 'turning point' for Deleuze; more specifically, in what ways Deleuze's 'method', 'principle' and 'practice', as we have portrayed them in this volume, were forced to undergo essential changes.

The Encounter with Guattari

According to François Dosse's exhaustive intellectual biography, *Gilles Deleuze and Félix Guattari: Intersecting Lives* (2011), the first time the two men met was in June 1969 (Dosse 2011: 5/16).[2] Prior to this, they had already exchanged correspondence on several occasions. Deleuze had in the previous year published *Difference and Repetition*, and earlier that year *The Logic of Sense*; Guattari had leafed through these works, as he himself mentions in the letters. At the time, Guattari was employed at the La Borde psychiatric clinic, founded by Jean Oury (1924–2014); these were not happy times for him however, with his colleagues irritated by his utter inability to conform, and Guattari himself frustrated by the difficulty of finding a suitable environment for his writing projects, overloaded as he was by his duties at the clinic. Though it is not widely known, behind the encounter of the two men lies the figure of Jean-Pierre Muyard, a doctor then working at La Borde. Muyard, who knew Deleuze personally, endeavoured to introduce Guattari to a philosopher who was just then in the process of making a name for himself, whether out of concern for Guattari's well-being, or perhaps because he was getting tired of Guattari's freewheeling tendencies. Either way, the meeting was a felicitous one. The two were to extend their dialogue beyond this initial encounter: Guattari as the ever-flowing fountain of discourse, and Deleuze as the hawk-eyed scribe, scribbling down everything he heard, tying up the loose ends, identifying the difficulties, and establishing resonances with the history of philosophy. As previously noted, Deleuze had just published two works of immense scope in close succession, and had passed a certain peak both theoretically and in his publishing schedule. (Deleuze had undergone a substantial operation to remove one of his lungs only the year before, and was in recuperation; worse, he was at the time a borderline alcoholic. It would not be fantastical to say that he had passed a certain peak in his life as well.) In this way, the coincidence of certain fortunate contingencies laid the groundwork for their collaborative work.

Deleuze and Guattari were extremely reluctant to go into detail about exactly how their collaboration progressed, leaving room for much speculation into this mystery, even a hint of sanctification. Since the publication of Dosse's biography and Stéphane Nadaud's *Anti-Oedipus Papers*, however, the way this work came to be has become less opaque. Having said that, knowing how something was done, and understanding its significance, are two completely different things.

To begin with the facts though, the first book published under their twin hands, *Anti-Oedipus*, was written in the following way. Deleuze had been fascinated by the way Guattari was able to come up with radically new ideas and concepts. He thus instructed Guattari to sit at his desk first thing in the morning, jot down everything that came to mind, and send the resulting scribbles to him without reading them over and without editing them. No doubt this was a tough ask of Guattari, but it seems that Deleuze had prescribed this bitter pill as the only possible remedy for Guattari's deep writer's block (Dosse 2011: 7/18). Guattari stuck to the prescription, and an unending stream of notes would appear on Deleuze's doorstep (the *Papers* edited and published by Nadaud are none other than a selection of these extraordinary scribbles). Deleuze in turn would read this ream of words over and over again, carefully extracting the parts he deemed usable. Thus saturating his brain with Guattari's ideas, he transformed the chaos he received into something resembling what we have today as *Anti-Oedipus*. As Nadaud states explicitly, the authoritative text of *Anti-Oedipus* was physically written by Deleuze and Deleuze alone (AOP, 17/19). Guattari re-enters at the editing process, and following extensive revision both independently by Guattari and then collaboratively, the final version of the manuscript was completed on New Year's Eve, to be published three months later in March 1972.

Looking back at the composition of *Anti-Oedipus*, the two reflected that the crucial thing was to reach a point where it no longer mattered whether they would refer to themselves in the first person or not (TP, 3/9). And this assessment we ought to take at face value. Deleuze would forage in the monumental volume of fragments sent to him by Guattari, in the process becoming as it were a shaman possessed by him. And presumably the moment this possession had passed a certain threshold, Deleuze took up his pen. Who then was it that wrote the work *Anti-Oedipus*? Certainly not Félix Guattari; but it was not Deleuze either, or, more precisely, not the man who up to then had gone by the name of 'Gilles Deleuze'. It was a monstrous hybrid that wrote *Anti-Oedipus*, a 'something' that can only be referred to as Deleuze-Guattari. We have here an experiment in the very act of *écriture* itself. Deleuze had prophesied in the 'Preface' to *Difference and Repetition* that an age was upon us where it would no longer be possible to write a book of philosophy in the traditional style (DR, xx/4). And the experiment of 'dual writing (*écrire à deux*)' was the practical fulfilment of this prophecy.

Having said that, there is also no need to emphasise the experimental nature of the text unduly. For in reality, it is possible to see the method of *Anti-Oedipus* as an application of what Deleuze had been doing for his whole academic career. We have already seen in Chapter 1 that Deleuze's monographs are written in 'free indirect discourse', where the judgements of the object of study appear as if they were the judgements of the writer him or herself. The subject and object of discourse are no longer clearly demarcated. One could say, the subject of discourse undergoes a becoming into its own object. Deleuze had always employed this unique method to compose his studies in the history of philosophy. From this perspective, we can understand Deleuze and Guattari's experiment of 'dual writing' as an adaptation and extension of free indirect discourse. Objectively speaking, since it is Deleuze who is rearranging Guattari's notes into coherent prose, Guattari is the 'object' of discourse, and Deleuze the 'subject'. Indeed, as many commentators have already pointed out, the vast majority of concepts put forward by the two in fact hail from Guattari (see the 'Prologue' to the present volume, p. 6). It would however be incorrect to imagine that Deleuze positioned himself outside of 'Guattari's thought', reporting its content like an external observer. For the discursive subject Gilles Deleuze has long since 'become' his discursive object, Félix Guattari. And this is precisely why, as they explained, it no longer matters at all whether one occupies the first person singular or not. There is simply no activity more futile than speculation as to which sections were written by Deleuze, and which by Guattari. Hence our suggestion, that the experiment of 'dual writing' ought to be understood as a radicalisation of the compositional method Deleuze had employed all these years.[3] The only difference is this: whereas hitherto Deleuze had limited his attention to bodies of work which had already been completed, now he was setting wire traps to capture alive a body of thought still in development.

Needless to say, our intention in asserting this is not to downplay the significance of this remarkable experiment. The reason we stress the continuity between Deleuze's method and Deleuze-Guattari's experiment is to oppose both the ubiquitous interpretative attitude which fuses the works of Deleuze with those of Deleuze-Guattari and the equally extreme stance which treats the two as entirely separate bodies of work (as can be seen in Alain Badiou, for example). For this experiment was planned, performed and completed all in accordance with Deleuze's designs. And the result was a genuine transformation in Deleuze himself, as we are about to demonstrate. These facts readily lend themselves to the assessment that we are dealing here with an experiment conducted under Deleuze's method, for the sake of revitalising Deleuze's philosophy.

Structure and Machine

If the biographical details surrounding the encounter of Deleuze and Guattari were a play of contingencies, we must admit that, in terms of theory, there existed a certain necessity. And the theoretical knot was Guattari's piece 'Machine and Structure', which he had been preparing around the time of their meeting in June of 1969.[4] This text was written under the grand banner of an overcoming of 'structuralism', which in those days had reached the pinnacle of its influ-

Transition: From Structure to the Machine

ence. Guattari envisioned that this overcoming could be achieved by putting forward the new concept of 'machine' to replace the old concept of 'structure'. The text even references *Difference and Repetition* and *The Logic of Sense*, both of which had been published very recently. It seems that Guattari had intuited something irreducible to the thematic of 'structuralism' coursing through Deleuze's work, though Deleuze, for his part, had only a vague awareness of this. At the other end, Guattari himself was struggling to reach an adequate conceptualisation of the machine. The concept of 'machine' was to become the centrepiece of *Anti-Oedipus*, but not before the two had entered into their collaborative work.

Let us now brave the actual text of 'Machine and Structure' itself. Guattari immediately focuses on the distinction between generality and repetition developed in *Difference and Repetition* (MS, 111n2/240n). Structure belongs to the dimension of generality, for each of its elements is readily replaceable. By contrast the machine is located in the dimension of repetition, because repetition concerns itself with singularities unamenable to replacement and exchange. This analysis we have already dealt with in greater detail in the previous chapter (see p. 73): each repetition is rigorously unique; it is impossible for an absolutely identical situation to return again. In this sense each event of repetition is irreplaceable and unexchangeable. And as we saw, it is only by subtracting the 'new', by 'eliminating difference' from repetition, that 'habit', belonging to the level of generality, can come about. The fact that Guattari places structure-generality in opposition to machine-repetition implies that the machine is conceived on the basis of *real* repetitions. Structure can only deal with normalised generalities, while the machine is concerned with repeating singularities. *Though as yet a nebulous image*, something along these lines is budding in Guattari.

This is followed by analyses of the machine from the perspective of 'time', and then the 'event'. We quote: '[t]emporalisation penetrates the machine on all sides and can be related to it only after the fashion of an event. The emergence of the machine makes a date, a change, different from a structural representation' (MS, 112/241). Guattari's prose style is exceptionally abstract, frequently making its comprehension a great toil, but what is being said here is not especially challenging. Structure, which resides in the dimension of normalised generalities, has nothing to say about time, dates, events and hence about history. Guattari's aim is to arrive at a model which can treat of these factors, in other words a model which in Deleuzian terms would belong to the level of repetition. And the provisional label for this model is here the 'machine'. For the event is necessarily dated; and the same date will never come again. The machine will concern itself with events occurring on a determinate date, and by implication it will be able to encompass time and history. Now it is a common criticism of structuralism that it cannot deal with time, history and hence ultimately change itself; Guattari wants to overcome this theoretical limitation through his new concept of the machine.[5]

However, at least at present one would be hard-pressed to say that the 'machine' has been sufficiently constructed into a concept. For the 'machine' to take the place of 'structure', it must have attained a comparable level of abstraction, and in this Guattari has not succeeded. For instance, out of the blue he starts to talk about 'human labour' and 'machine labour', with the (somewhat *passé*) observation that human behaviour has been incorporated into the order of the machine as a component part.[6] The discussion moves on to the solid printing and processing machines one finds in factories, and from here to the alienation of the labourer under capitalism. One cannot help feeling that in 'Machine and Structure', the 'machine' as an abstract model and the material machine (in the sense of 'machinery') are overlaid, without an adequate justification as to why such a move would be theoretically legitimate. As a matter of fact, though Deleuze reportedly showed great interest in the piece, as for the crucial concept of the 'machine', he remarked that he would need more time to digest it (Dosse 2011: 13/16). Tellingly, even though *Anti-Oedipus* ended up basing its concept of the 'desiring-machine' on Guattari's machine idea, Deleuze would have to reiterate over and over again that the machine is 'not mere metaphor' (AO, 1, 36 et passim/7, 43 et passim). We can understand this as a symptom of the inherently ambiguous position the concept of the 'machine' occupies, between the abstract and the concrete (indeed, from *A Thousand Plateaus* onwards, Deleuze-Guattari will replace the 'machine' with alternative concepts).

There also seems to be some confusion over the precise understanding of the concept of 'structure' as distinguished from the machine. In his definition of structure, Guattari refers to the eighth series 'On Structure' in *The Logic of Sense*, where Deleuze lists the three conditions which define structure: 1) the existence of at least two heterogeneous series; 2) the terms of these series exist only through the relations they maintain with one another; 3) the two series converge towards a paradoxical element (LS, 60/65–6). Now

Transition: From Structure to the Machine

Guattari states that of these three, only the first two ought to be considered as definitions of structure, with the third to be associated rather with the concept of machine (MS, 111n2/240n). However, as we shall soon see, this third condition will constitute the core doctrine of the 'ideology of lack' so vehemently attacked in *Anti-Oedipus*. The reason why the element towards which the two series converge is called 'paradoxical' is that it belongs to neither series, 'its proper place is lacking (*manquer à sa place*)'. In the terminology of Lacanian psychoanalysis this would be the phallus, which Lacan had analysed in great detail in the course of a reading of Edgar Allen Poe's *Purloined Letter* (1845). It thus seems that here Guattari has misallocated a structural criterion, which the concept of machine must by right see as its adversary, onto the side of the machine itself.

Let us read further into 'Machine and Structure', in order to investigate the relation of Guattari to Lacanian psychoanalysis. The machine aims to concern itself with repeated singularities, lest it neglect events and history. To this list Guattari adds the element of 'detachment'. To quote the relevant section in full:

> Though it is true that this unconscious subjectivity, as a split which is overcome in a signifying chain, is being transferred away from individuals and human groups towards the world of machines, it still remains just as un-representable at the specifically machinic level. It is a signifier detached from the unconscious structural chain that will act as *representative* to represent the machine.
>
> The essence of the machine is precisely this function of detaching a signifier as a representative, as a 'differentiator', as a causal break [*cette opération de détachement d'un signifiant comme représentant, comme 'différenciant', comme coupure causale*], different in kind from the structurally established order of things. It is this operation that binds the machine both to the desiring subject and to its status as the basis of the various structural orders corresponding to it. The machine, as a repetition of the particular, is a mode – perhaps the only possible mode – of univocal representation of the various forms of subjectivity in the order of generality on the individual or the collective plane. (MS, 114/243; original emphasis)

Truly a passage of suffocating density. And context will not help here either, for in the immediately preceding section Guattari concerns himself with the fate of the individual in the 'sphere of scientific research', where the proper name of one who makes a great discovery is elevated into a general noun, in lieu of the individual him/herself. What mental acrobatics were performed for this topic to lead onto this extremely abstract discussion of the signifier in psychoanalysis is unfathomable, but here amidst the thicket of words there does exist a genuinely novel idea. In order to understand it, however, we must first grasp the basics of Lacanian psychoanalysis, which was Guattari's intellectual formation.

Jacques Lacan (1901–1981) combined a fidelity to the Freudian inheritance with the concept of the 'signifier' (in its most basic usage, the phonetic aspect of the linguistic sign) borrowed from Saussurian linguistics, which he in turn transformed extensively into a unique psychoanalytic system. If one were to come up with a grandiose slogan for this body of work, it is an account of how the human being becomes a human being.[7]

According to Lacan, the infant attempts to overcome the helplessness of the years immediately following birth by entering into an imaginary relation with its mother, and for a time this strategy succeeds. However, its imaginary union with the mother is radically asymmetrical, insofar as the mother's desire is in excess of the organismal needs of the child. For the mother is already a bearer of language, the child not yet: it cannot understand the enigma of the mother's desire. The infant is thus forced to accept the impossibility of a narcissistic total union with the mother in this imaginary relation. Lacan then links this non-reciprocation of the respective desires of mother and child with the function of the 'father' in the Freudian Oedipus Complex, and calls the destruction of this phantasmatic relation 'castration'.

In its original Freudian version, the Oedipus Complex stages the child's desire to lie with its 'mother', and its hatred of the 'father' who stands in its way. Lacan elevates this tale to the summit of abstraction – crucially however, he retains the original terminology of 'mother' and 'father' – and imports the aforementioned asymmetry as that which the 'father' has but the 'mother' does not, namely the phallus. The infant thereby desires to 'be' the phallus (here designated by a small φ), but this desire is immediately forced to renounce itself by the 'Name-of-the-Father (*Nom-du-père*)'. When the desire to 'be' the phallus (φ) is renounced, it is transformed into the desire to 'have' the Phallus (Φ); and it is this Φ that is stored away in the unconscious as the primordial signifier. This is how Lacan explains the process of 'primal repression (*Urverdrängung*)' posited by Freud.[8]

Freud had generalised the myth of Oedipus Rex to portray the 'complexed' desire of the infant who wishes both to murder its father (hatred) and to be like him (love). To this narrative Lacan would go on to add that this is none other than the process by which the primary signifier of Φ is imprinted upon the unconscious, upon the id. And it is by virtue of this process that the human being can become human at all. Man will seek this Φ without end, but it is always beyond his reach. It is the 'eternal lack'. Hence we begin to look for a substitute. In the jargon, man begins to search for a certain signifier that can adequately signify the primary signifier Φ as its signified, as its sense. And to introduce yet another piece of jargon, the Φ as the elusive eternal primary object of desire is named the 'object a (*objet petit a*)'.[9] The dyadic linguistic unit of the signifier-signified is henceforth the by-product of man's futile grail quest to recover the object a. And from the primary signifier extends the 'signifying chain (*chaîne signifiante*)' of language, through whose inauguration man is said to enter into the linguistic order of the 'Symbolic'.

Within the traditional framework of Saussurian linguistics, the signifier and the signified constitute the inseparable dual components of the *signe* (just like the two sides of a sheet of paper), hence it is impossible to theorise the signifier in independence from its signified. From a Lacanian perspective, however, such a conceptualisation of the sign ignores the genesis of the sign itself. If one is to inquire further into that genesis, one must conclude that it is desire that attaches a signified to a given signifier; or quite simply, that 'the signified *is* desire' (Kaufmann 2003: 527; original emphasis). Such a definition might seem far-fetched from the perspective of linguistics, but in effect what is being proposed is *to locate desire as the ground of the sign's sense function*. Oversimplified, the reason something means something is that the subject desires for it to mean thus. From here, Lacan will define the signifier as follows: 'My definition of the signifier (there is no other) is as follows: the signifier is what represents the subject to another signifier. This latter signifier is therefore the signifier to which all the other signifiers represent the subject . . .' (Lacan 2006: 819). The reason a signifier can represent (and one ought to understand here both the philosophical sense of figuration and a more common sense, as in the representation of one's interests by a lawyer) the *subject* is that *the significative function of the signifier is always none other than the desire of the subject itself*. The reason this representation is directed *to other signifiers* is that *the signified of any given signifier is itself always a signifier in its turn*. Say we have the Phallus as signifier (call this s1), which is in turn the signified of another signifier (call this s2). It should be clear from the above analysis that s2 can only occupy such a position as the signifier of s1 because of the subject's desire. As a result, we can say that, here, s2 represents the subject for s1. For the representative function is the subject's desire itself, no less.

Returning to Guattari's text, we recall that there it was stated that at the machinic level the subject – 'unconscious subjectivity' – is no longer a possible object of representation. When the signifying chain arises, and desires are endlessly replaced one after another, or equivalently when the object a slides without arresting its motion, one signifier represents the subject for another signifier. But why can we say this? Why, in other words, can we say that a *single* signifier can represent the subject *itself, in its entirety*? This is because there is an implicit assumption being made here that there is in the last instance only ever *one* Desire. There exists a unique monolithic Desire for the object a, for the Φ, which seeks to make good the originary non-reciprocity of desires between mother and child, to compensate for the primordial loss, which is nothing less than the wellspring of humanity itself. It is this assumption that justifies the claim that a single signifier represents the subject itself. We can thus see that the problematic surrounding this significative representation concerns a core theoretical axiom of Lacanian psychoanalysis, which seeks to explain all desires according to a single unique cause. In turn, if as Guattari says the deployment of the machine will render the representative function ineffectual, a corresponding modification will be needed at the level of the fundamental axioms. To cut a long story short, this modification will reject any reduction of desire to a singular causative 'lack', instead understanding desire as the coagulation of multiple flows and streams. In time, *Anti-Oedipus* was to critique the 'ideology of lack' in order to affirm the multiplicity of desire. The first tentative step in this direction is already contained here, a ray of light amidst the opacity of Guattari's prose.

Next, Guattari had stated that '[t]he essence of the machine is precisely this function of detaching a signifier as a representative, as a "differentiator", as a causal break'. We can reasonably suppose 'a signifier' to refer to the Phallus. The meaning of 'detachment' is as yet unclear; in the light of the preceding discussion, however, it seems that with this term Guattari was seeking in some way to leave behind the theoretical universe in which all desire was explicable by a singular lack. Moreover, he asserted that the function of this 'detachment' will link the concept of machine to the 'desiring subject' and its 'status'. It is significant that the machine is here associated not with the subject *per se* but with the *desiring*-subject: for the implication is

Transition: From Structure to the Machine

that the model of the machine is one which locates desire at the very centre of its analytical framework.

Really though, what, after all this, is 'detachment'? In Lacanian psychoanalysis, the renunciation of the primary Phallic signifier is termed 'foreclosure (*forclusion*)', and it is at this point that psychosis (not neurosis) may take place. According to this theory, the Phallus has to be tucked away into the unconscious as the first signifier, in 'primal repression'; in other words, psychosis is diagnosed as the result of a failure in the 'normal' functioning of primal repression. Guattari's 'detachment' of 'a signifier' cannot but remind us of this mechanism of 'foreclosure'. In other words, Guattari seems to be trying to say (in so few words) something like the following: yes, Lacanian structure can posit a neat unidirectional process whereby the correct functioning of primal repression launches man into the Symbolic, but what if primal repression does not function as rigidly as Lacan thinks, what if the Phallus is readily 'detachable', and what if it is not architectonic structure but the fluidity of the machine that can truly explain this? The implication is that from the standpoint of the machine, the Imaginary (the phantasmatic relation of mother and infant) and the Symbolic (the order of language) begin to merge, such that it will no longer be possible to draw a clear line of demarcation between the two.

Such inspirations exist here but in a germinal state. And, one must point out, as it stands the seeds have fallen onto rocky soil, quick to germinate but equally quick to wither and die. For there is precious little here in the way of convincing explanation regarding the concept of the machine. But say we succeed in raising this insight up to a comparable level of abstraction as the concept of structure. What emerges is a perspective that does not have to bundle together multiple flows of desire into a single lack (the paradoxical element), but sees each flow as it is in itself. Guattari's gaze is directed towards such a new model, beyond the confines of structuralism. And this new framework will be able to treat events which occur with a determinate date, repeated singularities, history and even temporality, reality as it really is. It is easy to imagine Deleuze being drawn magnetically to this idea. But he 'needs more time', if all he has to go on is the word 'machine'. Hence the necessity of Deleuze's theoretical labours. It seems that this was the task posed by the 'theoretical' encounter of Deleuze and Guattari.

Structure and Structuralism

Why then was Deleuze drawn so strongly to these ideas of Guattari's? We sense that this is not unconnected to Deleuze's great theoretical affinity with structuralism in his work prior to the collaboration with Guattari, as is abundantly clear from his essay, 'How Do We Recognise Structuralism?' Though this essay was first published in 1972 – in Volume VIII, '20th Century Philosophy', of *History of Philosophy* compiled under the direction of François Châtelet – it had been completed in 1968, crucially before his meeting with Guattari (Deleuze had sent the essay along with a cover letter to Louis Althusser, dated February 1968 (Dosse 2011: 227–8/273)). What unfolds therein is an astonishingly acute series of definitions of the philosophical tendency loosely known at the time as 'structuralism'; but importantly among these definitions are interspersed insights unavailable to someone who merely looks upon the movement as an external observer, and only to one who has thought along its intellectual waves.

The opening of the essay is an inscription of the date: '*This is 1967 (Nous sommes en 1967)*' (DI, 170/238). And this even italicised for emphasis. The protagonists in this veritable diary entry are those thinkers known at the time as practitioners of 'structuralism' (whether they were in fact so notwithstanding), namely Claude Lévi-Strauss, Jacques Lacan, Michel Foucault, Louis Althusser and Roland Barthes. Structuralism was very much a movement in progress. That is not to say that Deleuze wanted to preface his essay with a convenient excuse, to the effect of 'structuralism is ongoing, my review may well be superseded'. Rather, what is expressed here is Deleuze's awareness that his essay cannot be situated outside of the movement it discusses, that it is itself infused through and through with a structuralist inspiration. And this is not hubris on Deleuze's part, for as we shall see, the explication of structuralism undertaken here owes a great deal to the concepts he had proposed in *Difference and Repetition* and *The Logic of Sense*. In other words, Deleuze himself had thought alongside the contemporary vector of structuralism, and consciously so. The essay succeeds to a hitherto unparalleled extent in extracting six or seven necessary conditions for structuralism to be recognised as such, from the works of writers who differ completely in both object of study and style of thinking. Now undeniably Deleuze was a philosopher who was extraordinarily proficient at such tasks. But that is not all: the fact that a substantial

Transition: From Structure to the Machine

part of Deleuze's own thinking had set off from within structuralism, the fact that he himself was a part of this movement – these are equally crucial factors which made possible the composition of this remarkable essay.

Deleuze's objective here is a one by one explication of the conditions of possibility of structuralism. In what follows, we shall consider each of these in turn, in Deleuze's original order, with some additional clarification here and there.

The first criterion is the discovery of the 'Symbolic (*le symbolique*)'. Structuralism concerns itself neither with the Real (*le réel/ réalité*) available to the senses, nor with the Imaginary (*l'imaginaire/ image*) which forms in our heads, but with a third level, the order of the Symbolic. Take Lacan's 'father': this does not refer to the real father in the flesh, nor is it the image of the father in our mind. Within the framework of Lacanian psychoanalysis, which locates the Event of primal repression at the origin of the process whereby the human being truly becomes human, it is the 'Name-of-the-Father' that commands this repression, and the 'father' is named as the structural agent of this prohibition. It is not the case that one's biological father utters the 'No', nor does he hand down imaginary 'No's in one's head.

From this we arrive at the perspective that, within the Symbolic order, a given element does not possess any positive consistency of its own, but only exists as the bearer of a structural function/ meaning. In other words, it is not that the father exists first of all, and then proceeds to declare the prohibitive 'No'; rather, the structural element imbued with the prohibitive function is subsequently given the name of 'father'. This is the second criterion: 'local or positional (*local ou de position*)'. The Symbolic element has its sense and function determined at all times according to its position within the structure. As Lévi-Strauss (1908–2009) would say, 'sense is always a result, an effect' (DI, 175/244). In sum, both 'father' and 'mother', as structural elements, are assigned a function befitting their structural position.

The next step is to identify the precise mechanism by which this determination takes place. Structuralism's answer is that the sense and function of each structural element is determined by its interrelations with the surrounding elements. The example chosen by Deleuze to illustrate this is the 'phoneme (*phonème*)'. The phoneme is the most basic unit of all language, and it is the phoneme that allows us to distinguish between, for example, the words '*billard*' and '*pillard*'. Though the phoneme is materialised in the form of letters and syllables, it is not reducible to them; and crucially, a given phoneme cannot exist independently of a phonemic relation, such as the one that holds between '*b*' and '*p*'. Such inter-phonemic relationality is here termed the 'differential relation (*rapport différentiel*)', a term first introduced in *Difference and Repetition*. Deleuze terms 'differentiation' the process through which the value of an entity, entirely determined by its interrelations with its surroundings, is fixed.[10]

The value of a structural element is dependent upon its differential relations. This time the example given is Lévi-Strauss's theory of kinship systems. According to this theory, there are two pairs of oppositions, brother/sister, husband/wife on the one hand, and father/son, maternal uncle/sister's son (nephew) on the other, and collectively these constitute the 'elementary structures of kinship', or in Deleuze's terminology the 'differential relations' in kinship structures. Lévi-Strauss had realised, based on his studies of the kinship systems of 'many' societies (six, to be exact; judge that number as you will . . .), that there was a certain regularity in the emotional dynamics between each of the above oppositions, in what he called the 'kinship attitudes (*attitude entre parents*)'. Namely, if father and son are close emotionally, son (nephew) and maternal uncle are distant, and so too the reverse. And if husband and wife enjoy proximity, conversely the wife will be on frigid terms with her brothers, and vice versa (Lévi-Strauss 1963: 213ff./235ff.).

In this way the 'kinship attitudes' follow the laws of the 'elementary structures of kinship'. Such 'functions' between relatives are not at all an expression of spontaneous, humanistic feelings of affection and enmity, they are rigorously determined according to the differential structures of kinship. Nevertheless, such determination is contingent upon the underlying social 'attitude' of each society; and the differential relations of structure are unable to explain which 'attitude' is selected in a given society. For Lévi-Strauss, 'the elementary structures of kinship' constitute a universality; but even if we understand these structures inside out, we will not be able to predict the exact 'kinship attitudes' that will come to be actualised in a given society. It is for this reason that Deleuze calls what the 'kinship attitudes' come to realise a 'singularity', or a 'singular point'. For the singular point is that which is not amenable to any further mathematical differentiations. Hence singularity points towards a force that cannot be exhausted by the set of differential relations.[11]

Transition: From Structure to the Machine

We thus have our third criterion: 'the differential and the singular (*le différentiel et le singulier*)'.

We saw above that the third criterion had pulled structuralism into great proximity with the concerns of *Difference and Repetition*. The fourth, 'the differenciator, differenciation (*le différenciant, le différenciation*)', goes ever further in this direction, so much so that the explication of the conditions of structuralism merge into an exposition of Deleuze's own theories, as if Deleuze himself is a bearer of the structuralist mantle. Here we are told that the 'structure' according to structuralism is always something unconscious, always the 'Virtual'. And virtually, the totality of elements in a given structure 'coexist' in mutual interdependence. Whence, a select set of relations are 'actualised (*s'actualiser*)' in the 'here and now'. Word for word this is the formulation for an ontology of the Virtual that Deleuze had set forth in *Difference and Repetition*.

One can understand the sense in which not the whole, but only a part of Virtual structure comes to be actualised, if one considers the case of language. It is impossible that every possible phoneme actualise in a stroke before our eyes and ears. For language is necessarily something spoken, and what is spoken is only ever (the most miniscule) part of the totality of language. Nevertheless, this speech presupposes the existence of a Virtual structure, a structure where all phonemes do coexist in mutual interdependence. Each time a phoneme is actualised 'here and now', the Virtual totality of structure, that is, the language as a whole, is reaffirmed; correlatively, the individual phoneme appears as a partial realisation of this totality. Deleuze calls this process of partial realisation 'differenciation (*se différencier*)'. This term was used in connection to Leibniz's 'minute perception' in *Difference and Repetition*, to provide a general characterisation of the concept of the Virtual (see p. 48 above), and here Deleuze revisits it to explicate the concept of structure in structuralism. Combine this with the third criterion, and we have the formulation that Virtual structure is 'undifferenciated (*indifférencié*)', but 'differentiated (*différentié*)' (in that it is made up of differential relations), which should be familiar to all readers of *Difference and Repetition*.

That Deleuze has begun to avow structuralism as his own philosophy can also be gleaned from the fact that by this point he no longer needs to scour for examples from the works of the structuralists, so-known (DI, 179/252). And that is not all. Deleuze now begins to construct hypothetical objections to the structuralist enterprise, and answers these with his own counterarguments. This main objection concerns the problem of genesis, or the problem of time. Deleuze writes that 'one can no more oppose the genetic to the structural than time to structure' (DI, 180/252). This is because '[a]s regards time, the position of structuralism is ... quite clear: time is always a time of actualisation, according to which the elements of virtual coexistence are carried out at diverse rhythms' (DI, 180/251–2). The criticism that structuralism excludes genesis and temporality is not lifted from some external source; it is as if Deleuze has here inscribed his own personal doubts regarding structuralism and his own response thereto, in order to defend structuralism from himself, so to speak. We have here the physical documentation of Deleuze's self-questioning.

Moreover, from this perspective it becomes apparent that the response Deleuze had provided to his own doubts has nonetheless left some questions unanswered. It is true that structuralism does concern itself with the sort of temporality that Deleuze has described, and to that extent it does provide an adequate solution to the problem of genesis. However, to borrow a term used in *The Logic of Sense* to characterise structuralism, it ultimately limits itself to an 'ideal' conception of time.[12] And this is a truly bizarre temporality indeed, a strange time which *moves backwards only to fall back upon us*, a mysterious time which *first regresses and then progresses*. For example: we saw earlier that each time a word is uttered, the virtual differential relation between phonemes is actualised. At the moment of its materialisation, language as the totality of differential relations is *posited* in the background (regression), following which the materialisation of the specific differential relation is correlatively understood as a differenciation of the part from the whole (progression). It is much the same for the genesis of the subject in Lacanian psychoanalysis discussed earlier. When we investigate within its framework the process whereby the human being becomes human, we hit upon the Event of primal repression, and the 'father' is named as its structural agent (regression). In this way man is said to enter the order of language, the Symbolic (progression). So yes, structuralism does not ignore time and genesis. Nonetheless, its concern is strictly limited to an ideal time, and this only within the pre-delimited confines of structure itself. It is possible to read Deleuze's internal monologue as inadvertently exposing this limitation. And we must remember that the concept of structure is being explicated using Deleuze's own terminology, as if it constituted Deleuze's own thinking.

We can consider the fifth criterion of the 'serial (*sériel*)' and the

Transition: From Structure to the Machine

sixth criterion of the 'empty square (*la case vide*)' together. According to Deleuze, the foregoing exposition of structuralism is still only half the story. For it is only once the Symbolic elements grasped within their constitutive differential relations are arranged into a 'series (*série*)', that we can be said to have arrived at a complete definition of structuralism. For example, in Lévi-Strauss's analysis of totemism we have on the one hand an animalistic series determined by the differential relation, and on the other hand a societal series determined Symbolically, and these two series enter into a relation of correspondence with each other. Or, for Lacan, the unconscious is neither something individual, nor is it a collective phenomenon, but it is intersubjective. What this means is that the unconscious does not form according to pre-defined wholes, whether individual or collective, but rather forms by being strung into a series in relation to Symbolic functions such as the 'father' and the 'mother'. The 'empty square' of the sixth criterion is what relays between these otherwise disparate series, allowing elements within a structure to exchange positions at any time. The reason it is described as 'empty' is because with regards to itself it is a non-entity. Take Lacan's 'Phallus', or equivalently the 'object a': since this is no more than a substitute elected in an attempt to fill the originary absolute lack which by definition cannot be filled, it is literally irrelevant what this object in fact happens to be. It is 'that which does not coincide with its own identity (*ce qui manque à sa propre identité*)' (DI, 187/263). Which is why Deleuze also refers to it as the 'object = x'.

Harking back to the position Deleuze-Guattari occupies in relation to psychoanalysis, it is easy to see that this sixth criterion corresponding to the 'Phallus' should be of immense significance. For it is precisely through a problematisation of the absolutism of this criterion that the two tried to lay the groundwork for an alternative theoretical framework. And Deleuze as a matter of fact had already expressed certain reservations regarding the necessity of this final criterion. The relevant passage is worth quoting in full:

> We can nevertheless remain a bit doubtful: what Jacques Lacan invites us to discover in two cases [Poe's *Purloined Letter* and the case of *The Rat Man* reported to us by Freud], the particular role played by a letter or a debt – is it an artifice, strictly applicable to these cases, or rather is it a truly general method, valid for all the structurable domains, a criterion for every structure, as if a structure were not defined without assigning an object = x that ceaselessly traverses the series? As if the literary work, for example, or the work of art, but other *oeuvres* as well, those of society,

those of illness, those of life in general, enveloped this very special object which assumes control over their structure. And as if it were always a matter of finding who is H, or of discovering an x shrouded within the work. Such is the case with songs: the refrain encompasses an object = x, while the verses form the divergent series through which this object circulates. It is for this reason that songs truly present an elementary structure. (DI, 184–5/8–9)

No doubt it would be possible to gloss over this passage as no more than a compositional technique, that is, 'doubt' rhetorically formulated for the sole purpose of propelling the debate. We feel, however, that the way the query is set up here is too substantial to be brushed aside as mere technique. Indeed, the inevitable consequence of thinking in terms of the object = x that Deleuze draws here is quite momentous. To wit, if we accept the function of the object = x in holding together a structure, this means that any given 'structurable' domain is determined by its specific paradoxical object, the object = x (even if the question of whether a given domain is 'structurable' in the first place is also briefly problematised here).

Furthermore, the phrase 'life in general (*la vie en général*)' carries weight precisely because it is written by Deleuze. For in effect we are concerned here with the entire world, and the totality of objects therein. The world as a whole is determined by the object = x . . . The first part of the above passage gives indications that there is reason to suspect the external validity and applicability of Lacanian theory, utterly dependent as it is on the object = x for its integrity. Lacanian psychoanalysis 'discovers' this paradoxical object everywhere and anywhere. But what if this is the result of forcibly imposing an extant framework indiscriminately onto heterogeneous domains? What if it is only because we have set off from the theoretical axiom that all desires encircle the object a/Phallus, that we keep stumbling across the object a, the object = x, in each and every domain we care to turn our attention to?

Following this passage, Deleuze will reply affirmatively to the necessity of the object = x for structure: '[t]he whole structure is driven by this originary Third, but that also fails to coincide with its own origin' (DI, 186/260). The final word of this essay is thus the assessment that the discovery of the object = x, which quilts into a whole the structural series, is 'a general method, valid for all the structurable domains'. Even so, one must hear in Deleuze's explication of the sixth criterion an almost pained expression of his crisis of faith. That is, Deleuze has already noticed the major difficulty

Transition: From Structure to the Machine

inherent in the structuralist system; however, he himself occupies a position not all that far from this system, and he has yet to see a way out of it. The proximity is so pronounced, indeed, that what was in the first place begun as an introduction to structuralism could not help but be swept up by concepts and terminology of his own creation ...

To summarise the order of proceedings hitherto, Deleuze's essay moves from:

1. Basic, general conditions of structuralism (criteria one and two); to
2. A fulfilment of the most radical potential of structuralism, through an exposition that approaches his own theories (criteria three and four); to
3. An all-out plunge into the depths of structuralism, which (unwittingly) brings to the surface its difficulties (criteria five and six).

In this way one can see that there was a sort of continuity all along. And the problems which come into the open in phase 3) are just as much criticisms raised against Deleuze's own work, a fact of which he himself is aware.[13] From here Deleuze will move on to the final criterion, to provide a conclusion, *for the time being*, concerning the transformation of structure (final criterion: 'from the subject to practice (*du sujet à pratique*)'). Deleuze's answer is simple. The empty square, or the object = x, has two characteristics: one, it is always affixed to a subject, and two, it is empty, lacking its own 'self-identity' and its proper 'place'. Therefore, for there to arrive some 'accident' which is capable of engendering a change in structure, all we need is a modification in one or other of these characteristics.

First: we recall that the signifying chain extends without end in search of the signifier with the Phallus as its signified, and that each time there is signification, we have a representation of the subject. Contrary to general opinion, structuralism is not a thought which eliminates the subject; rather it defines the subject in a different way.[14] In other words, if a situation were to arise where the object = x ceases to be affixed to a subject, the whole chain will fall apart. In particular, this means that 'the "signifier" has disappeared, that the stream of the signified no longer finds any signifying element that marks it' (DI, 190/267). In this state, raw material for the object a can no longer be supplied. The 'emptiness [of the empty square] becomes *a veritable lack, a lacuna*' (DI, 190/267; my emphasis).

The other possibility is in effect the reverse. The empty square, the object = x, must always be lacking in its own self-identity, its own proper place, in order to function. In other words, *when this is filled*, it will no longer be able to fulfil its role. 'Or just the opposite, *it is filled, occupied by what accompanies it, and its mobility is lost* in the effect of a sedentary or fixed plenitude' (DI, 190/267; my emphasis). As such, 'the "signified" has faded away . . . the chain of the signifier no longer finds any signified that traverses it' (DI, 190/267).[15]

Such a conclusion is the inevitable consequence for one who has portrayed a structuralism which requires the object = x as its centrepiece; at the same time, it cannot but feel like a cul-de-sac, a conclusion one has been driven into. And needless to say, as a conclusion it is the height of abstraction. If Deleuze appends at the end of the essay that structuralism cannot be thought apart from a certain practice in each of the domains it deigns to interpret, this only sounds like a faint-hearted excuse. For it is quite obvious that the practical attitude put forward here is none other than that of *waiting* for an accident to befall structure, which will miraculously eliminate the signifier or the signified. In other words, this conclusion can be subsumed completely under the model of Deleuzian practice which we developed in the previous chapter, *the seeking of failure*, with all its concomitant difficulties. And to top it all off, astonishingly Deleuze himself declares that '[t]hese last criteria, from the subject to practice, are the *most obscure* – the criteria of the future' (DI, 192/269; my emphasis). He had even written, in the cover letter to Althusser, that '[m]aybe the last part has to be cut' (Dosse 2011: 228/273). It is clear that for Deleuze, the problem with this conclusion was only too apparent.

What is even more interesting is that *The Logic of Sense*, despite its extensive deployment of Lacanian psychoanalysis, avoids the above conclusion (the disappearance of the signifier or the signified) in its discussion of structural transformation, instead opting for a more basic model of the excess of the signifying chain in relation to the chain of signifieds (in case one has forgotten, 'How Do We Recognise Structuralism?', contrary to the order of publication, was written before *The Logic of Sense*).

To delve into a somewhat technical discussion, there is a certain ambivalence in the exposition of the 'empty square' in 'How Do We Recognise Structuralism?', in that it combines the Lacanian theory of the Phallus with the theory of the 'floating signifier' explicated by Lévi-Strauss.[16] The latter refers to the lack of coincidence between at least two different series (DI, 186/261). Let us read a direct discussion of this theory in the eighth series 'On Structure' in *The Logic of*

Transition: From Structure to the Machine

Sense. Whenever we have the twin series of the signifier and signified, there is always an excess in the series of the signifier, and correspondingly a lack in the series of the signified. Deleuze explains this as a problem pertaining to the social, and in a broad sense to Law and rules. Law – not only of the state, but religion, politics, economics, even love and labour, kinship and marriage, obedience and freedom, life and death ... – law in its widest possible sense constitutes one single system, and is therefore given in one go, all at once. However, the actual social 'conquest of nature' only takes place in increments. Simplistically, society comes across new things one after another. As a result, Law is always deployed as a totality, all at once, without, however, it being known in advance how and upon what domains it will come to be handed down. In the jargon, between the signifier (Law, rules) and the signified (its objects of application), there is an irreducible lack of correspondence. According to Deleuze, it is precisely this irreducibility that is the potential cause of social change.

> It is this disequilibrium that makes revolutions possible. It is not at all the case that revolutions are determined by technical progress. Rather, they are made possible by this gap between the two series, which solicits realignments of the economic and political totality in relation to the parts of the technical progress. There are therefore two errors which in truth are one and the same: the error of reformism or technocracy, which aspires to promote or impose partial arrangements of social relations according to the rhythm of technical achievements; and the error of totalitarianism, which aspires to constitute a totalisation of the signifiable and the known, according to the rhythm of the social totality existing at a given moment. The technocrat is the natural friend of the dictator – computers and dictatorship; but *the revolutionary lives in the gap which separates technical progress from social totality, and inscribes there his dream of permanent revolution*. This dream, therefore, is itself action, reality, and an effective menace to all established order; it renders possible what it dreams about. (LS, 59/64; my emphasis)

A moving passage. And the account of law is one that harks back to the theory of law and institution that Deleuze had frequently concerned himself with early in his career, and there is ample scope for further analysis and development in this avenue. And yet, it is imperative for us to point out that this passage is testament to a sort of theoretical regression: for Deleuze was thoroughly versed in the Lacanian object = x, with its higher degree of abstraction, and yet chose to bury this theory in favour of the 'safer' option of the floating signifier. Though Deleuze does mention the Lacanian object

= x in *The Logic of Sense*, he does so only to pay his respects to it as 'Lacan's paradox' (LS, 50n6/55n6); the theory of structural transformation through the disappearance of either the signifier or the signified, which we found in 'How Do We Recognise Structuralism?', is not even tacitly implicated. And this even though the theory of the object = x is deployed extensively in this book, especially in the final three series.

One cannot help but read in this a strong vacillation on the part of Deleuze. For he understands that his own thinking is situated in great proximity to a certain structuralist inspiration. Equally, however, he is aware of the difficulties this inspiration entails (at least insofar as it has been laid out systematically by Deleuze himself), and most radically in the domain of practice. But he cannot see a way out of them. 'How Do We Recognise Structuralism?' had entrusted the solution to the future; *The Logic of Sense* covered over the issue by simply bypassing the practical difficulties altogether.

Series, Phallus, Primal Repression

Let us stick to the texts written by Deleuze in the singular for a moment longer, in order to understand the turmoils more theoretically. In *Difference and Repetition*, Deleuze takes an ambiguous stance as regards the concept of the Phallus in Lacanian psychoanalysis. The crux of the issue is the problem of the genesis of the ego from the id, which we have touched upon in Chapter 2.

We recall that Deleuze had explained the id and the ego idiosyncratically as follows. First, it was stated that '[t]he id is populated by local egos (*Le Ça se peuple de moi locaux*)' (DR, 120/129). These 'local egos' in the plural are a bundle of disparate partial desires each seeking a partial object. In contrast, he calls the 'so-called' ego, generated in being split off from the id, which 'unite[s] all its small composing and contemplative passive egos' and synthesises them 'actively', the 'global ego (*moi global*)' (DR, 122, 124/131, 133).

Roughly speaking, these two egos correspond to the pleasure principle and the reality principle. With respect to the local egos, the repetition of the blockage of excitation gives rise to pleasure as a determinate principle (Deleuze considers the pleasure principle as itself something generated). The genesis of this principle is termed 'passive synthesis'. On the other hand, the global ego is one which has learnt to delay the realisation of pleasure (reality principle). Since this is linked to the genesis of the 'active ego', so to speak, it is termed 'active synthesis'. In sum, the former triad (local egos/ pleasure principle/passive synthesis) is prior to the latter (global ego/ reality principle/active synthesis). At the same time, however, there is a simultaneity and continuity between the two states; it is emphasised that the predominance of the latter over the former is itself founded on this continuity and simultaneity (DR, 122/131).

Now Deleuze had understood the genesis of the global ego from the local egos as the actualisation of virtualities, borrowing from Leibniz's theory of minute perception (see above, p. 52). Each individual minute perception is 'distinct' yet 'obscure'; only when they are taken together *globally* do they become 'clear', and at the same time something 'confused'. Deleuze reformulates this as each minute perception being 'differential (*différentiel*)' but not 'differenciated (*différenciée*)', and in this way developed his theory of the actualisation of virtualities. In this terminology, the local egos are indeed the 'small passive egos', hence they belong to the level of the Virtual; and their corresponding partial objects are likewise to be classed as virtualities. 'The virtual object is a *partial* object' (DR, 125/133; original emphasis). And the earlier condition appended to the relation between local egos and the global ego (that although the former precedes the latter, the two be at the same time simultaneous and continuous) is also explained as follows, using the alternative terminology: 'the virtual is never subject to the global character which affects real objects. It is – not only by its origin but by its own nature – a fragment, a shred or a remainder. It lacks its own identity' (DR, 125/133).

Such an explication of the genesis of the global ego from local egos, using the theory of minute perception, is a progressive development (to use the legal term) of Freudian scholarship. This exposition is admittedly unorthodox, but it is hardly an extravagant interpretation. Having said that, one must realise that this version has deliberately excluded a core creed of the Freudian tradition: castration within the dynamic of the Oedipus Complex, otherwise known as primal repression. Why does this step, which occupies the place of honour in orthodox psychoanalytic accounts of the genesis of the ego, not make an appearance in Deleuze's reformulation? It is because Deleuze refuses to accept any generative model which is put into motion by a one-off Event. However ideal, however figurative this Event is claimed to be, he will not accept such an originary Act. It is likely for this reason that *Difference and Repetition* does not so much as *mention* the Oedipus Complex. Given how extensively psychoanalysis is dealt with in this work, this should be a cause for surprise.

Primal repression was the underlying mechanism that had been posited by Freud in order to explain repression as such, as it is used in common parlance (what Freud calls 'repression proper'). Repression, in its ordinary usage, means the exile of a certain representation from consciousness, and its burial in the unconscious. For such repression to be possible, however, there ought to be some force of traction from some already unconscious content; hence one is inexorably led to posit an originary repression always-already at work, or so the reasoning goes.[17] But this logic is only necessitated so long as we situate repression as something originary in the first place. And because Deleuze is intransigent in his rejection of the one-off primeval Event, this 'origin', he will explain repression in the following way: it is repetition that gives rise to repression. 'I do not repeat because I repress. I repress because I repeat, I forget because I repeat [*Je ne répète pas parce que je refoule. Je refoule parce que je répète, j'oublie parce que je répète*]. I repress, because I can live certain things or certain experiences only in the mode of repetition' (DR, 20/29). What Deleuze is referring to here is the phenomenon of the 'repetition compulsion', where the repressed content returns again and again, as if man is actively seeking to put himself in an unpleasant situation. As is clear from the fact that Freud describes this phenomenon as the 'return of the repressed', the general understanding is that there is first the repression of a certain representation for external reasons, but because repression requires the constant exertion of psychic energy, the repressed representation will resurface into consciousness whenever the energetics falls short of the requisite level. Deleuze however turns this order of proceedings on its head: man represses because he repeats. He goes so far as to say that repetition is the *condition to live a certain experience*. Indeed it is worth noting that Deleuze even extends the discussion from repression proper to oblivion in general: repetition is given a highly privileged position at the foundation of a wide spectrum of human experience.

The immediate consequence of this reversal of hierarchy is that Deleuze admits the existence of repression *per se* (it is observed all the time in treatment), but *will not admit the existence of primal repression*. For if it is repetition that causes repression, we no longer need to posit any singular repression at the origin, which is precisely what primal repression is. In any case this foundational repression is not observed empirically, but something arrived at by deducing

Transition: From Structure to the Machine

backwards from the end result.[18] Indeed, as late as the 1922 work *Inhibitions, Symptoms and Anxiety*, Freud states explicitly that very little is understood about primal repression.[19] In which case one can paraphrase Deleuze's point as follows: the reason so little is known about primal repression is not that there has been insufficient research on it, but that we have been circling around trying to get to the bottom of a phenomenon which does not even exist in the first place. For what lies at the origin is not some mythical act of foundation, but just good old repetition. Only when we compress repetitions into a monologic global perspective do we fantasise the primal repression into a pseudo-origin.

Thus reversed, then, the problem becomes the following: whence does repetition, such as is capable of bringing about repression, arise? The above quotation is taken from the preface to *Difference and Repetition*, where the discussion has yet to be developed in full; this task is left to chapter II of the same work, where an almost identical formulation is proposed, except that now repetition appears as a *concept which is in turn encompassed by another concept*:

> We do not repeat because we repress, we repress because we repeat. Moreover – *which amounts to the same thing* – we do not disguise because we repress, we repress because we disguise (*On ne répète pas parce qu'on refoule, mais on refoule parce qu'on répète. Et,* ce qui revient au même, *on ne déguise pas parce qu'on refoule, on refoule parce qu'on déguise*) (DR, 130/139; my emphasis).

Here Deleuze pits 'disguise' alongside repetition in an effort to explicate repression, and 'disguise' is presented as a worthy substitute for repetition. Disguise is being used here in a broad sense, encompassing the general psychoanalytic mechanisms of condensation and displacement (DR, 18/27). Let us, following Deleuze, explain this process with reference to the case of Dora (DR, 19/27). During his analytic sessions with Dora, who had been displaying symptoms of hysteria, Freud discovered among her complex and disparate emotional elements her love for her father (Freud 1905). This was in turn used by Freud to explain her troublesome behaviour, well beyond what was acceptable for a daughter, as well as physical symptoms such as her cough. More precisely, the former implied that Dora had been conducting herself not as a daughter but as a wife to her father, while the latter was an expression of her response to the oral sex acts which she had fantasised between her father and his lover, Frau K. In other words, Dora was disguising (masquerading) herself at times as her mother, whom her father had once loved, and at times as Frau K, the current object of his affection.

According to the usual interpretation, we have first the repression of Dora's love for her father, which then results in the reappearance of the repressed content in its various guises. Not so with Deleuze, however, who considers the disguises to be primary, and repression to be nothing more than their *effect*. This is best visualised not chronologically as repression coming after disguise, but topologically, with disguise and repression being two perspectives on the same underlying phenomenon.[20]

Now that we have understood the relation between disguise and repression in Deleuze, the next task is to understand why repetition and disguise are equivalent. How is it that 'one represses because one repeats' 'amounts to the same thing' as saying that 'one represses because one disguises'? This is because Deleuze understands disguise according to the structuralist theory of the 'empty square'. The process whereby the object = x, namely the Phallus, is chased after relentlessly as the object a and displaced by successive signifiers one after another, is being equivocated with disguise. And this is in turn how repetition comes about. It is thought that disguise, as the *displacement* of successive representations of the object = x, is what constitutes repetition.

> It is because this object constantly circulates, always displaced in relation to itself, that it determines transformations of terms and modifications of relations, both imaginary, within the two real series in which it appears, and therefore between the two presents. *The displacement of the virtual object is not, therefore, one disguise among others, but the principle from which, in reality, repetition follows in the form of disguised repetition.* (DR, 129/138; my emphasis).

It is true that, provisionally, 'displacement (*déplacement*)' and 'disguise (*déguisement*)' are distinguished here, with the former used in association with the level of the Virtual, and the latter with the level of the Actual; but equally the two are equivocated, so much as to declare that the 'displacement' of the Virtual object, in other words the object = x, is the principle of repetition. It is none other than the sliding in the object = x that gives rise to repetition. Indeed, elsewhere Deleuze writes that repetition is a consequence of disguise and displacement, and does not pre-exist these processes, or that disguise is the proper internal genetic element of repetition.[21]

The inference to be drawn here is clear: *in these sections of*

Transition: From Structure to the Machine

Difference and Repetition *at least*, the 'repetition' that Deleuze speaks of coincides for all practical purposes with the theory of the 'signifying chain' in Lacanian psychoanalysis. Let us be unequivocal: *it is the Phallus that causes repetition*. Or with marginally more nuance (but really only marginally), Deleuze is here revamping the structuralist theory of the signifier, according to which the Phallus generates the signifying chain in the futile attempt to discover an adequate substitute for the object a, in an almost undiluted form. Indeed, even the critique of the Freudian model of the unconscious is being conducted from this basic standpoint.[22] And to top it all off, Deleuze goes on to declare explicitly that the Phallus is 'indistinguishable from' this space of displacement.[23]

But we must pause here and think back a little, since *the concept of the Phallus is inseparable from the logic of primal repression*. At the moment of Symbolic castration, when the imaginary interrelation of mother and child is irrevocably destroyed by language, the phallus as that which was lacking in this relation from the beginning ($-\varphi$) is translated into the Phallus as eternal lack (Φ). It is this Φ that is primordially inscribed into the unconscious as the signifier of lack, and it is precisely because of its status as lack that it is able to function as the traction attracting all further instances of repression (this is the mechanism of the signifying chain). But was it not Deleuze's avowed intention in *Difference and Repetition* to refute the hypothesis of primal repression decisively, in favour of an explanation of repression as the effect of repetition? One cannot avoid the sense that there is a contradiction here, or at least a certain lapse in rigour. For the reason Deleuze refuses to admit of primal repression is that he is suspicious of all explanations of the genesis of structures and principles based on the efficacy of a one-off Event. Instead, he finds the principle of genesis in repetition: for the construction of a transcendental empiricism, this is a fundamental commitment. Nevertheless, at least one version of the conceptualisation of repetition by Deleuze seems to have been re-inscribed unwittingly into the orbit of the monology of the primordial Event.

Deleuze, for his part, has of course taken account of this situation. He is wary that the introduction of the Phallus would reopen the door to a theoretical position anchored in the one-off Event. It is for this reason that he repeatedly stresses that the Phallus is lacking in its own proper place, its self-identity, unequivocally that the Phallus is not an 'ultimate and original term'.[24] It is as if Deleuze hopes in this way to neutralise the Phallus, so to speak. But in doing so he has only come full circle: for it can just as well be said that it is precisely because the Phallus lacks self-identity and its proper place, that it qualifies as an ultimate and original term. Indeed, it was for this very reason that Deleuze has termed it 'paradoxical' in the first place.

Where then did Deleuze's reasoning go astray? Let us trace back our steps for a second. Deleuze had distinguished the unary global ego and the multiplicity of local egos. The inspiration behind this introduction of multiplicity was a criticism of the original Freudian version of the id, to the effect that this model had been an obfuscation, constructed from the perspective of the already pre-formed consciousness/self, the global ego. Deleuze calls this an unconscious of 'opposition' (DR, 133/143). Turning a blind eye to the reality of countless elements disparately seething and writhing, Freud had bundled them altogether indiscriminately into the 'id', and opposed the latter abstractly to the (global) ego; this opposition was then deployed in order to explicate the unconscious and its vicissitudes. By contrast, Lacanian psychoanalysis had succeeded in constructing a serial model of the unconscious, based on structuralist principles. And Deleuze was extremely favourable towards this serial model of the unconscious, for the simple reason that it is capable of overthrowing the earlier oppositional model.

However, we recall that the inspiration behind the introduction of local egos had never been serialism, but the Leibnizian model of minute perception. For the local egos had originally been conceived as 'minute' selves, situated in the Virtual domain. Moreover, Deleuze had recognised that Freud himself was not an unquestioning advocate of the oppositional model, that he displayed proximities to the model of minute perception: if not, 'why did he pay so much homage to the Leibnizian Fechner' (DR, 133/143)?

From the preceding analysis, it thus becomes clear that there are in fact three competing models of the unconscious at work here:

1. A Freudo-Hegelian oppositional model.
2. A Freudo-Lacanian serial model.
3. A Freudo-Leibnizian minute perception model.

However, in reading Deleuze's exposition one cannot avoid the feeling that he has collapsed 2) and 3) in a none too clear way.[25] Minute perceptions have never in themselves been serialised. For serialisation presupposes the prior structuralisation of a given domain; the sound of waves frolicking constitutes neither structure nor series. In other words, the problem lies in the fact that Deleuze became too bogged down in the structuralist theory of the series, and as a result tried to derive even the model of minute perception from it. In psychoanalytic jargon, what was required was a perspective which could treat disparate partial objects prior to their serialisation by the object a, and partial desires prior to their systematisation by the Phallus. Only then could the hypothesis of primal repression be overcome.

That is not to say that Deleuze has nothing to say at this stage about pre-serialised repetition. The relevant section is the discussion of the 'harnessing [*liaison*][26] of excitation' which we considered in Chapter 2. Freud had discovered, as a result of his investigation into the repetition compulsion found in post-traumatic neurosis, that repetition was a process to harness psychic excitation; further, he was led to posit the existence of an internal excitation whose intensity can balance the external energetic influx behind neurosis. And to explain this internal excitation, Freud ultimately arrived at the concept of the 'death instinct (Thanatos)' as its fountainhead. What interested Deleuze in all this was the fact that a genetic origin of the pleasure principle was being proposed, vis-à-vis the harnessing of excitation. In effect, the almighty experiential principle with dominion over the psychic apparatus is revealed to have been generated through the *repetition* of the process of excitation-harnessing. Such a mechanism of psychic harmonisation Deleuze links to the concept of habit: 'habit, in the form of a passive harnessing synthesis, precedes the pleasure principle and renders it possible. The idea of pleasure follows from it in the same way that . . . past and future follow from the synthesis of the living present' (DR, 121/129).[27] Crucially, the repetition of harnessing giving rise to 'habit', with which we are concerned here, is a pre-serialised repetition. For it is this repetition that gives rise to the pleasure principle presupposed by disguise and repression in the first place. In this way, it is not the case that Deleuze only deals with repetition as conceptualised by the inter-serial flitting of the object = x.

Indeed, Deleuze would even go one step further, to say that the repetition of harnessing is itself derivative: for 'there is more profoundly a passion of repetition' (DR, 120/129). What he means here is that '[e]xcitation as a difference was *already* the contraction of an elementary repetition' (DR, 120/129; original emphasis) in the first instance. That is, Deleuze understands the excitation brought about by external/internal impetus as in itself a sort of repetition, a seismic compression. Harnessing and investment are functions secondary to this primary repetition within the psyche (DR, 120/129); instinct in turn is but a tertiary stage arising from these secondary repetitions. In his words, 'instincts are nothing more than harnessed excitations' (DR, 120/129). And the theoretical circle is closed when we observe that these in their turn come to ground the multiple 'local egos' which we considered in some detail earlier. Each time a harnessing takes place, a new 'ego' is born within the id, an ego which is subject to partial desire, passive, itself partial, fragmentary and larval. Such Virtual egos arise one after another inside of the id, a veritable witch's cauldron.

It would therefore be wrong to claim that Deleuze reduced repetition to a serial model. He is at pains to explicate a repetition prior to serialisation, which will not require the Phallus to bestow upon it its theoretical integrity. Hence a modest suggestion on our part, that the dual theses traversing repetition and repression ought in the last instance to have been conjoined as follows: 'We repress because we disguise, and we disguise because we repeat' (*On refoule parce qu'on déguise, et on déguise parce qu'on répète*). The reason Deleuze could state that repression was founded on repetition, but was nonetheless forced to equivocate this with the proposition that repression is founded on disguise, is precisely because of this indistinction of the serial and minute perception models in his mind. This is the reason repetition had to succumb to disguise at this crucial juncture.[28] This, however, is not the only thought-train discernible here: indeed we have a highly developed two-stage theory of pre-serialised repetition, which is even situated as the genetic principle behind the whole armoury of psychoanalytic concepts, including ego, desire and even the pleasure principle itself. This goes to show that Deleuze had all the requisite materials to think repetition without reference to the concepts of series and Phallus (at the end of the day, serial repetition is but a tertiary derivation of the derivation). But ultimately this insight could not be rigorously deployed. Now we are not saying that serialism and the concept of the Phallus are erroneous; the point is rather that the moment Deleuze decided to reject primal repression, he ought to have forbidden himself from incorporating these Lacanian inspirations into his thinking. And yet, in the last instance, the Deleuze of *Difference and Repetition* could not shake off his dependence on these concepts. This contradiction is, as it were, the physical theoretical manifestation of the vacillation we found in 'How Do We Recognise Structuralism?'

Transition: From Structure to the Machine

Anti-Oedipus and Schizoanalysis

One detour led to another, but here we are at last. Let us finally direct our attention to the collaboration between Deleuze and Guattari.

Against the Lacanian concept of structure, Guattari had pitted a novel concept (or rather, figure) of the machine. From the point of view of the latter, it is no longer possible that the subject of the unconscious be represented by a signifier. For the Phallus, the primordial signifier, has been 'detached', and the very idea of a 'normal' functioning of primal repression is now under question.

The Deleuze of the late 1960s vacillated between the magnetic attraction of structuralism on the one hand, and an acute recognition of the problems besetting it on the other. *Difference and Repetition* had sought a renewal of the concept of repression through repetition, in the process profoundly problematising the hypothesis of primal repression. There is even an attempt to construct a concept of repetition that is no longer dependent on the structuralist theory of the series. But all this is finally cast to the flames, and we are back to the sphere of a serialised structure whose consistency draws from the object = x (Phallus).

The theoretical necessity of the encounter has thus been definitively established. And the common aim is to construct a model with which to think beyond the confines of a structuralist, serialised structure, a structure quilted by an object = x given the monolithic name of 'Phallus'. One man was having difficulty making the decisive step, while the other had taken it, but was struggling to follow it up with the requisite conceptual labour. The two decide to join hands. It is evident that at the forefront of their concerns was the hypothesis of 'primal repression'; for the Phallus is ultimately the self-same hypothesis, abstracted a hundredfold. When *Anti-Oedipus* criticises psychoanalysis's fixation with the Oedipal family, proposing to extend this to a generalised social critique, it is indubitable that a basic task the two had set for themselves was to think social repression outside of an analytical perspective founded upon primal repression. Hence the title of their collaborative debut, *against* the Oedipus and its omnipresence. For it is precisely the doctrine of 'primal repression' that lies at the heart of the Oedipus Complex. We can also situate in this vein the programme of 'schizoanalysis (*schizoanalyse*)', which the pair advanced as an antidote to psychoanalysis. The latter had conducted its analysis from the base-hypothesis of primal repression; schizoanalysis by contrast questions the very idea of the 'normal' operation of primal repression, indeed this question constitutes its starting point.

The theoretical significance of primal repression as the central antagonist in *Anti-Oedipus* is contained in the following remark: 'Is there a frontier between the Imaginary and the Symbolic? (*La frontière passe-t-elle entre l'imaginaire et le symbolique?*)' (the title of the final subsection of AO, chapter 2, section 4; translation modified). Deleuze-Guattari declares that one cannot admit of any essential difference between the Imaginary and the Symbolic, there is no border or frontier separating them.[29] And when the two worlds melt into indistinction, the consequence to be extrapolated is that the ideal stage of primal repression, as fantasised by psychoanalysis, *never* in fact takes place in reality. True, there is an ego that emerges from the id, inserting itself into the reality principle through active synthesis. Nevertheless, this is only half the story, a mere descant, for on the underside of this global ego is the dissonant chorus of local egos, incanting in devil's intervals. In the collaborative works, Deleuze's terminology of the local/global will be transformed into the opposition between the 'molecular' and the 'molar', coined by Guattari, to be employed henceforth for years to come. Moreover, Deleuze's staunch refusal of the reduction of the local-molecular to the global-molar in *Difference and Repetition* is absorbed unaltered into the collaborations, to become an indispensable aspect of their work. The famous opening lines of *Anti-Oedipus* are, as it were, a declaration of war on this front:

> It is at work everywhere, functioning smoothly at times, at other times in fits and starts. It breathes, it heats, it eats. It shits and fucks. What a mistake to have ever said *the* id. (*Ça fonctionne partout, tantôt sans arrêt, tantôt discontinu. Ça respire, ça chauffe, ça mange. Ça chie, ça baise. Quelle erreur d'avoir dit le ça.*) (AO, 1/7; original emphasis)

The relentless repetition of 'it' of course renders the impersonal pronoun '*ça*', but at the same time it is also the French translation of the psychoanalytic 'id'. What is being asserted here is that the id is not something which can be grasped globally under the auspices of the definite article, it is rather a bundle of multiplicitous and disparate partial desires. The problematic has definitively shifted to the local egos, in the indefinite plural.

Returning to primal repression, when this is cast into doubt, the general psychoanalytic attitude founded on the strict demarcation of psychosis (*psychose*) and neurosis (*névrose*) is forced to undergo a major modification. For psychoanalysis has always treated these two conditions as clinically distinct.[30] Neurosis is a disorder of the psychic apparatus traceable to an internal conflict rooted in the life history of the individual, and here there is no disorder of personality. Only in psychosis is there such a radical disorder, for here the ego is under the command of the id.[31] Lacanians explain this difference by saying that the 'Name-of-the-Father' has been 'foreclosed (*forclusion*)' in psychosis, and not in neurosis. In other words, in neurosis there has been a 'normal' functioning of primal repression, while in psychosis this has failed to take place. The failure of primal repression implies that for the affected subject the signifying chain is fragile; as a result, for the psychotic 'the totality of the world appears to the subject as one gigantic piece of nonsense, as an "enigma"' (Matsumoto 2012: 32). By contrast, in neurosis the signifying chain operates 'normally', such that the individual is able to live and breathe in a world of sense. In effect, the neurotic's trouble is the exact opposite, (s)he is overwhelmed by the excess of sense.

As is clear from the above, the vision of the 'normal' human being according to psychoanalysis is that of the patient suffering from mild neurosis. For your bog-standard man on the street is one who has repressed some figure or other 'in' primal repression, and subsequently lives through a world of sense burdened, *within reason*, by a certain psychic struggle. All of which necessitates the following assessment: the end of the psychoanalytic cure is to turn the patient into a moderate neurotic, the paragon of 'normality'. What then happens the moment one ceases to believe in the ideal functioning of primal repression? The spurious image of the 'normal' moderate neurotic is thrown out of the window. In other words, psychoanalysis is exposed to have been striving towards an image of 'normality' which is pure fiction. Whereas schizoanalysis, which suspected all along that there was something fishy about the 'normal' operation of primal repression, 'throughout its entire process of treatment ... schizophrenises, instead of neuroticising like psychoanalysis' (AO, 362/434). The sense in which psychoanalysis is an enterprise of 'neurotisation' should by now be clear. The sense of 'schizophrenisation' is as yet obscure, but either way it involves a critique of the mild neurotic as the moving image of 'normality'.[32] And if some close relative of this 'normal' man is our present social pandemic, if this figure of 'normality' (adulthood?) has covered the face of the Earth, the abstract concept of 'primal repression' is already far out of its depth. What we need henceforth is to analyse the systemic social (in the widest sense of this term) mechanisms of 'neurotisation' and repression, of which the nuclear family will be an expression. Herein lies the necessity for *Anti-Oedipus* to expand into an analysis of capitalism and politics via the work of Marx. It is also why the goal of schizoanalysis is characterised as follows: 'to analyse the specific nature of the libidinal investments in the economic and political spheres, and thereby to show how, in the subject who desires, desire can be made to desire its own repression' (AO, 105/124–5).

If we recall, Guattari had rounded off his image of the machine by affirming that this new model would be able to concern itself with actual, dated histories. Deleuze, for his part, had expressed his doubts regarding the concept of structure in structuralism, to wit, when one thinks upon the bannister of structure, the problem always boils down to searching for the appropriate object = x, wherever, whenever. Schizoanalysis bids farewell to this monology by analysing, without recourse to the hypothesis of primal repression, societies which exist as a part of history, with a determinate set of dates, and the real people who live in them. Deleuze 'and' Guattari, in their union as Deleuze-Guattari, finally managed to achieve what they had long sought to do in vain on their own.

To conclude this chapter, let us give a more detailed account of their joint project. In the preceding quotation, they stated that the aim of schizoanalysis is to reveal how a desiring subject comes to desire its own 'repression'. Deleuze-Guattari proposed to step out of the suffocation of structure, which explained all desires according to the lack of the Phallus, by surgically extracting the hypothesis of primal repression. With this slice of the scalpel, desire is reimagined as something determined more broadly in the realm of the social. And in observing desire thus reconceived, the very first question that imposes itself with the utmost urgency is how it is possible that man repress himself, why ever in the world he would call for his own enslavement. The Marxism of the time, by contrast, had stubbornly upheld the discursive dualism of rulers and the ruled; against this, Deleuze-Guattari offer a more refined vantage point, yet one which had at the same time been hinted at by certain predecessors. The perspective deployed in the following quotation is precisely this vantage point, rediscovered in modernity by the fusion of Marxian political economy with a critical extension of psychoanalysis, which is veritably the proper lighthouse of political economy.

There is only desire and the social, and nothing else. Even the most repressive and deadly forms of social reproduction are produced by

Transition: From Structure to the Machine

desire within the organisation that is the consequence of such production under various conditions that we must analyse. That is why the fundamental problem of political philosophy is still precisely the one that Spinoza saw so clearly, and that Wilhelm Reich rediscovered: 'Why do men fight *for* their servitude as stubbornly as though it were their salvation?' How can people possibly reach the point of shouting: 'More taxes! Less bread!'? As Reich remarks, the astonishing thing is not that some people steal or that others occasionally go out on strike, but rather that all those who are starving do not steal as a regular practice, and all those who are exploited are not continually out on strike: after centuries of exploitation, why do people still tolerate being humiliated and enslaved, to such a point, indeed, that they *actually want* humiliation and slavery not only for others but for themselves? (AO, 29/36–37; original emphases)

Everything is here, right in this passage: all the problems which political philosophy must confront to be worthy of its name.

In the next chapter, we will consider this question of Deleuze-Guattari in greater detail. Centre-stage will be the concept of power.

Notes

1. The three books are, in order of publication, *Anti-Oedipus* (1972), *Kafka: Towards a Minor Literature* (1975) and *A Thousand Plateaus* (1980). In addition to which the two have several essays penned under their dual signatures. In 1991 *What is Philosophy?* was published under both their names, but as already discussed, it has since been established that it was written by Deleuze in the singular (Chapter 1, n3). Indeed, this is all but clear from the actual content of the book itself; as such we insist on classing it as a work of Deleuze's, not Deleuze-Guattari.
2. For the provenance of this and other biographical details touched upon in this chapter, please refer to the 'Prologue' of this book.
3. From which it is quite clear that the process of 'dual writing' was undertaken entirely under the directive of Deleuze. It would indeed be no exaggeration to say that Deleuze, who was suffering from a literary and theoretical writer's block, made use of Guattari for his own purposes. As a matter of fact, following the publication of *Anti-Oedipus* Guattari was to experience a period of vacuity and inferiority. Dosse lifts remarks such as these from the diaries of Guattari: 'I feel like curling up into a tiny ball and being rid of all these politics of presence and prestige . . . The feeling is so strong that I resent Gilles for having dragged me into this mess'; 'Deleuze works a lot. We're really very different . . . I'm a sort of an inveterate self-taught man . . .'. All of

which culminates in this striking confession: 'I don't really see myself in the *A-O*' (quoted in Dosse 2011: 12/24).
4. This piece had originally been a spoken address to the École Freudienne de Paris founded by Jacques Lacan. Roland Barthes gave this text rave reviews, and urged Guattari to submit it to the journal *Communication*. Lacan felt slighted by this, and demanded to know why Guattari would not publish the text in his journal *Scilicet*. Guattari would obey Lacan, informing Barthes of his decision, but Lacan went back on his word; publication suffered postponement after postponement, until it finally saw the light of day in Jean-Pierre Faye's journal *Change* in 1972 (no. 12, Seuil) (see Dosse 2011: 71/92 for the sensational coverage). It is worth pondering the fact that Guattari had been involved in the foundation of the École Freudienne back in 1964, and was at first highly regarded by Lacan himself. However, as Lacan began to favour the group led by Jacques-Alain Miller, so Guattari would gradually lose any hope of receiving Lacan's blessing as the chosen successor. Also noteworthy is the fact that Lacan had thought extremely highly of Deleuze. Upon hearing that Guattari, whom he believed to be his disciple, was collaborating with Deleuze, Lacan briefly attempted to repair matters between Guattari and himself in an effort to find out what it was that the two were up to theoretically. It was at this fateful meeting that Guattari would recognise that there was no turning back. He had already broken irreconcilably with Lacan's way of thinking. This was October of 1971 (Dosse 2011: 184/223).
5. Since this book has for its object of analysis Gilles Deleuze, we are unable to delve into the problem of structuralism in its wider implications.
6. 'Human work today is merely a residual sub-whole of the work of the machine. This residual human activity is no more than a partial procedure that accompanies the central procedure produced by the order of the machine. The machine has now come to the heart of desire, and this residual human work represents no more than a point of the machine's imprint on the imaginary world of the imaginary' (MS, 113/242).
7. This grandiose phrase is adapted from the words of Hiroshi Fujita, who sums up Lacanian psychoanalytic theory thus: 'the truth of the Φ [Phallus] born of symbolic castration is no less than the *ultimate condition which renders a human being a human being*, and it is none other than this truth which Freud succeeded in extracting from the course of his experience in analysis: "the historical truth (*die historische Wahrheit*)"' (Fujita 1990: 80; my emphasis). No doubt any explanation in terms of the 'human being' is plagued by an ambivalence; nevertheless, it is valuable in highlighting that Lacan's psychoanalytic theory does have recourse to a certain image of what the 'human being' is. Deleuze-Guattari's critique is not unrelated to this aspect of his thought.

Transition: From Structure to the Machine

8. The foregoing explanation owes much to the expositions in Fujita 1990 and Hara 2002. In particular we refer the reader to chapter IV of Hara's book. In what follows, in addition, we have turned to Laplanche and Pontalis 1973 as and when appropriate.
9. Incidentally, in Lacan's theory the 'object a', contrary to its appellation, is understood not as the simple object of desire but as its object-cause. 'To call the *objet a* an "object of desire" is, as far as Lacan's teaching goes, a transitionary nomenclature' (Ogasawara 1989: 69).
10. It seems that Deleuze's understanding of differentiation was heavily marked by the post-Kantian philosopher Salomon Maimon (1754–1800), who tried to interpret Kant's thing-in-itself as a sort of derivative of differentiation.
11. Deleuze extends this to the renewal of Marxism undertaken by Althusser and his collaborators. According to this, relations of production are determined as differential relations. That is, relations of production do not subtend between concrete human individuals, rather they exist between the 'object' and the 'agent' determined as bearers of symbolic value. And each mode of production is characterised by singularities corresponding to the relations of production (DI, 178/249).
12. Vis-à-vis not time but the event, *The Logic of Sense* states: 'it is imprecise to oppose structure and event: the structure includes a register of ideal *events*, that is, an entire *history* internal to it' (LS, 60/66; original emphases). Here too one can sense Deleuze's hesitation. Yes, structure concerns itself with events. But only provided they are 'ideal' events. Yes, structure encompasses a history. But only a history that is 'internal to it'. Against this, Guattari was trying to deploy his concept of the 'machine' in order to treat events and history in themselves.
13. In his highly noteworthy book on Derrida, Hiroki Azuma narrated Derrida's intellectual journey as a protracted battle against negative theology. In the course of this Azuma takes up the case of Deleuze, to point out that his thinking too is apophatic (1998: 196ff). But as Azuma himself discovers from his detailed reading of *Difference and Repetition* (1998: 205ff), the relation of Deleuze to an apophatic mode of thinking should be seen as *ambiguous*.
14. Deleuze is explicit on this point: '*[s]tructuralism is not at all a form of thought that suppresses the subject*, but one that breaks it up and distributes it systematically, that contests the identity of the subject, that dissipates it and makes it shift from place to place, an always nomad subject, made of individuations, but impersonal ones, or of singularities, but pre-individual ones' (DI, 190/267; my emphasis).
15. Slavoj Žižek, in an intentionally provocative application of Lacanian psychoanalysis to the realm of social analysis, has managed to explicate this difficult theory in an impressively comprehensible way. His first domain of application was ideology. Contrary to how it is ordinarily

theorised, ideology works precisely by not being believed (Žižek 1989). For example, no one believes a pinch in the greatness of Stalin: everyone knows that he came to occupy the position of the 'great comrade' at the end of a bloodthirsty battle for power and a hypochondriac purge. Now it is not in spite of but precisely because of this that Stalinism functions. And the reverse is true too: when the people genuinely begin to believe in an ideology, the ideology disintegrates. For once there exists genuine belief, the people cannot but face up to the rift between what they believe and the reality that they live. It is this that Deleuze would call the filling of the object = x.

16. Following Hiroki Azuma's taxonomy, we can class the former as a 'transcendental signifier' and the latter a 'transcendental signified' (Azuma 1998: 101n26).
17. 'We have reason to assume that there is a *primal repression*, a first phase of repression, which consists in the psychical (ideational) representative of the instinct being denied entrance into the conscious. With this a *fixation* is established; the representative in question persists unaltered from then onwards and the instinct remains attached on it' (Freud 1915: 148/250; original emphases).
18. 'Primal repression is postulated above all on the basis of its effects' (Laplanche and Pontalis 1973: 334).
19. 'As I have shown elsewhere, most of the repressions with which we have to deal in our therapeutic work are cases of *after-pressure*. They presuppose the operation of earlier, *primal repressions* which exert an attraction on the more recent situation. Far too little is known as yet about the background and preliminary stages of repression' (Freud 1926: 94/121; original emphases).
20. To paraphrase further still: when one imposes the opposition of 'consciousness on the surface' and the 'unconscious deep down' onto disguise, we end up with what is called 'repression'. For example, little Hans (one of Freud's patients) had a pathological fear that he would be 'bitten by a horse', which rendered him incapable of venturing out into town. Now analysis reveals that this fear is a modification of his enmity towards his father; normally, however, this is interpreted as a repression of this enmity, which subsequently resurfaces under the disguise of a fear of horses. However, in Deleuze's analysis there is simply the disguise practised by the father with whom little Hans used to play horsey, which process would elsewhere be explained as the effect of repression.
21. Repetition 'is woven from disguise and displacement, without any existence apart from these constitutive elements' (DR, 137/148). As a matter of fact, already in the 'Introduction' Deleuze had written: '[t]he disguises and the variations, the masks or costumes, do not come "over

and above": they are, on the contrary, the internal genetic elements of repetition itself, its integral and constituent parts' (DR, 19/27).
22. 'For Freud, it is not only the theory of repression but the dualism in the theory of instincts which encourages the primacy of a conflictual model. However, the conflicts are the result of more subtle differential mechanisms (displacements and disguises)' (DR, 131/140). That Deleuze describes 'displacement' and 'disguise' as 'differential' indicates that he is here thinking under the auspices of structuralism.
23. 'The phallus as virtual object is always located by enigmas and riddles in a place where it is not, because it is indistinguishable from the space in which it is displaced' (DR, 131/141).
24. To that effect, the following passage is surely decisive. We have emphasised the crucial phrases. 'As for this [virtual] object itself, *it can no longer be treated as an ultimate or original term* [...] If it can be "identified" with the phallus, this is only to the extent that the latter, in Lacan's terms, is always missing from its place, from its own identity and from its representation. *In short, there is no ultimate term* – our loves do not refer back to the mother; it is simply that the mother occupies a certain place in relation to the virtual object in the series which constitutes our present, a place which is *necessarily filled by another character* in the series which constitutes the present of another subjectivity, always *taking into account the displacement* of that object = x' (DR, 130/139; my emphases).
25. For instance, in the following passage the model of the unconscious is subjected to an either/or, but by opposing both the serial and minute perception models to the oppositional model, the former models are made to overlap ambivalently (we have italicised the relevant phrases for visibility): 'To ask whether the unconscious is ultimately oppositional or *differential*, an unconscious of great forces in conflict or *one of little elements in series*, one of opposing great representations or *differentiated minute perceptions*, appears to resuscitate earlier hesitations and earlier polemics between the Leibnizian tradition and the Kantian tradition' (DR, 133/143).
26. Translator's note: on the decision to render Freud's '*Bindung*' (*liaison* in French) as 'harnessing', please see above Chapter 2, note 26.
27. In a similar vein: '[t]his harnessing is a genuine reproductive synthesis, a Habitus' (DR, 120/128). The term 'Habitus' is used in *Difference and Repetition* to mean disposition, or proclivity.
28. Following this proposition, it would be possible to reinterpret Deleuze's interpretation of the case of Dora as such. According to Freud, Dora bore a love towards Frau K, which she attempted to deny by reviving her childhood love for her father. Dora, however, simultaneously harboured this homosexual longing for Frau K. Now, these are states of 'love' that have already been circumscribed globally. However, prior to

this there is the criss-crossing of partial desires for all varieties of partial objects bubbling away in the id (for instance, Dora is strongly attracted to Frau K's 'white body'). And each one is repeated within the id as an excitation. Only when these are grouped together globally, do we find such complex and inconsistent vectors of emotions as the above. Disguise takes place along these lines, and as a result, repression comes about. As such, an explanation framed in terms of the serial model is effective only once circumscription into grand states of love has already taken place.

29. 'How many interpretations of Lacanism, overtly or secretly pious as the case may be, have in this manner invoked a structural Oedipus to create and shut the double impasse, to lead us back to the question of the father, to oedipalise even the schizo, and to show that a gap in the Symbolic would bring us back to the Imaginary, and inversely that imaginary drivel or confusions would lead us to the structure! As a famous predecessor said to these creatures, you've already made this into an old refrain. As for us, that is why we were unable to posit any difference in nature, any border line, any limit at all between the Imaginary and the Symbolic, or between Oedipus-as-crisis and Oedipus-as-structure, or between the problem and its solution' (AO, 82–3/98).
30. On neurosis and psychosis, we have had occasion to rely on the many secondary sources cited in this chapter, but above all we have gained much invaluable insight from Matsumoto 2012.
31. '[I]n neurosis the ego obeys the requirements of reality and stands ready to repress the drives of the id, whereas in psychosis the ego is under the sway of the id, ready to break up with reality' (AO, 133/145).
32. Incidentally, the mild neurotic as the image of the 'normal man' is being overturned by an interesting case study. According to Matsumoto (2012), in recent years Jacques-Alain Miller has proposed a new concept of psychological structure which goes by the name of 'ordinary psychosis'. As the name implies, this describes clinical cases where the state of psychosis is lived with normalcy. France today has in place an experimental scheme where one can be psychoanalysed for free in a state institution; apparently, many of those who come to visit display the structure of 'ordinary psychosis'. Based on these considerations, Matsumoto suggests that '"ordinary psychosis" may well be the dominant psychological structure of the twenty-first century' (2012: 38). This might seem a little forced, but to me it seems that this fact demonstrates the prophetic power of Deleuze-Guattari's schizoanalysis.

Research Note IV: The Individual Soul and the Collective Soul

Towards the end of his life, Deleuze would compose several essays on literature. Of these, the most widely disseminated is probably his piece on Herman Melville's (1819–1891) novella *Bartleby, the Scrivener*, titled 'Bartleby, or the Formula' (CC, 68–90/89–114). Here, however, we wish to take up a different essay, which deserves more attention: 'Nietzsche and Saint Paul, Lawrence and John of Patmos', on D. H. Lawrence's (1885–1930) *Apocalypse*.

In this book Lawrence discusses the 'Book of Revelation according to John'. There were no fewer than three people who went by the name of John in the early Christian community: John the Baptist, baptiser of Jesus; the apostle John, author of the fourth gospel; and John of Patmos, author of the Book of Revelation, who was incarcerated on the island of Patmos for religious crimes against the Roman Empire. Though today almost completely discredited, there once existed a theory which claimed that the gospel author John was the same person as this John of Patmos. It is into this debate on authorship that Lawrence makes his intervention: '[i]t's not the same [person], it can't be the same [person] . . .' (CC, 36/50).

For the Book of Revelation tells of the apocalypse and the Last Judgement, the victory of the believers over the unbelievers; its thematic is a tribunal upon this world, a verdict which thirsts for revenge. Its content is diametrically opposed to that of the gospels, which trade in human and spiritual love. Revelation gasps for fulfilment of the rights of the 'poor', the 'weak'. However, these 'are not who we think they are'. Permeating its pages is what Deleuze calls the 'collective soul'. These 'are not the humble or the unfortunate, but those extremely fearsome men who have nothing but a collective soul' (CC, 38/53).

The collective soul desires power as vehemently as it seeks its destruction, impelled as it is by hatred for power and those in power. Deleuze also quotes the words of the painter Gustave Courbet (1819–1877) to explain it like this: these cry out, 'I want to judge! I have to judge!' Moreover, the collective soul is a 'carnivorous lamb'. This lamb wails, 'Help! What did I ever do to you? It was for your own good and our common cause.'

Contraposed to this collective soul is the 'individual soul'. The collective soul would like to *be given to the ends of time without ever giving anything in return*. In contradistinction, the individual soul would like to *give to the ends of time without ever being given in return*. The John of Revelation would be a paradigmatic figure of the former, Christ of the latter soul. 'Christ's enterprise is individual' (CC, 38/52). Unquestionably, this enterprise was an extremely valuable one. Nevertheless, Christ was prey to a serious misunderstanding. For he did not see that the collective and individual souls reside within each of us, side by side. 'He thought a culture of the individual soul would be enough to chase off the monsters buried in the collective soul' (CC, 38/52).

Jesus in fact never wished to become a leader, nor did he wish to reach out to his disciples with a helping hand. He never actually interacted with his disciples in a genuine sense, much less did he ever act in concert with them. As Deleuze points out: '[i]n Christ's love, there was a kind of abstract identification, or worse, *an ardor to give without taking anything*. Christ did not want to meet his disciple's expectations, and yet he did not want to keep anything, not even the inviolable part [soul] of himself. There was something suicidal about him' (CC, 50/52; original emphasis).

Undoubtedly, the individual soul must be saved. However, the collective soul too must be saved (CC, 51/68). Soteriology is incomplete if it only disdains and abhors the collective soul; nor is it complete if it concerns itself only with burnishing the individual soul. And this is hardly a problem limited to the Christian religion. For what Christ and John together exemplify is that which has cursed man, fated as he is to live collectively, at the very foundation of his being.

5

Politics: Desire and Power

In the previous chapter, we situated the collaborative works of Deleuze and Guattari theoretically. For Deleuze, who had been building up his own philosophic thought in the context of 1960s France, structuralism was in the air as a revolutionary theory, opening up unprecedented ways of thinking about hitherto unexplored fields. Yes Deleuze had realised that structuralism was beset by numerous difficulties; but perhaps due to this theory's radical novelty, he had been unable to find a way out of them. It is precisely this complicated relationship between Deleuze and structuralism that can be read between the lines in his 1972 essay 'How Do We Recognise Structuralism?' From the perspective of this essay, one can discern that a strong structuralist element pervades *Difference and Repetition* as well, which gives rise to the infelicitous consequence of a theoretical inconsistency (the conflation of the serial and minute perception models of the unconscious).

It is none other than this inconsistency that was overcome through the collaboration with Guattari. Lacanian psychoanalysis was held high in Deleuze's esteem as one of the pinnacles of structuralist achievement; Guattari for his part had absolute command of this theory's subtleties and intricacies, and moreover had instinctively recognised its problematic aspects. When Deleuze learnt of this, he set off on the work of turning Guattari's intuitions into fully-fledged concepts. Through this collaboration, Deleuze arrived at a new psychoanalysis (schizoanalysis) which no longer sought to explain all things from the hypothesis of primal repression, instead explaining repression itself from a wider social vantage point. Both the object of study and the way of studying it have undergone an irreversible change. In technical terminology, we are no longer interested in 'the' global-molar ego and id, but in a multiplicity of local-molecular egos and desires; and this no longer according to an idealised scene of primal repression and castration, but henceforth through socially constituted repressions in the indefinite plural. What is thus allowed to appear is an entirely new theoretical domain, emerging out of the union of Freudo-Lacanian psychoanalysis and Marxist political economy: a philosophy which sees the world in terms of desire. The problematic that lies at the foundation of this new philosophy is formulated by Deleuze-Guattari as follows: '[w]hy do men fight for their servitude as stubbornly as though it were their salvation?' (AO, 29/36–37; emphasis removed).

If we look back at the tentative beginnings of this present volume, we discussed the problem of the widespread confusion of Deleuze and Guattari, with reference to Slavoj Žižek's assertion that theoreticians who wish to extract from Deleuze a political programme merely read a 'Guattarised' Deleuze ('Prologue'). In an attempt to frame a response, we started by examining where, in the first place, we ought to locate Deleuze's philosophy (Chapter 1). Having explicated Deleuze's philosophical project (Chapter 2), we proceeded to illustrate the practical philosophy this thinking would engender (Chapter 3). What this investigation revealed was that there is a clear difficulty in Deleuze's vision for philosophical practice: for what it requires of us is to seek to fail. Then in Chapter 4, we tasked ourselves to provide the requisite theoretical context for this limitation in Deleuzian practice, while simultaneously situating the collaboration with Guattari as a gamble to overcome this weakness *in theory*. In other words, not only is there a theoretical gulf that cannot be brushed away between the works of Deleuze proper and those of Deleuze-Guattari, the leap from the former to the latter in fact constitutes an attempt to overcome the impasses of the former: this dual fact more than validates Žižek's reading. For when Žižek identifies Deleuze as an apolitical philosopher, there are aspects of his practical programme which justify this assessment. If one is to obfuscate this point, one risks pick-and-choosing convenient out-of-context quotations from the works of Deleuze and Deleuze-Guattari in order to advance a spurious image of a 'political Deleuze'.

Having said that, as noted above it is true also that Deleuze's work in itself contains a certain vacillation. The 'apoliticity' (the seeking of failure) in Žižek's sense is the heritage of the structuralist inspiration which *Difference and Repetition* and *The Logic of Sense* depend upon so heavily, but Deleuze himself had definite doubts about this inspiration, doubts that come through in 'How Do We Recognise Structuralism?', and which introduce into his work of this period a torsion of sorts, a lack of consistency. Through his collaboration with Guattari, Deleuze was able to transform his speculative doubts into concrete criticisms, to gain a powerful impetus in the construction

Politics: Desire and Power

of a philosophy capable of moving beyond structuralism. Thus, in one sense Žižek is right to see Deleuze as an elitist, apolitical thinker. Nevertheless, such a summary judgement can only be upheld so long as one averts one's eye from the wavering in Deleuze's works themselves (though it is true that this can only be brought to light through a tireless attention to detail in one's reading). And needless to say, an interpretive stance like Žižek's will result in a mis-assessment of the true value of the works of Deleuze-Guattari.

The obvious task now is to understand this new perspective Deleuze attained by overcoming the problems he was plagued by. What does this philosophy, which redefines the basic unit of political philosophy as desire, aim at? What indeed might it mean to look at society from the point of view of desire?

We propose to answer this question after first taking a detour via a book of Deleuze's to which we have accorded little attention thus far, his 1986 work *Foucault*. This work, whose object of study is his contemporary, the philosopher Michel Foucault (1926–1984), holds a unique place in the Deleuzian canon in its very explicit treatment of concepts to do with the political realm. What is, however, surprising is the fact that this work has been all but neglected by those theoreticians who wish to interpret Deleuze as a philosopher with genuine political sympathies. Foucault is of course best known for his tireless investigations into 'power (*pouvoir*)', in the process transforming everything we previously thought we knew about this concept. And naturally, the book *Foucault* is written with this concept of power at its core. For those of us engaged in trying to locate the hideaway of the 'political Deleuze', this is a book we simply cannot afford to bypass.

But there is more to it than this. This work holds a decisive place for our purposes in a more restricted sense as well. Foucault had attempted to theorise society from the standpoint of 'power'; by contrast, Deleuze looks at society through the lens of 'desire'. What are we to make of this difference? How did Deleuze understand Foucault's efforts in this sphere, and what was his final assessment of his project? Our wager is that we will finally be able to understand what it means to analyse society from the vantage of desire when we have found an answer to the foregoing questions.

Michel Foucault's Historical Studies

The vast majority of Foucault's works are studies in history. His first book, *The History of Madness*[1] (1961), a work of truly astounding scope, revealed that the 'experience' of so-called 'madness' had undergone a major modification at least twice in history, first at the start of the seventeenth century, and then again at the end of the eighteenth/beginning of the nineteenth century. *The Order of Things* (1966), which became a bestseller and made Foucault's name, observed that the seventeenth- and eighteenth-century disciplines of 'general grammar', 'natural history' and 'analysis of wealth', which had seemed to be the direct predecessors to 'linguistics', 'biology' and 'economics', had in fact been grounded on an entirely different system of knowledge (or 'episteme' as Foucault calls it). *The Archaeology of Knowledge* (1969) was a critical reflection on his own works up to that point, redefining his own methodological attitude of 'archaeology' towards historical research. And probably the most influential of all his works is *Discipline and Punish* (a more literal rendering of the original French title would be 'Surveillance and Punishment'), published in 1975, which honed in on the fact that the preferred method of punishment shifted at the end of the eighteenth/beginning of the nineteenth century from violence to surveillance, to illustrate vividly the shift in the functional form of power from 'sovereign power' to 'disciplinary power'. Continuing this line of thought, in the 'History of Sexuality' series, initially announced as a pentalogy but veering in a vastly different direction during the writing process, the first volume of *The Will to Knowledge* (1976) at least was an analysis of the great modification undergone by sexuality, and the emergence of a new modality of power in 'biopolitics'.

Now what is singular about Foucault's studies in history is the fact that with each new work a new domain of research was established.[2] For *History of Madness* is not a history of psychiatry, *The Order of Things* is not a piece of intellectual history, *Discipline and Punish* is not a history of criminology, and the 'History of Sexuality' series is certainly not a cultural-anthropological study in the history of sex. What each of these works achieved was to pioneer an area of research which had not existed before then, but which became the epicentre of a concomitant seismic shift in all the regions adjoining it. In addition, Foucault was a writer who moulded each new piece of work out of a sustained reflective engagement with his previous works, never hesitating to critique or even override them when

Politics: Desire and Power

necessary. Indeed, one could read *The Archaeology of Knowledge* as the materialisation of this very style of composition. For *stricto sensu* this book was neither an overview of the method employed hitherto, nor was it a 'looking ahead' to the method to be taken up henceforth.[3] What these quirks of the man and his works amount to is a difficulty in trying to isolate a unified project for this body of writing. Not only did Foucault traverse a myriad domains in his work, he did not even apply the same base method in dealing with these domains. Nevertheless, a close textual comparison of the major works, it seems to us, can reveal one common theme within the sprawling verbal architecture, and an extremely specific one at that. This is the historical break that took place in all these domains at the end of the eighteenth/beginning of the nineteenth century. Foucault wrote as if possessed by the singularity of this particular period. And more than likely, this was in turn with a view to situating correctly the 'present' epoch, which Foucault himself lived. Where his works allocate a vast number of pages to the study of the age immediately preceding this break (the seventeenth and eighteenth centuries, which he calls the 'Classical Age'), this was his attempt to establish a proper run up to the time that we call the 'present'.

At a first glance, Foucault's primary point of reference is history; this fact may well lead one to classify him as a historian. Against this, Deleuze emphasises that Foucault is a philosopher; indeed, he even names a specific philosophical school for his endeavours, 'a sort of Neo-Kantianism'.[4] As a word of warning, Deleuze does not intend, in so categorising Foucault, to force his works into the framework of Kantian philosophy. Through his transcendental philosophy, Kant had inquired into the conditions of possibility of experience. What has to underlie experience in order for it to take place? It was these ideal conditions that Kant had tried to excavate. In contradistinction, Foucault is concerned with the conditions of *real* experience (F, 51/67). For there are as many conditions of experience as there are epochs, and each epoch has its own unique condition of experience. The condition of possibility of experience is not, as Kant had imagined, something universal, something *a priori*; rather it forms and morphs with its own historicity. Foucault, using history as a method, is as it were attempting a rigorous deepening of Kantian philosophy; at least, this is Deleuze's take on things.

Take madness for example. In seventeenth-century Europe, it was common for madmen to be consigned into the 'general hospital (*'L'Hôpital Général*)'. Now this is something entirely different from, say, hospitalising a patient suffering from a psychological disorder in a psychiatric ward. For in the general hospital were also confined beggars and wanderers, alongside criminals, spendthrifts, the slothful, even atheists, all lumped together into one. And what was thought to justify this hodgepodge was that all these people were marked by the taint of 'unreason (*déraison*)', an idea which had first appeared at that time. In the 1600s, 'reason (*raison*)' had yet to achieve an unchallengeable position for itself. And when reason began to be intimidated by unreason, it resorted to imprisoning unreason through the use of violence. Yes, unreason was not an adequately differentiated concept, among the clouds in its obscurity; but reason for its part did not have anything like the requisite level of luminosity to shine through this nebulousness. In this connection Foucault points out that philosophers of the seventeenth century (specifically Descartes and Spinoza) never seem to tire of expressing their *decision* to embark upon the enquiry of truth (Foucault 2006: 138–40/186–8). What this shows is that the philosophers of the period thought always in fear of the ever-present possibility of man falling into the badlands of unreason, if his steadfast decision to enquire after truth should ever falter. But since the nineteenth century, reason has ceased to live in fear. For it has built for itself an impregnable fortress upon the rock of positivism.[5] Correspondingly, unreason was sub-divided into such fields as crime and mental illness, losing its unific force. As a matter of fact, the very word '*déraison*' falls into oblivion in its noun form, only surviving adjectivally in '*déraisonable*' (just as in English, where 'unreason' is a linguistic relic but 'unreasonable' is still used every day). In effect, unreason ceased to exist in itself as a substantial entity, fading away into a mere image. As for madness itself, henceforth it would be given a new place of confinement in the psychiatric hospital, isolated in 'compassion'. Now clearly, it is impossible that the 'experience of madness' would have remained unaffected through this immense change. How madness is treated, how madness is articulated – everything is different when we compare the post-nineteenth century with the Classical Age. Foucault, commanding a vast bibliographical reference, in this way brought to light the condition of experience for each epoch.

For a time, Foucault termed such historical research 'archaeology (*archéologie*)'. Archaeology takes as its elementary unit of analysis the 'statement (*énoncé*)', which means nothing more mysterious than 'what has been said'. According to Foucault, what is spoken, what is narrated within a given objectile domain, obeys certain rules, which

Politics: Desire and Power

is what the archaeologist seeks to unearth. When a multiplicity of statements is arranged according to a certain set of rules, this totality will be called a 'discourse (*discours*)'. For this reason, it is common to see Foucault's work being characterised as 'discourse analysis'. Let us listen to Foucault's own lucid exposition of the discourse and its rules:

> Let us take a very simple example. In France, until the end of the eighteenth century, between the discourse of the *charlatan* and the discourse of the *doctor*, the difference was marginal. The difference was rather in the success or failure [of treatment], in the studies undertaken or not undertaken; the nature of the things that they were *saying* was not so different: the type of discourse was, for all intents and purposes, the same. But there came a time when medical discourse organised itself according to a certain number of norms and rules such that one could know immediately, not, if a doctor is good or no good, but if he is a doctor or a charlatan. For he will not speak of the same things, he will not refer to the same type of causality, he will not use the same concepts . . . Of what must a discourse, for example the medical, speak, so as to be really a scientific discourse and recognised as a medical discourse, what concepts must it make use of, to what type of theories must it refer itself, these were the problems which I tried to resolve in The Order of Things, in any case that I posed in The Order of Things and The Archaeology of Knowledge. (Foucault 1978 (1994): 584–5; my emphases)

Any discourse is constructed according to a given set of rules. Until the end of the eighteenth century, a set of rules which made no distinction between the discourse of the doctor and that of the charlatan had been dominant in medical discourse. However, at the end of that century, a new set of rules arose which introduced a line of demarcation between the former and the latter, emancipating medical discourse as legitimate scientific discourse. It was this set of rules that Foucault was interested in, investigating how a determinate discourse could come into being, and how it could be modified.

Nonetheless, as is hinted at towards the end of the above quotation, this method of Foucault's was in time to undergo a major change. What Deleuze focused on above all in his *Foucault* was this methodological turn, and its concomitant theoretical problems. As this point spans the entirety of the Foucauldian *corpus*, the discussion is necessarily intricate; let us go through it step by step.

In *The Archaeology of Knowledge*, Foucault terms any domain of discourse composed according to a determinate set of rules as, collectively, the 'discursive formation'.[6] Up to this point, the problematic of the discursive formation had been at the forefront of Foucault's concern. Somewhat simplistically, it was the level of 'saying (*dire*)' that constituted the centrepiece of his research. As such, the aim was to discover what was being said in a given domain, what sort of concepts were being employed, and what theoretical forms lay at its basis. The impression of 'Foucault's discourse analysis' in common circulation roughly corresponds to this early stage of his work.

However, if the *Archaeology* is the culmination of this attitude, it simultaneously ventures a step beyond its confines. For this work of methodology makes explicit the existence of an alternate formation, parallel to the discursive, lying outside of its sphere of competence, which he termed the 'non-discursive formation'. Simplifying once again, one could say that this new formation belongs to the domain of 'seeing (*voir*)', the level of *things* which is irreducible to that of the word. Now as Deleuze points out (F, 28/40), it is not the case that the works up to the *Archaeology* had exclusively problematised the discursive at the expense of the non-discursive formation. Take for instance, the 1963 work *Birth of the Clinic*, which investigates clinical medicine at the end of the eighteenth century: though this work is very much a study in the medical discourse of the period, trivially this discourse cannot exist apart from the existence of such 'beings' as the masses and the population (explosive population growth, and so on) contemporaneous with it, and in this sense even this early book had the non-discursive within its peripheral vision (F, 27/38–9). Nevertheless, as Foucault himself admits, the non-discursive had yet to be elevated to the status of a genuine object of study in its own right. The *Archaeology* went beyond this in recognising the non-discursive as a proper object of research, paving the way towards an investigation of extra-discursive 'reality'.

Having said that, the express purpose of the *Archaeology* was never any more than to define rigorously the statement, based on a self-critical survey of the implicit method employed hitherto. As such, it is ultimately an exhaustive treatment of the discursive formation, and as for the non-discursive, Foucault goes no further than to define it negatively as that which is *not* capable of being subsumed into the discursive (the clue is in the name). In other words, the efforts in this book are commendable to the extent of positing the discursive and the non-discursive as a paired analytic matrix, but stopped short of being able to provide a full substantiation of the latter formation. It is in this sense that Deleuze situates the *Archaeology* as a transitionary work, playing the 'role of a hinge (*un rôle de charnière*)'.[7] For a

Politics: Desire and Power

proper investigation of what Deleuze, giving a positive nomination to the 'non-discursive', calls the 'formation of environment (*formation de milieu*)', one would have to wait until the next work in Foucault's oeuvre, which Deleuze rates the most highly of all: *Discipline and Punish*. Deleuze explicates this as follows:

> *Discipline and Punish* marks a new stage. Let there be some 'thing' like a prison: this is an environmental formation (the 'prison' environment) . . . It refers to completely different words and concepts, such as delinquency or delinquent, which express a new way of articulating infractions, sentences and their subjects. (F, 27–8/39)[8]

The terms 'delinquency' and 'delinquent' will be explained in the next section. For the time being we note Deleuze's assessment, that *Disciple and Punish* discovered a new question pertaining to the relation between the discursive (words) and the non-discursive (things, or the environment), beyond the narrow focus on the rules which constitute a given discourse. The prison is a 'thing', connected to such words as 'delinquency' and 'delinquent', which in turn renew the force of such statements as 'illegalism' and 'punishment'. Schematically, the environment begets the statement, and correlatively the statement determines the environment. Henceforth a given epoch, a given society, will be understood as essentially comprised of the twin levels of the discursive and the non-discursive.[9]

To repeat, it is true that these two formations, the discursive and the non-discursive, had always been present in Foucault's work. Indeed, the opposition between the 'visible' and the 'articulable' in *Birth of the Clinic*, or that between 'madness as seen in the general hospital' and the 'folly . . . as it is described in medicine' in *The History of Madness*, are clear forerunners (F, 28/40). Nevertheless, as stated above, the non-discursive had yet to achieve a positive theoretical formulation of its own. 'What *The Archaeology* recognised but still only designated negatively, as non-discursive environments, is given its positive form in *Discipline and Punish*' (F, 28/40). This shift in Foucault's analytic standpoint from one centred almost exclusively on the level of discourse to one actively concerned with that which lies outside of discourse is lauded by Deleuze. One suspects that somewhere in Deleuze is a firm conviction that reality cannot be adequately grasped solely through linguistic functions, so that one has to confront directly the entities lying outside of language. With *Discipline and Punish*, Foucault had become equal to this conviction.

And no sooner has Deleuze indicated the discovery of the non-discursive formation in Foucault, than he turns his undivided attention to the theoretical problem of the precise relation between the two formations. For the discursive and non-discursive formations (which Deleuze, in an effort to provide substantive appellations for both, also calls the 'form of expression' and the 'form of content' respectively) exist in a uniquely subtle causal interrelation with each other. 'There is no correspondence or isomorphism, no direct causality or symbolisation' (F, 27/39). What, then, is the relation which encompasses them? As usual, Deleuze assumes that his reader is familiar with *Discipline and Punish*, hence his explication is rather concise. Therefore, we shall be taking a brief detour away from *Foucault*, so as to think through this problem along the concrete lines of investigation undertaken by Foucault himself.

The Two Formations in Discipline and Punish

Discipline and Punish is divided into four parts. The first of these introduces the mode of 'torture' – which existed right up to the end of the eighteenth/start of the nineteenth century, and was then consigned to historical oblivion as if overnight – in an effort to theorise the characteristics of the mechanisms of power at work there. The opening account of the 1757 execution of Robert-François Damiens is painted in scarlet with prose befitting a horror novel. Upon the scaffold, the executioner is tasked with the expert performance of the 'spectacle' of excessively cruel punishment for the criminal, and the whole affair is put on as a show for the audience of spectators. At the time, execution was a public affair, and it was perfectly ordinary for the people to gather to watch the proceedings. The execution was designed as a display of violent power for those who came to watch; and this exemplary power was of course none other than the power of the sovereign him or herself.[10] In other words, it was precisely by thus publicising its own boundless capacity for force that power maintained its rule over the populace. It was a vulgar and overt expression of the threat that all those who did not obey would invariably suffer the same fate. Power which functions in this way is termed 'sovereign power'. In this first part, the relation between the discursive and non-discursive formations has yet to come to the fore as a problematic in its own right. For this we will have to wait for the second part onwards.

In Part II, Foucault turns his attention to the discourse of the 'reformers' of the penal system in the eighteenth century such as Cesare Beccaria (1738–1794), who tried to reform this violent and excessive exaction of punishment. The meticulous attention to contemporary documents makes it evident that this part is very much a work of discourse analysis. In the process, Foucault clarifies that these 'reformers' were not at all motivated by humanistic considerations, arguing that such excessively cruel spectacles were incompatible with the 'innate dignity of man'; far rather they pressed for reform on 'economistic' grounds, for it was thought that such displays were inefficient in terms of exercising power over criminals, and that therefore they ought to be replaced by more efficient methods.[11] Punishment had taken the form of torture under sovereign power because it was conceived as retribution against the criminal. By contrast, the 'reformers' turned their attention to how one could deter people from committing crimes in the first place. Beccaria for instance – the father of early modern criminal law and most famous for his theory advocating the abolition of the death penalty – had proposed the punishment of so-called 'perpetual slavery'. In this way one kills two birds with one stone, for there will no longer be the need to inflict cruel suffering on the criminal, which requires years of wasteful training on the part of the executor, and the people who observe such unending servitude will be privy to an even more frightful sight than before. Minimum effort for those exacting punishment, maximum impact for those who imagine this eventuality: such economism is the great advantage of this new method of punishment (Foucault 1979: 95/113). Or take the eighteenth-century French jurist François-Michel Vermeil (1732–1810), who pushed for the punishment to fit the crime: for the abuse of privileges, their removal; for theft, dispropriation; for corruption, a fine; and for arson? Burning at the stake. He stressed the need for such a strict correspondence in the methodical application of punishments (1979: 105/124). To cut a long story short, the 'reformers' sought to inculcate the people with the notion that any crime whatsoever will without fail have its rightful consequences, so as to deter the committing of crimes in the first place. A great many jurists in the eighteenth century had advocated such a view, and it was assented to far and wide.

At this point, however, we encounter the greatest historical enigma dealt with in *Discipline and Punish*. As we know today only too well, out of these weird and wonderful forms of punishment put forward by the eighteenth-century 'reformers', *not a single one ended up being taken on board by subsequent criminal law*. And this despite the fact that the discourse of these 'reformers' had been widely disseminated and accepted; by stark contrast, their concrete proposals have been all but forgotten. And the prison, having appeared *out of the blue* as a novelty form of punishment, in the blink of the historical eye had come to cover every form of punishment more severe than the fine and less severe than the death penalty. The astonishing fact is that as a form of punishment the prison had been really rather unpopular among the reformers themselves, guided as they were by the principle of 'economism'. Confinement does not in fact constitute a punishment at all – limitation of bodily freedom through imprisonment is 'to hold the person as security, not to punish him [*ad continendos homines, non ad puniendos*]' (Foucault 1979: 118/139) – or so it was argued. In other words, at the close of the eighteenth century there existed three competing modes of punishment – the sovereign form, the reformers' model, and the prison – of these the second, widely believed to be the preferred candidate, was for some reason rejected, overwhelmingly in favour of the third. Now it is not as if this fact had been hidden under the velvet carpet of history; yet nobody before Foucault was able to draw attention to it, and with such great analytic precision at that. And from here, Foucault goes on to explain *how* it came about that the third option was eventually to become hegemonic (1979: 131/155).[12]

Needless to say, it is here that the problem of the relation between the discursive and non-discursive formations is thrown into the clearest focus. For what this historical fact tells us is that the two formations do not progress in a facile correspondence with each other. The discourse of the 'reformers' ultimately failed to win out in the selection of a new method of punishment. But that is not to say that the discursive is always at the mercy of developments on the side of the non-discursive. For it is equally undeniable that the discourse of the 'reformers', for all their dismissal of the prison as a viable form of punishment, was indeed widely accepted. Hence Deleuze's summary assessment: '[w]hat counts is that *Discipline and Punish* marks the heterogeneity between the development of penal law and the rapid rise of the prison in the eighteenth century' (F, 117n22/255n14). 'Heterogeneity' here refers to the lack of correspondence between the discourse of the 'reformers' and the actual developments in the system of punishment. The fact that Foucault was able to pinpoint this historical enigma implies that in his work, non-discursive events which cannot be reduced to the discursive formation have come to occupy a positive, substantive role. It is this shift in Foucault that Deleuze focuses on.

Politics: Desire and Power

Let us provide an overview of the remaining two sections as well. In Part III, Foucault formalises the mode of administration that, just as the prison began to be adopted as the principal form of punishment, came into ascendance in the factories, the schools and the hospitals, as one of 'discipline'. The definition of this new technology of power as the most minute control of the body through surveillance and normalisation is one of the most well-known analyses of the book.[13] The famous account of the panopticon comes at the end of this section as well. This is the concrete apparatus of a mode of power no longer dependent on sovereign violence, instead enforcing its rule through the act of surveillance, of 'seeing'. It is this dissemination of discipline that is tasked to explain the rise of the prison in such a short period of time. To wit, the prison was able to go from wildcard to uncontested hegemon because the disciplinary mode of rule had already permeated through society.[14] In other words, Part III clearly trades in the analysis of the non-discursive formation. That is, it explicates the autonomous vicissitudes of the non-discursive formation, which is not determined by the discursive formation analysed in Part II.

In Part IV, Foucault goes on to point out the scandalous fact that the 'delinquent (*délinquant*)' – or 'thug', in street-language – created by the prisons was in turn fed back into the ruling power. Henceforth, apparatuses tasked with the administration of punishment (the prisons) are required to punish not the abstract being who happened to transgress the law (the offender, *infracteur*), but the concrete individual 'delinquent', who bears within his or her life history and attitude towards life the latent potential for criminality. Or, somewhat simplistically: systems of punishment are in place no longer to 'make you pay for your bad deeds', but to ask (in one sense 'compassionately') 'how come you've ended up becoming such a bad person?' The system of punishment has come to depend on an unprecedented discourse structured around the novel concept of 'delinquency (*délinquance*)'.

This shift entails yet another consequence. When it is the life story of the criminal that is at issue, the underlying assumption is that their offence is not a contingent occurrence, but one necessitated by the very logic of their life. In other words, those sent to prison are understood as thugs 'at the level of essence', fulfilling what is the only possible way of life for them. 'Naturally' then, in the vast majority of cases they will never again be able to return to be respectable members of society. And as if to prove this, they will offend again.

This new mode of punishment, ostensibly designed to support the 'rehabilitation' of the offender, ended up actively contributing to the reverse: recidivism.

Does this then show that post-nineteenth-century systems of punishment, centred around the prison, have failed on their own terms? Not so according to Foucault. For to label the criminal as 'delinquent' allows the ruling classes to restrict these 'types' to the periphery of society, where they are readily placed under observation. And that is not all: the ruling classes gain such 'delinquents' as disposable bodies available for use. Foucault gives the example of their historical use as spies, informants and decoys, or as instigators of factional strife in political parties and labour unions. Karl Marx's analysis in *The Eighteenth Brumaire of Louis Bonaparte* (1852) of the deployment of the lumpenproletariat as stormtroopers during the 1848 Revolution, for example, is adduced (Foucault 1979: 280/327). The 'delinquent', invented by the criminal-legal concept of 'delinquency', is swiftly placed into the prison environment, and in the process becomes a disposable tool for the ruling classes.

Now this analysis of the success *qua* failure of the prison is absolutely not an exaggeration on Foucault's part, the philosopher who cannot restrain himself from piercing down to the bottom of things. 'Prisons do not diminish the crime rate'; 'detention causes recidivism'; 'the prison invariably produces delinquents'; 'the prison makes possible, even encourages, the organisation of a milieu of delinquents, loyal to one another, hierarchised, ready to aid and abet any future criminal act'; 'the conditions to which the freed inmates are subjected (surveillance by the police, assignment to particular residences or interdiction from others) necessarily condemn them to recidivism'; 'the prison indirectly produces delinquents by throwing the inmate's family into destitution' . . .: such criticisms of the prison have existed since at least the start of the nineteenth century, when the prison system first got off its feet (Foucault 1979: 265–8/309–13). In other words, the ruling classes have maintained the prison system despite being perfectly aware of all these difficulties. Whatever the case may be, the concluding assertion of the book is that as the whole of society came to be subsumed under the disciplinary matrix, deployment of the 'delinquent' petered out (1979: 305–6/357–8).

We must now inquire into the relation between the discursive and non-discursive formations as it emerges in this fourth part. The key notion is that of 'delinquency'. 'Delinquency' is on the one hand a concept, one that establishes the direction towards which the criminal system was to shift, treating those who break the law as 'delinquents'. In that sense therefore, 'delinquency' veritably belongs to the discursive formation which structures the discourse of law. And yet, the word 'delinquency' is equally used to signify the 'delinquent' positioned within the prison environment in its materiality. In other words, this 'delinquency' dealt with in the fourth part traverses both the discursive and non-discursive formations; or to phrase it differently, the two formations blend into each other, mediated by this nodal point. Deleuze for his part renames the discursive aspect 'illegalism-delinquency', and the non-discursive aspect 'object-delinquency'.[15] What these 'two delinquencies' point towards is the extremely subtle causality at work between the two formations. True, the discourse surrounding the word 'delinquency' functions determinatively with respect to the prison environment. At the same time however, it is the crime without end committed by the 'delinquent' which serves up the objects for the discourse of the penal system. The prison 'as a form of content' (belonging to the non-discursive formation) and penal law 'as a form of expression' (belonging to the discursive formation) 'continue to come into contact, seep into one another and steal bits for themselves: penal law still leads back to prison and provides prisoners, while prison continues to reproduce delinquency, make it an "object", and realise the aims which penal law had conceived differently' (F, 28–9/40). What is therefore decisive for Deleuze is the way in which the two formations take two completely different modalities, yet proceed in influencing each other.

If one is to follow Deleuze's lead in *Foucault*, which interprets Foucault's work through the lens of the relation between the discursive and non-discursive, identifying *Discipline and Punish* as the apex of this line of analysis, then one can reasonably (though Deleuze does not in fact go so far) organise the second, third and fourth parts of *Discipline and Punish* as follows:

- The second part is concerned with the discursive formation.
- The third part is concerned with the non-discursive formation.
- The fourth part is concerned with the interpenetration of the two formations.

Power and the Two Formations

Discipline and Punish understands the relation between the discursive and non-discursive formations as one where neither determines the other unilaterally – at least *according to Deleuze's interpretation*, we can indeed read this book in this way. Put this aside for the moment though, and we can wonder why Deleuze obsesses over this relation quite so much. After all, Foucault himself utters not a word in *Discipline and Punish* about any such relation, and yet, Deleuze's *Foucault* discusses it throughout. The study itself is composed of 'six studies, relatively independent' (F, 7[16]): namely, two separate review essays published in the journal *Critique*, 'A New Archivist (*Archaeology of Knowledge*)' and 'A New Cartographer (*Discipline and Punish*)'; three essays newly composed for the volume, on 'Knowledge', 'Power' and 'Subjectivation'; and a final 'Appendix'. Astonishingly, the relation between the discursive and the non-discursive is discussed in all five essays excluding the 'Appendix', though of course the distribution is not even across the board. 'A New Archivist' was first released in the 1970 volume of *Critique*, which means that it was written before the publication of *Discipline and Punish*; yet here already, it is highlighted that the discursive is determined in a relation with that which lies outside discourse. It would be no exaggeration to say that the book *Foucault* is written as an extended response to this problem.

Now I confess the following is no more than a gut instinct of mine, but it seems that this excessive fixation on Deleuze's part is not unrelated to Foucault's links to Marxism. In introducing the Foucauldian conception of power, Deleuze stresses its difference from the Marxist conception of the same. As a matter of fact, he goes so far as to claim that Foucault's new theory is a response to the 'New Left (*gauchisme*)', who were struggling to move beyond the framework of orthodox Marxism (F, 22/32). *Discipline and Punish* itself is situated as the long-awaited successor to the Marxist problematic ('[i]t is as if, finally, something new were emerging in the wake of Marx' (F, 27/38)). No doubt speculations based on biographical details must in all cases be kept to a minimum, but nonetheless the fact that Foucault had for a period been a member of the Communist Party cannot be overlooked. Moreover, Dosse relates that Deleuze had in fact met Foucault as early as 1952, where he felt that the man 'clearly reflected a Marxist perspective' (Dosse 2011: 307/365). When one rethinks the relation between the discursive and non-discursive formations in the light of these subsidiary considerations, one realises that this opposition is remarkably reminiscent of the dualistic schema of the superstructure and infrastructure upheld by traditional Marxism. In the Marxist conception, it is the infrastructure that determines the superstructure, *tout court*. Now up to the *Archaeology* Foucault had stressed the determinative force of the discursive.[17] Does this not then amount to a mere reversal of the Marxist conception, according to which it is the base that determines the superstructure? When on the other hand Deleuze insists that neither the discursive nor the non-discursive determines the other unilaterally, was it not perhaps the difficulty of the theoretical mechanism of unilateral determination itself that he had in mind? As for Foucault, with *Discipline and Punish* he definitively succeeds in moving beyond such a mechanism. Isn't this the reason for Deleuze's unreserved admiration for this work? So I venture to suggest.

But enough now of speculations, back to the text itself. According to Deleuze, Foucault had been thinking from the outset within a dualistic schema of the discursive and non-discursive formations. However, up to the *Archaeology* he had accorded to the latter no more than a subsidiary role. By contrast, *Discipline and Punish* accords to the non-discursive a substantive role, portraying the interpenetrative relation between the two formations.[18] This is an overview of Deleuze's reading of Foucault as we have traced it thus far. What, though, does it mean to say that the two formations 'interpenetrate'? For instance, Deleuze writes that though the two interpenetrate, 'there is no correspondence or isomorphism, no direct causality or symbolisation' (F, 27/39). This tells us much about what this two-way relation is not, but nothing about what it in fact is, positively speaking. In an effort to find an answer, Deleuze pushes the problem of the relation in an even more theoretical direction, posing questions such as the following (F, 29/41):

1. Beyond these two forms, does there exist a common cause immanent to the social domain?
2. What makes possible the variable ways in which this interpenetration manifests itself in each particular case?

Again, these are questions which Foucault himself has not dealt with in any capacity, at least not explicitly. And yet, Deleuze fixates his gaze thereupon. Having posited two formations, Deleuze cannot help but inquire into their relation, and whether there exists a shared cause common to both. Foucault for his part had been interested primarily in analysing and portraying how the two formations function in reality. But as for Deleuze, he is compelled by the urge to determine the relation between the two. And this is his answer:

> This, then, is the reply made to the two problems posed by *Discipline and Punish*. On the one hand, *the duality of forms or formations does not exclude a common, immanent cause* which works informally. On the other, the common cause envisaged in each case or in each concrete mechanism will go on measuring the mixtures, captures, and interceptions taking place between elements or segments of the two forms, even though the latter are and remain irreducible and heteromorphous. It is not an exaggeration to say that every mechanism is a mushy mixture of the visible and the articulable ... *Discipline and Punish is the book in which Foucault expressly overcomes the apparent dualism of his earlier books* (although even then this dualism was already moving towards a theory of multiplicities). (F, 33/46; my emphases)

This passage is lifted from the review essay on *Discipline and Punish*, 'A New Cartographer'. The answer to our first question is categorical: there does exist for the two formations a *common immanent cause*. In other words, Foucault's dualism of the discursive and non-discursive posits a *single* common cause at their foundation – or so Deleuze claims. If there is a dualism at work in Foucault, this is but an *apparent* dualism ... However dualistic Foucault may seem, he was working to *overcome* this tendency ... For Deleuze, that is, dualism cannot but be a *provisional* stage of investigation.

What then is this common cause traversing the two formations? The reply to this necessarily brings us to the second of our questions. We can find Deleuze's answer in the three essays newly composed for this volume; and his answer is as simple as it is enigmatic. It is 'power (*pouvoir*)' that constitutes this common cause, the 'third dimension' (F, 58–9, 68/75–7, 88).[19] Power is 'the common cause envisaged in each case or in each concrete mechanism [which] will go on measuring the mixtures, captures, and interceptions taking place between elements or segments of the two forms, even though the latter are and remain irreducible and heteromorphous' (F, 33/46). To penetrate to the bottom of this answer, we must first familiarise ourselves with the Foucauldian theory of power in its Deleuzian reformulation.

It is said that Foucault revolutionised the theory of power. And the place where this took place most acutely was none other than in *Discipline and Punish*. According to Deleuze, *Discipline and Punish* was a response to the re-posing of the problem of power by leftism, a re-posing 'directed against Marxism as much as against bourgeois conceptions' (F, 22/32). Here we must note that terms like 'bourgeois conception' and 'Marxism' are used not as vague imageries, but in their precise significations. In explicating Foucault's theory of power,

Deleuze employs six postulates as targets which this new conception has overturned (F, 22–6/32–8); of these, the first five correspond (though Deleuze is not explicit on this point) to 'Marxism', and the last to 'bourgeois conception'. Let us first follow each of these six postulates, so as to understand what it is that the Foucauldian theory opposed, what it must be distinguished from.

The first and second postulates are those of 'property' and 'localisation' respectively. It is typical of power to be conceived as if it were a piece of property belonging to the class who won it, but this is not legitimate. For power is not possessed, it is exercised. From which it follows that it is just as illegitimate to situate power as 'localised' within the state apparatus. For disciplinary power, characteristic of the early modern period, works by tactically positioning the objects to be ruled (labourers, students, soldiers) within a determinate space (the factory, the school, the military); thus invigilating them, it *makes* them act in a certain desirable fashion. For this reason power is not only non-local but also non-global; it is diffuse (*diffus*).

The third postulate is that of 'subordination'. It has been thought that the power made manifest in the state apparatus is 'subordinated' to the infrastructure. However, even if it is undeniable that the superstructure displays an element of responsivity to the infrastructure, it is illegitimate for the latter to be elevated into a 'determination in the last instance'. Quite the contrary, specific wholes of economic practice such as the workshop and the factory assume the prior functioning of disciplinary power. From this we can derive the fourth postulate of the 'essence or attribute'. It is believed that power, either as 'essence' or 'attribute', somehow characterises the powerful as one who rules, demarcating them from those who are ruled. But power does not originate from 'on high' with the ruler, it is a relation. Just as in the workshop or the factory, where disciplinary power flows through the nexus of relations between the strategically positioned elements. Deleuze also cites Foucault's analysis of the *'lettres de cachet'* (a document furnished with the sovereign seal, by whose authority it was possible to arrest or exile someone without trial) as an example.[20] Relations of power cannot be explained by a simplistic model from 'on high'. They are rather supported by the properly humble lives of the everyman himself, 'down below'.[21] And this 'down below' in its turn explains the fifth postulate of 'modality'. We are inclined to think that power is enacted through its various modalities: threats backed up by violence, lies propagated by ideology, subordination enforced by suppression. Now of course violence, ideology and suppression are all undeniably realities. And yet, it is impossible to capture adequately the notion of power through them. For power is 'an action upon an action': it need not threaten with violence, deceive through ideology or suppress with subordination, all it need do is position people tactically and watch over them, so as to *make* them act. No doubt violence exists 'in the room or out in the street' (F, 25/36), yet it is impossible to reduce the concept of power to that of violence. As for ideology or suppression, these exist but as effects of power: 'repression and ideology ... do not constitute the struggle between forces but are only the dust thrown up by such a contest' (F, 26/36).

The preceding are clearly criteria which correspond to the 'Marxist' understanding of power. By contrast, the sixth and final postulate corresponds to 'bourgeois conception', or more precisely (though again Deleuze does not mention these by name) to social contractarian political philosophies which take their cue from Hobbes. This is the postulate of 'legality'. In the social contractarian tradition, the rule of law is understood as 'a state of peace imposed on brute force' or 'the result of a war or struggle won by the stronger party' (F, 26/37). It is said that in the state of nature men live a perpetual state of lawless war, which is why peace has to be established by means of the social contract (in Hobbesian terms, this corresponds to 'commonwealth by institution'); or else that intra-state peace is achieved when the real annexation of a weaker group by a stronger group has progressed to some degree (again in Hobbesian terms, this is 'commonwealth by acquisition'). However, such an abstract opposition between the rule of law and lawlessness is overly simplistic. According to Deleuze, Foucault would replace this with 'a subtle correlation between illegalism and law (*une corrélation fine illégalisme-lois*)'. For the law does not stand in opposition to illegality: the law is rather bespoke for the specific needs of the ruling classes of any particular time, displaying clemency for one illegal act, sophistically reserving it as the exclusive privilege of the ruling classes, while pardoning some other illegal act as a compensation to the ruled classes. Indeed Deleuze's remark is of pinpoint precision: '[w]e need only look at the law of commercial societies to see that laws as a whole are not contrasted with illegality, but that some are actually used to find loopholes in others' (F, 26/37; translation corrected).[22] We see the extent to which the notion 'rule of law' obscures the 'strategic maps' immanent in society. The following passage, among the words of Deleuze giving expression to Foucault's thought, is surely one of the most penetrating and at the

Politics: Desire and Power

same time the most beautiful: 'Foucault shows that the law is now no more a state of peace than the result of a successful war: it is war itself, and the strategy of this war in action, just as power is not the property of the dominant class but the strategy of that class in action' (F, 26–7/38).

These six postulates were formulated to clarify what it was that the Foucauldian theory of power sought to overcome. And for Deleuze, it is power characterised thus which acts as the common cause underlying the two formations. Let us next investigate the ways in which this common cause functions.

First, power is defined as the 'relation between forces'. '[P]ower is a relation between forces, or rather every relation between forces is a "power relation"' (F, 59/77). Nevertheless, these power relations on their own 'would fade and remain embryonic or virtual without the operations that integrate them' (F, 68/88). As a result, they have need of a partner by the name of 'knowledge (*savoir*)'. Take the school: to deal efficiently with students, one needs a working knowledge of pedagogy. Or to rule over and utilise a patch of land, one needs a knowledge of the practice of surveying. The complicity of power and knowledge had been a theme of Foucault's work practically from the outset. Regarding this complex, Deleuze would say that power works flexibly, passing through a myriad of 'points', whereas knowledge constitutes rigid 'forms' (F, 61/80). Knowledge after all needs to have a certain fixed structure as theory or technique, which is capable of being passed on or down. For this purpose knowledge generates textbooks and manuals, and departments dedicated to its teaching. It is in this sense that knowledge is said to possess semi-permanent *rigid forms*. By contrast, power must flow through each individual student in a school, each individual worker in a factory, understood as *points*, always *supple and flexible*.

This modality of power which functions by connecting otherwise disparate points with a line, Deleuze terms the 'diagram (*diagramme*)'. By diagram we should understand, for example, the railway schedule, a 'diagram' made up of points and lines representing stations and the operations between them respectively. In thus connecting the stations (points) with the service (lines), the schedule is administered and regulated. Now when accidents and other shocks to the system cause delays in this running, the intervals between each line are tightened; the command centre responds by loosening ever so slightly these intervals, gradually restoring on-schedule operations. In this way, the diagram deals with the ever-changing rail situation *supplely and flexibly* (quite literally), in order to submit the whole to a determinate objective. As such, we feel that this concept is a term of art to explain the Foucauldian mechanism of power, whose preferred mode of exercise is precisely regulation through allocation and distribution. Deleuze notes that Foucault himself had termed the panopticon a 'diagram' (F, 30, 61/42, 79), which is indeed the case (though, as far as I can see, it occurs only twice across the entire text of *Discipline and Punish* (Foucault 1979: 171, 205/202, 239)), but it is hardly as if Foucault had invested specially in this term. And yet Deleuze draws out this concept of the diagram with a view to resolving the perplexity of the relation between the two formations: they are tied together by power in its diagrammatic functioning.

We have already noted that Deleuze categorised Foucault as a philosopher of a 'neo-Kantianism'. In this vein, he claims that the diagram corresponds to the role of the 'schematism' in Kant (F, 68/88). The schema for Kant is a function of the imagination, which mediates between the passive faculty of the senses and the active faculty of the understanding, between which there exists an unbridgeable abyss. What the senses receive is infinitely diverse, yet the understanding hems them in to pre-made concepts. The role of the imagination is therefore to schematise this diversity into something conceptually manipulable. Now according to Deleuze, the diagram of power performs a comparable function in Foucault. Having renamed the non-discursive formation as 'receptivity to light' and the discursive formation as 'spontaneity of language' (F, 51/67) – that is, having linked the former to the senses and the latter to the understanding – Deleuze states: 'Foucault's diagrammaticism, that is to say the presentation of pure relations between forces or the transmission of pure particular features, is therefore the analogue of Kantian schematicism: it is this that ensures the relation . . . between the two irreducible forms of spontaneity [discursive formation] and receptivity [non-discursive formation]' (F, 68/88). And the Kant-Foucault connection does not end there. Deleuze pushes the very concept of the power relation in a Kantian direction: '[p]ower relations are therefore not *known*' (F, 62/80; original emphasis). The intention to equate the Foucauldian power relation with the Kantian 'thing-in-itself' is palpable. Which means: yes, power relations are ubiquitous in reality, but in just the same way that the 'thing-in-itself' is not a possible object of cognition, only the 'phenomenon' as its manifestation, so it is not possible to know the power relation 'in itself'. All we can know is the diagram of this relation as its 'presentation'.

Politics: Desire and Power

To summarise, then. Power, aided by knowledge (whose form is rigid), functions diagrammatically as the schema to traverse the gap between the discursive and non-discursive formations, in this way having the last say in their interpenetration. This is Deleuze's answer to the theoretical problem of the relation between the two formations of Foucault.

Monism and Dualism

It seems that we are approaching the crux of Deleuze's reading of Foucault: reality cannot be grasped through the discursive formation (linguistic reality) alone. Therefore, we must rate *Discipline and Punish* most highly among the works of Foucault, because this is where he takes up the non-discursive formation (extra-linguistic reality) in a positive sense. Now that we have two formations before us, we must inquire into the relationship between them. Indeed, we must discover whether there is a common cause underlying the two. This common cause is power. Power always exists in complicity with knowledge; its mode of functioning is diagrammatic . . .

Deleuze had *for some reason* set out Foucault's dualism as something to be overcome. Hence the book *Foucault* obsessed over the relation between the two formations, aiming to arrive at the common cause underlying them. And this aim was realised. The distaste for dualism however does not end there. It is said that power is complicit with knowledge. In a famous passage in *Discipline and Punish* which explicates the relation between the two, Foucault writes that 'power and knowledge directly imply one another', and reiterates that there can be no knowledge which does not assume some power relation, and vice versa.[23] But Deleuze will not sanction such a dualistic equality between knowledge and power; he will flex all of his interpretive muscles to read into Foucault a 'primacy of power over knowledge, and of power-relations over relations of knowledge' (F, 68/88). No doubt that without the integrating function of knowledge, power relations will be fleeting, transient; even so, without there being first some power relation, there will be nothing to integrate in the first place, or so he claims. *In Deleuze's eyes*, what comes to the fore in Foucault's work is first of all the power relation in its supple and flexible diagrammatic functioning; this in turn gives rise to two distinct formations, which for their part are integrated into a rigid modality by the work of knowledge. *In Deleuze's eyes*, this is the story of reality as Foucault sees it.

Deleuze rejects categorically the dualism. The dualism is most likely the image of things after their genesis has already terminated, and as such it can be posited as originary only so long as one does not ask the question of genesis. If one does ask this question, then one must be able to determine the underlying force giving rise to the two components of the dualism; for Foucault, this is power. In discussing this 'dualism peculiar to Foucault' – needless to say, this 'dualism' is characterised as 'peculiar' so as to refuse the classification of Foucault as a dualist – Deleuze mentions that there are in fact three types of dualism (F, 69–70/89–90). The first (the only true dualism) emphasises the irreducible difference between two substances, as in Descartes, or between two faculties, as in Kant. The second initially appears to be a dualism, but the twin elements are only a hypothetical stage on the way to their eventual transformation into a monism: this is the dualism of Spinoza and Bergson. Finally we have the dualism of Foucault, which only employs dualism as a preparatory stage in an analysis blossoming out into multiplicities. For the two formations in Foucault relate, each in their own way, to real multiplicities: the labourer in the factory, the soldier in the military, the student in the school. And it is the diagrammatic relation of power composed of points and lines that integrates all of this. Hence Deleuze concludes: the Foucauldian 'dualism' always leads on to a multiplicity.

The discursive and non-discursive formations – that is, words and things, expressibility and visibility, language and light, to say and to see ... – two distinct orders, and the twin forces of knowledge and power that motivate them: nobody would berate you for imagining that Foucault's thought is fundamentally dualistic. And our assessment of this dualism notwithstanding, nobody can deny that Foucault has, through the dualistic framework of his thinking, left behind an enduring series of thematic analyses of the age. For Foucault himself, the dualistic tendency of his thinking is not an issue. A certain 'pragmatism' suffuses the whole of his work: to penetrate to the heart of each epoch, to bring to light the set of rules which determines each epoch.[24] In stark contrast, Deleuze fixates upon the dualism in Foucault fiercely, declaring that it is only apparent, and moreover that Foucault has indeed overcome this tendency. What seems to be a dualism is but a preparatory and hypothetical distinction, underlying which one can unearth a monistic principle: power ... Deleuze is, in other words, a rigorous, verging on puritanical, monist. If so, then this book *Foucault*, written by this unwavering monist, interpreting and reformulating the work of a colleague whose thinking cannot

Politics: Desire and Power

help but appear dualistic – would this book not be (on a light-hearted note) a 'one-point-five-dimensional' portrait of Foucault, somewhere in between one and two . . . ?

Why then did Deleuze decide to read Foucault in this way? No doubt his own stringent monism had something to do with it, but that is not all. In moving beyond the quasi-pragmatic attitude suffusing Foucault's writings to dig down into its theoretical foundations, Deleuze was likely attempting to illuminate a certain difficulty existing at this most fundamental stratum, a certain cul-de-sac. And we have evidence that Deleuze had been aware of this from a remarkably early stage. In time, Foucault was to run up against this dead-end, as it were, through his own thinking, experiencing a mid-life crisis of sorts. To see the relevant issues in greater relief, let us follow *Foucault* for a little while longer.

A year after publishing *Discipline and Punish*, Foucault released the first volume (of a projected five) of *The History of Sexuality*, subtitled *The Will to Knowledge* (1976). In one sense at least, this work was the crowning achievement of the Foucauldian theory of power. By saying that '[p]ower is everywhere; not because it embraces everything, but because it comes from everywhere', he is compressing and formalising the concept of power which his works hitherto had presupposed. To summarise the main points:

- Power is not a possession, it is rather exercised in the interplay of non-egalitarian and mobile relations.
- Power relations are not in a position of exteriority with respect to other types of relationships (economic processes, knowledge relationships, sexual relations), they are immanent in them.
- Power comes from below, there is no binary opposition between rulers and ruled at the root of power relations.
- Power relations are intentional but non-subjective: there is no power that is exercised without a series of aims and objectives, but this does not mean that it results from the choice or decision of an individual 'powerful' subject.
- Where there is power there is resistance: resistance is never in a position of exteriority in relation to power. (Foucault 1978: 92–6/123–7)

This time it is 'sexuality' that is investigated on the basis of such a concept of power. It is commonly supposed that since the seventeenth century discourse about sexuality has been strictly repressed in European society. The reality however is the exact opposite, says

Foucault; in fact we see a veritable explosion of discourse on sexuality from that period on. Now this proliferation cannot be understood apart from the fact that since the eighteenth century sexuality has become an object of administration by the body politic. In this era, the people become rechristened the 'population', conceived as an object of quantitative study according to variables like birth rates, rates of infection, average lifespan, measures of health, frequency of illness, types of food and housing, etc. Enter a form of power which organises the people as a population. A mode of power which manages the very life of its populace, moulding it into a form conducive to the powers-that-be, replacing the old sovereign power that claimed the right to put the person under its dominion to death. 'One might say that the ancient right to *take* life or *let* live was replaced by a power to *foster* life or *disallow* it to the point of death' (Foucault 1978: 138/181; original emphases). Foucault terms this a power which coordinates/administers the specific variables of the populace, the 'biopolitics of the population' (1978: 139/183).

The concept of biopolitics (and biopower) was received favourably by theorists worldwide enthused by the study of power, giving rise to a great number of acolytes. But as for Foucault, not only does he abandon any further development of this concept, he is about to experience a crisis. The books stop forthcoming, and the projected *History of Sexuality* pentalogy is forced to undergo a seismic change of direction. Now this is not because of Foucault's personal, domestic encroachments – at least according to Deleuze. As if to say that he knew all along this would happen, Deleuze highlights Foucault's proverbial 'hitting the wall' that became apparent in *The Will to Knowledge*. '*The History of Sexuality* explicitly closes on a doubt. If at the end of it Foucault finds himself in an impasse, this is not because of his conception of power but rather because he found the impasse to be where power itself places us ...' (F, 79/103).

Foucault had inquired into the concept of power meticulously. So meticulous indeed was this inquiry that he was led to discover a certain cul-de-sac. Power is everywhere, and it arises from everywhere. If so, that which lies 'outside' power is no longer thinkable. Even the resistance to power is generated within the frame of the power relation. As quoted above, '[w]here there is power, there is resistance, and yet, or rather consequently, this resistance is never in a position of absolute exteriority in relation to power': all action, whatever it be, is drawn out by some action of power. Power as the

Politics: Desire and Power

'action on action' colours every conceivable action from the outset . . .

The opening of the third of the essays newly composed for *Foucault*, 'Foldings, or the inside of thought (subjectivation)', makes reference to this problem, albeit phrased extremely cautiously. The idea that Foucault 'had . . . trapped himself within the concept of power relations' is a misunderstanding, says Deleuze (F, 78/101). As justification, he cites Foucault's 1977 text on 'The Lives of Infamous Men', which he praises as a beautiful piece of writing. Here Foucault had written: 'the most intense point of lives, the one where their energy is concentrated, is precisely where they clash with power, struggle with it, endeavour to utilise its forces or to escape its traps' (F, 78/101). Quite. Resting on Foucault, one has every right to say: 'the diffuse centres of power do not exist without points of resistance that are in some way primary; and that power does not take life as its objective without revealing or giving rise to a life that resists power; and finally that the force of outside continues to disrupt the diagrams and turn them upside down' (F, 78/101). But to this Deleuze adds, in a gentle tone: 'but what happens, on the other hand, if the transversal relations of resistance continue to become restratified, and to encounter or even construct knots of power?' (F, 78/101). What if it is resistance that 'construct[s] knots of power'? This is Deleuze's open question. Quietly, he makes a passing remark on the 'failure' of Foucault's prison information group (the G.I.P.).

Skipping ahead, it will be eight whole years before Foucault breaks his silence in 1984. Having published the second and third volumes of *The History of Sexuality* (titled *The Use of Pleasure* and *The Care of the Self* respectively), he will pass away as one of the earliest victims of AIDS. In these volumes Foucault's thinking had undergone an ostensibly major shift. The concept of biopolitics proposed in *The Will to Knowledge* has vanished without a trace. The two books concern themselves instead with Graeco-Roman ethics, in an attempt to rediscover a 'subjectivity' which is not brought on by the 'action on action', but through a 'care of the self'. If it is necessary to spell it out, this development implies that Foucault had ultimately abandoned the theory of power which he had been building up till then.

That Foucault turned his back on the theory of power in favour of an ethics is surely a development of momentous significance. In this light we must re-approach Deleuze's earlier remark: it is not Foucault's conception of power which is the problem, rather the 'impasse . . . into which power itself places us' (F, 79/103). This appears to be an insight of immense acuity and profundity. What Deleuze means to say, in other words, is that *as long as we think within the framework of power, we cannot but end up in the same place as Foucault sooner or later*. The theory of power leads inexorably to a dead-end. And if there happens to be some theorist of power who does not tread the same path as Foucault, this can only be because (s)he has only skirted the surface of power. Only because (s)he is not as meticulous as Foucault can (s)he chatter away idly about power without misgivings.

Recall that what Deleuze's 'one-point-five-dimensional' interpretation of Foucault had revealed was that each of Foucault's works, whether explicitly or otherwise, develop along the axes of a dual formation, which are in turn sustained at their foundation by the shared common cause of power. Yes knowledge might be an indispensable accomplice, but in the last instance it is power that determines everything: this is Foucault's veritable 'philosophy'. In which case, the cul-de-sac we are forced into by the theory of power is not restricted to an internal difficulty with *The Will to Knowledge*. Rather Foucault's works had always been afflicted by the virtuality of crisis, a crisis related to the limits of conducting one's thinking in terms of power. Deleuze's discussion of Foucault, which unwraps the pragmatic attitude to organise the purely theoretical coordinates of his work, brings this to light for us. The 'one-point-five-dimensional' interpretation teaches the crisis of Foucault.

Desire and Power

And yet, one gets the impression that in *Foucault* Deleuze is not really being candid with the reader. In this book, he situates the *Archaeology* as a liminal work, finds an 'apparent dualism' in Foucault's *oeuvre*, and finally points out the 'impasse' of the theory of power. The reason is of course that Deleuze, though holding Foucault's work in the highest esteem, ultimately disagreed with the basic underlying motivation inspiring that work as a whole. For Deleuze questions *the very Foucauldian programme of attempting to portray society through the concept of power*. Now as it happens, a text survives in which Deleuze states this quite plainly: the letter he addressed to Foucault in 1977 following the publication of *The Will to Knowledge*, titled 'Desire and Pleasure (*Désir et plaisir*)' (TRM, 122–34/112–22). This letter is a ten-page document, essayistic in tone. According to François Ewalt, who orchestrated the publication of the piece, Deleuze had only ever intended to show his support for Foucault (TRM, 408/112): by expressing his doubts explicitly he sought to encourage Foucault, who was embroiled in crisis at the time. Be that as it may, this text hands down to us in no uncertain terms what it was in Foucault that Deleuze disagreed with. Though of course such misgivings can be intuited in *Foucault*, the letter provides full explanations on details which could previously only be reconstructed. To that extent, it is of immense interpretive value.

In the opening lines, Deleuze quickly summarises the sense of the 'apparatus of power (*dispositif de pouvoir*)' in *Discipline and Punish*. By and large, this squares with what we have been discussing in detail up to this point. After which, without further ado we are treated to his queries regarding *The Will to Knowledge*. In *Discipline and Punish*, Foucault paved the way for a 'micro-analysis' of power: casting off the imprecise image of an all-inclusive power which rules over society, he opened up the possibility of analysing the diagrammatic function of specific 'micro-apparatuses' such as the factory, the school and the prison. Of course, 'micro' here is *not a matter of size* (TRM, 123/113). For instance, the family is a micro-apparatus even though it exerts a pervasive influence. By 'micro' we must therefore understand a name for *each specific* apparatus in its diagrammatic function. However, with *The Will to Knowledge* Foucault will leave behind this perspective curtly, in favour of a commonplace opposition between the macro and the micro, and allocate the macroscopic to a strategic model, the microscopic to a tactical model. This, says Deleuze, 'bothers me': 'it seems to me that Michel's micro-arrangements have a wholly strategic dimension' (TRM, 124/114). In other words: the great merit of *Discipline and Punish* had been the way in which specific micro-apparatuses involve themselves in the strategic totality of the social. But this perspective has, by *The Will to Knowledge*, fallen into retreat. A little later it will be clarified that this query is not unconnected to the concept of 'biopolitics' (TRM, 132/121). For *The Will to Knowledge*, building on this opposition, further allocates the microscopic to the disciplinary and the macroscopic to the biopolitical. We have already seen that power is diffuse, and not global: but does not the concept of 'biopolitics' revive a global notion of power? For this is a model of power unconnected to the diagrammatic, rather something like the general orientation of a society. 'I felt the diagram notion was a very rich one', mourns Deleuze (TRM, 132/121).

To summarise briefly the relation of the micro-apparatus to the diagram (referring also to *Foucault*), the former names a specific apparatus (the family, the factory, the school, the military), and the latter the modality in which these function. The diagram is the way in which the power relation, which can never be known in itself, functions (F, 62/80), also termed 'the abstract machine that covers the whole social field' (TRM, 132/121). Specific micro-apparatuses exist ubiquitously in a segmented society, working diffusely. Abstracting from these workings, one can arrive at the functional modality of the diagram which infests the totality of the social domain. And the diagrammatic was in turn the 'presentation' of the 'power relation', definitely real but unknowable. All of which implies that micro-analysis traverses the concrete dimension of the apparatus and the abstract dimension of the diagram. It is this latter that Deleuze dwells on. Indeed, as he says quite pointedly to Foucault: you have given us many excellent analyses of the micro-apparatuses, but have you perhaps not given sufficient thought to the dimension of the 'power relation' itself in its diagrammatic manifestation? 'But Michel, I believe, has not yet developed this point: his original conception of relations of power must be as new a concept as all the rest' (TRM, 124/114). The diagrammatic is surely an extremely rich concept, but its analysis is still incomplete. And yet the perspective of the diagram retreats: with the entry onto the scene of the one-size-fits-all idea of 'biopolitics', the possibilities of micro-analysis are aborted, relegated to one wing of the uninteresting opposition between the macro and the micro. The query, in other words, is raised at the level of base principles.

And Deleuze presses even deeper. Instead of developing this query further, he pierces through to the very foundations of Foucault's thinking, that which motivates this work as a whole. The significance of the following passage in determining Deleuze's theoretical position cannot be overemphasised.

> I am getting to the first way in which I differ from Michel at the present time. If I talk about assemblages of desire with Félix Guattari, it is because I am not sure that micro-arrangements can be described in terms of power [*je ne suis pas sûr que les micro-dispositifs puissent être décrits en termes de pouvoir*]. For me, an assemblage of desire indicates that desire is never a natural or spontaneous determination. (TRM, 124/114)

In this way, Deleuze adds a question mark to the very attempt to illuminate the micro-apparatuses through the concept of power. It is the same reason why, together with Guattari, he probes into 'desire'

Politics: Desire and Power

(we will discuss the concept of the 'assemblage' shortly): in order to approach that which cannot be expressed adequately by the concept of power. In other words, Deleuze makes an active choice in favour of desire *instead of* power. The Deleuzo-Guattarian programme is one which seeks *to go beyond the concept of power, to attain what cannot be attained from the perspective of power*. What then is the meaning of this choice? We take leave of this text written in the interstice between 'desire' and 'power', in order to understand Deleuze's intent through an engagement with the works of Foucault.

Power is an action which works upon action, which armed with a certain strategy and a certain destination, makes people act. Take a step back, however, and we can ask: how is it that such a strategy, such a destination, arises in the first place? For example, the beginning of *Discipline and Punish* had staged the scene of the spectacle of the scaffold: the executioner deftly provides a piece of entertainment for the people, while the people respond by turning up *en masse* as onlookers. In this way sovereign power exhibits its violence to rule the people. Now, as Foucault himself notes, this apparatus of power will not function if the people do not in fact turn up to spectate. To that extent, the people who come to watch the scene of the scaffold exist in complicity with the power apparatus. Foucault had of course analysed the ways in which this apparatus functions in extraordinary detail. But in the first place, how is it that this apparatus can maintain itself in this function? For the people are not being forced to turn up. They turn up because they want to watch the gruesome display of excessively cruel punishment. Why? Why do they actively *desire* to look on this cruelty? And if a similar punishment were to be staged in the centre of town today, would the people still desire to spectate as they did in times of old? Recall that in the citation above, Deleuze says that 'an assemblage of desire indicates that desire *is never a natural or spontaneous determination*'. 'Assemblage (*agencement*)' is a term taken up by Deleuze and Guattari in *A Thousand Plateaus* (1980). With this work the two sought to give voice to the mechanism whereby multiple elements enter into a constellation (*agencer*), to constitute a holistic and organised '*agent*' capable of action.[25] In this way the assemblage of the people's desire is precisely determined by the constellation of a whole nexus of causes; it is neither 'natural' nor 'spontaneous'. For this reason, we must understand that first a particular assemblage of desire exists, which then gives rise to a particular mode of power.

Or take again disciplinary power. Here it is surveillance that makes people act. But why is it that people behave in a uniform way when they come under surveillance? Clearly, because they possess a *desire* to act in this way. After all, is it really the case that a group of people, under observation for a certain strategic purpose, will universally respond in an identical fashion? *Discipline and Punish* had for example emphasised the role of examinations and hierarchical observation in the school (Part III, chapter II: 'The Means of Correct Training'). By making academic achievement in schools visible, it makes the students act in a suitable fashion. But the reason why such visibility of academic achievement is capable of motivating students is that there is presumed to exist in each child a *desire* 'not to fall behind the others'. Only when such an assemblage of desire has overrun society can this apparatus of power function properly speaking. Or equivalently: as soon as the assemblage of desire shifts even minutely, this particular apparatus of power will cease to function.

Towards the end of his life, Deleuze caused quite a stir with his assertion that the 'disciplinary societies' of Foucault's *Discipline and Punish* were coming to an end, to be replaced in turn by 'control societies' (N, 178/236).[26] The word 'control' means here not 'rule', but 'check'.[27] Instead of making people act through surveillance, 'control societies' operate by installing 'check-points' along where people move and act, only permitting those who satisfy a determinate set of criteria to pass through.[28] Unsurprisingly, this remark has been taken up with inordinate enthusiasm by those who take exception to societies which 'control' high-handedly, but unfortunately its theoretical backbone is little understood. The reason Deleuze was able to make such an assessment is none other than the fact that for him *any given modality of power assumes a particular assemblage of desire as its ground*. As such, when, for example, the desire 'not to fall behind the others' ceases to be reproduced, the earlier disciplinary mode of power will no longer be able to function (and as a matter of fact, today its functionality is rapidly fading away).

To say that a determinate modality of power assumes a determinate assemblage of desire means that this power is for whatever reason being *desired* by the people. For sovereign power to work, rule under the sovereign has to be desired. Likewise for disciplinary power to work, disciplinary rule has in turn to be desired. And finally, with the advent of control societies, this new form of rule – not through discipline but through administration by means of the check-point – has to be desired by the people. In other words: 'Of course, an assemblage of desire will include the power arrangement

Politics: Desire and Power

... but *these must be located among the different components of the assemblage*... Power arrangements would therefore be *a component of assemblages*' (TRM, 125/114–15; my emphases).

Undeniably, apparatuses of power exist. Nevertheless, they assume in turn the prior existence of specific assemblages of desire. What is more, the apparatus of power is but an individual component part of this assemblage. For it is the specific desire which upholds an apparatus of power. From here, Deleuze will say that it becomes possible to 'answer a question that is necessary for me, but not for Michel: How can power be desired?' (TRM, 125/115). Undeniably, the work of illumining how power functions is indispensable. But one must not stop there. One must ask, *how is it that this power is being desired?* For wheresoever a certain power arises, this means that this power is being desired.

What then is power, thus conceived? Categorically, 'power is an *affection of desire*' (TRM, 125/115; my emphasis). 'Affection' here (presumably after the Spinozist usage [*affectio*]) means the state a thing comes to be in when it undergoes some stimulus. The assemblage of desire is at work here there and everywhere, motivating people and society. And when such flows of desire satisfy some set of criteria, there is an 'affection' of desire into a specific modality of force, namely 'power'. This force in its turn, always as a machine part constituted within the assemblage of desire, functions through the micro-apparatus diagrammatically, as 'action upon action'. Which is why one must not halt one's analysis at the level of power, even though it is perfectly true that power traverses and impels the entirety of society. One must ask where such power comes from in the first place. For at the end of the day, power is but an affection of desire.

Mid-letter, Deleuze takes pains to declare that he has always thought alongside Foucault (TRM, 125/115), which is certainly not him being polite for its own sake. Under consideration is the thesis that power is 'neither ideology nor repression [*ni idéologie, ni répression*]'. As seen above, in his *Foucault* Deleuze would write that 'repression and ideology ... do not constitute the struggle between forces but are only the dust thrown up by such a contest' (F, 26/36). Deleuze is in agreement with this idea. However, with regard to the Foucauldian theory of power, he feels that ultimately it cannot move in this direction. This is because as long as we locate power as the determination in the last instance, it is impossible to *rid ourselves completely of the perspective of repression*. Though Foucault believed that power cannot be grasped in the terms of ideology or repression, Deleuze thinks that a conception of power such as Foucault's clandestinely remains dependent on such a notion. Indeed he is quite explicit on this point:

> However, given that I emphasise the primacy of desire over power [*primat du désir sur le pouvoir*], or the secondary character that power arrangements have for me, *their operations continue to have a repressive effect* since they stamp out, not desire as a natural given, but the tips of assemblages of desire. (TRM, 126/115; my emphasis)

What does he mean here? Power *makes* people act. That which constitutes the source of the capacity to make people act is understood to be power. As a result, the concept of power, however subtly its tapestry is woven together, must necessarily presuppose a scheme according to which some determinate thing like the subject pre-exists, who is subsequently *made to* act. Power necessarily works *from somewhere, upon something else*. All of which implies that power exists on a different plane from that upon which it is exercised. No doubt power as Foucault sees it arises not only from 'on high' but also from 'down below'. Nevertheless, power must work *from somewhere* upon something. In more quotidian terms, this essentially means that a distinction between 'what one really wants to do' and 'what one is actually made to do' inevitably creeps into the concept of power. Whether from high or low, power comes from somewhere, tugs at the strings of the subject, represses what this subject 'really wants to do', and makes it act otherwise instead. Needless to say, the idea that there is something 'we really want to do' which is subsequently repressed is in the last instance unsustainable. For this something which 'we really want to do' is not at all some spontaneous generation, but something brought about by a specific and as yet undetermined set of causes. However, for as long as we are dependent on the concept of power – a concept of some force by which to *make* somebody do something – we can never rid ourselves of this way of thinking. For under the auspices of power, man is never just *doing* something, he is *being made* to do it.

This is why Deleuze chooses to focus not on power but on desire. Desire does not arise from somewhere to work upon something else; it is a force immanent to the subject itself. And this immanent force enters into a constellation with various other elements to constitute the assemblage of desire. The people who come to spectate at the scaffold are not being forced to attend. The labourer, the soldier, the student are not being forced to follow the surveillance of the

Politics: Desire and Power

disciplinary matrix. Rather, they are impelled by desire to act in this way. The notion of an assemblage of desire, then, furnishes us with a vantage from which to bring to light the real genesis of desire; whereas the concept of power can only concern itself with the final product of such a genetic process: 'the tips of the assemblage of desire'. Which is why, though the analysis of the power apparatus is indispensable, it possesses only a 'secondary' significance. Without an understanding of the 'primacy of desire over power', we cannot penetrate to the reality of social phenomena.

In *Anti-Oedipus*, Deleuze and Guattari expressed the objective of its work of 'schizoanalysis' in the following terms: 'the goal of schizoanalysis [is] to analyse the specific nature of the libidinal investments in the economic and political spheres, and thereby *to show how, in the subject who desires, desire can be made to desire its own repression*' (AO, 105/124–5; my emphasis). It is not that social repression does not exist – it is undeniably a reality – but we cannot be content to define it as something exercised by the apparatus of power. For any given repression presupposes a determinate assemblage of desire which alone can make possible this repression. Which is why it is even possible for people to come to desire their own repression. In fact, this is a phenomenon of the greatest banality. To remind ourselves of the problem *Anti-Oedipus* had posed as its political philosophical end:

> *There is only desire and the social, and nothing else.* Even the most repressive and the most deadly forms of social reproduction are produced by desire within the organisation that is the consequence of such production under various conditions that we must analyse. That is why the fundamental problem of political philosophy is still precisely the one that Spinoza saw so clearly, and that Wilhelm Reich rediscovered: '*Why do men fight for their servitude as stubbornly as though it were their salvation?*' How can people possibly reach the point of shouting: 'More taxes! Less bread!'? As Reich remarks, the astonishing thing is not that some people steal or that others occasionally go out on strike, but rather that all those who are starving do not steal as a regular practice, and all those who are exploited are not continually out on strike: after centuries of exploitation, why do people still tolerate being humiliated and enslaved, to such a point, indeed, that they *actually want* humiliation and slavery not only for others but for themselves? (AO, 29/36–37; first and third emphases original, second mine)

Having now passed through Foucault's theory of power and Deleuze's criticisms, we are in a position to understand this passage more precisely. The *raison d'être* of political philosophy is not to reveal how one could be *made* to do something. Much more, it must reveal how one can come *willingly* to do something. People willingly undergo exploitation, insult and slavery, and desire these not only for others but even for themselves. It is this that political philosophy must seek to understand. Until such time as it achieves this, political philosophy will not be able to move beyond the oppositional schema of repressor and repressed, ruled and ruler. Accordingly, it will also be unable to grasp this most blood-curdling form of power which arises from 'down below'. We will never be able to get to the bottom of the nauseating yet omnipresent phenomenon of a people desiring to be subjugated while also enforcing subjugation over others. *Nor will we ever see the end of it.*

Indeed, we can rephrase the question in this way: why is it that man cannot become free? Why does man not even seem to *want to become free*? How can man begin to *seek to become free*? This, finally, is the problem posed by the 'political Deleuze'. Deleuze-Guattari do not, for example, advance a practical philosophy which 'aims at failure', of the sort which Deleuze had developed in his self-penned works. That is, they do not propose an abstract model of action that can be applied to all possible circumstances. Instead, and in much the same way as a psychoanalyst orients themselves not towards patients in general but to the real, singular patient before them, Deleuze-Guattari propose to analyse each individual power apparatus, the diagram according to which it functions, and of course, most importantly, the assemblage of desire this presupposes. And from here, the question towards freedom is allowed to unfurl. A question which by definition is asked at the level of individual and specific situations.

The Assemblage of Desire and the Apparatus of Power: Situating A Thousand Plateaus *Theoretically*

To reiterate, the preceding mode of thinking inspired by the assemblage of desire does not in any way compromise the effectivity of the Foucauldian analysis of power, or the analysis of power more broadly. Although Deleuze was to construct with Guattari what could very well be termed a 'monist philosophy of desire', the analysis of power is sublated into this monism in much the same way as the micro-apparatus of power is sublated into the assemblage of desire. In this way, on condition that we abide by the principle of the

Politics: Desire and Power

'primacy of desire over power', the analysis of power is valid, even indispensable. For example, in *Foucault*, Deleuze expands the scope of the concept of the diagram, pointing out that its applicability is not restricted to the early modern era. 'Every society has its diagram(s)': 'a Greek diagram', 'a Roman diagram', 'a feudal diagram' . . . even a diagram for 'primitive societies' (F, 31, 71/43, 90–2). It is therefore possible to employ the concept of the diagram to illuminate the power apparatus of any given society. Moreover, such an investigation does not stand at odds with the maxim of the 'primacy of desire over power'. What matters rather is to ensure that one does not lose sight of the assemblage of desire whence the power originates, all the while one engages in pragmatic analyses of real power apparatuses. For no sooner does one lose sight of this fact than one falls back into the schema of ruler and ruled, and becomes blind to the reality of a 'desire desiring its own repression'.

When we situate Deleuze-Guattari's works within this perspective of the assemblage of desire and the apparatus of power, we start to be able to see the relation between *Anti-Oedipus* and *A Thousand Plateaus*, written as the first and second volumes of *Capitalism and Schizophrenia*. Because *A Thousand Plateaus* deploys a great deal of terminological fireworks (reterritorialisation/deterritorialisation, smooth/striated spaces, major/minor, war machine and the state apparatus, nomadism . . .), in one sense it has been the most enthusiastically received of the pair's works; and yet, little attempt has been made to situate this work theoretically. From the perspective built up in the course of our investigations hitherto, however, we can see that *Anti-Oedipus* critically takes up Freudo-Lacanian psychoanalysis and connects it to Marxist political economy in order to construct the principles of a 'monist philosophy of desire', while *A Thousand Plateaus* develops the analysis of the power apparatus in multiple directions, all the while grounded upon this principle of monism.

In stating the objective of an analysis of the power apparatus, Deleuze declares that he 'would distinguish territorialities or reterritorialisations, and movements of deterritorialisation that lead into an assemblage' (TRM, 125/114–15). 'Territoriality', 'deterritorialisation' and 'reterritorialisation' are all concepts introduced by Deleuze and Guattari in *A Thousand Plateaus* and employed extensively throughout the book. He continues: '[p]ower arrangements would surface wherever reterritorialisations, even abstract ones, take place' (TRM, 125/115). Reterritorialisation names, for example, the way a state encircles its inhabitants within a defined territorial limit and in this way governs them. Deterritorialisation in turn takes place when the circle is bust open. When *A Thousand Plateaus* draws on archaeological research[29] to posit a radically new theory of the state, we can infer that this later work has at its centre not so much the assemblage of desire as the analysis of power apparatuses. Indeed, the concept of the 'war machine' proposed by *A Thousand Plateaus* is defined as the 'diagram of lines of flight' (TRM, 133/121) *apropos* the state defined as the 'diagram of power'. Similarly, the distinction between 'smooth' and 'striated' spaces, corresponding to the war machine and the state respectively, can be understood along the same lines as an analysis of power. And when one reads the short concluding section to *A Thousand Plateaus* ('The Concrete Rule and the Abstract Machine'), one can see that practically the entirety of this vast tome is engaged in the analysis of power apparatuses. Such a perspective allows us to situate with precision *A Thousand Plateaus* (whose multiple topics apparently lack any unifying thread) among the works of Deleuze-Guattari, making it possible to interpret this work as part of a coherent *oeuvre*.

Having thus slotted the complete works of Deleuze-Guattari within one overarching perspective, we catch more than a glimpse of a Deleuze who never shied away from, indeed proactively pushed through with, pragmatic analyses of power, yet at the same time went beyond this towards the problem of desire, always at bottom problematising the possibility of human freedom. The diagnosis of contemporary society Deleuze handed down through his analysis of its power apparatus is not a rose-tinted one. Nevertheless, the very fact that his philosophy was through it all one which sought freedom does give us courage. A philosophy which began as the 'discovery of nature' is ever turned towards freedom. One thing we can say for certain is that Deleuze has taken a definite step towards this in the realm of philosophy.

Notes

1. Published originally as *Folie et Déraison* in 1961, its title was changed to *Histoire de la folie à l'âge classique* upon its reissue in 1972 (it is believed that Jacques Derrida's critique of the book had a hand in this). To avoid unnecessary complications we will henceforth cite only the title of the English translation.
2. Yoshiharu Ishioka points out 1) that each time Foucault released a new book of historical research, a new domain of study was established;

2) moreover that each of these books completely overturned existing research in these fields; and finally 3) that most probably Foucault conferred upon his work the form of a book only when he became certain that it was capable of thus overturning existing scholarship. Ishioka writes: 'even if a theme is potentially a fertile one, whether it will come into fruition in book-form rests entirely on his judgement as to whether it is capable of . . . constituting a new object of investigation' (2003: 94). We can glimpse here the reason why such fertile and frankly book-worthy work like his studies on Manet, governmentality, or neoliberalism, topics broached in his essays and lectures, were nevertheless abandoned before they left for the bookbinders.

3. When writing a book Foucault would first compose a full draft, which he would then discard; only then would he begin work on the actual manuscript. It is known that there exists an unpublished first draft of the *Archaeology*.
4. 'History's certainly part of his method. But Foucault never became a historian. Foucault's a philosopher who invents a completely different relation to history than what you find in philosophers of history' (N, 94–5/130).
5. 'If libertines, blasphemers, the debauched and the prodigal were thrown together with those whom we would describe as mentally ill, it was not because too little account was taken of the innocence or determinism of madness, but simply because unreason was given pride of place. When the time came to deliver the mad and "free" them from their shackles, it was not an indicator that the old prejudices had been done away with; all it meant was to let close one's eyes, and to hand over to a "psychological slumber" this nightwatch over unreason, which was what gave to classical rationalism its most pointed direction' (Foucault 2006: 157–8/210; translation substantially modified). In the nineteenth century, reason begins to proclaim for itself a solid foundation in positivism. The old 'nightwatch over unreason', as in the philosophies of Descartes or Spinoza ('classical rationalism'), is abandoned, and reason descends into a 'psychological slumber'.
6. For example, any 'statement' in a medical textbook in a given age is structured according to the rules governing this age's medical 'discourse'. The term 'discursive formation' names not individual discourses, but the domain to which discourses in general belong.
7. '*The Archaeology of Knowledge* therefore marked a turning point: it posited a firm distinction between the two forms but, as it proposed to define the form of statements, it contented itself with indicating the other forms in a negative way, as the "non-discursive"' (F, 27/39).
8. Translator's note: translation substantially modified.
9. The opposition between the discursive and non-discursive formations is rephrased by Deleuze as that between the 'statement (*énoncé*)' and

'visibility', the 'statable (*énonçable*)' and the 'visible'. Deleuze explains that this opposition makes up what Foucault conceives of as an 'epoch': '[a]n "age" does not pre-exist the statements which express it, nor the visibilities which fill it. These are the two essential aspects: on the one hand each stratum or historical formation implies a distribution of the visible and the articulable which acts upon itself; on the other, from one stratum to the next there is a variation in the distribution, because the visibility itself changes in style, while the statements themselves change their system' (F, 42/56). Stripping the terms 'statement' and 'visibility' of all theoretical subtlety, we can say that these two formations reduce ultimately to 'words' and 'things'. From 'statement' to 'word' there is no great leap, but wherefrom such a term as 'visibility'? This is because it is imprecise to presume the existence of an identical 'thing' perduring through history. For what is visible, what is capable of being seen, differs according to the rules of each epoch. The 'thing-in-itself' cannot be posited unproblematically. Hence, according to Foucault, an epoch must be thought from the interplay of the two factors: 'what is said and how it is said' (statability) and 'what is seen and how it is seen' (visibility).

10. In those days crime, the transgression of the law, was construed as an injury against the person of the sovereign him or herself. Punishment, correlatively, was an act of retaliation by the sovereign against the criminal. '[B]y breaking the law, the offender has touched the very person of the prince; and it is the prince ... who seizes upon the body of the condemned man and displays it marked, beaten, broken' (Foucault 1979: 49/60).
11. 'The criticism of the reformers was directed not so much at the weakness or cruelty of those in authority, as at a bad economy of power ... The true objective of the reform movement, even in its most general formulations, was not so much to establish a new right to punish based on more equitable principles, as to set up a new "economy" of the power to punish, to assure its better distribution, so that it should be neither too concentrated at certain privileged points, nor too divided between opposing authorities; so that it should be distributed in homogeneous circuits capable of operating everywhere, in a continuous way, down to the finest grain of the social body' (Foucault 1979: 79–80/95–6).
12. This 'how' is extremely important in recognising the singularity of Foucault's writings. Foucault is not concerned with the reason 'why'. For to ask 'why' something has happened runs the risk of reducing history to a unilinear chain of reasons.
13. The theory of 'discipline' is immediately comprehensible, and as such has been 'adapted' time and again by dilettante theoreticians. The flipside, it seems to me, is that not enough attention has been paid to the structure of *Discipline and Punish* as a whole. In particular the problem

Politics: Desire and Power

of the non-correspondence between the discourse of the 'reformers' in Part II and the birth of the prison, in spite of its axial position in the work, is barely discussed at all. Further, because many commentators have not bothered to read the book in its entirety, the ambiguities in Foucault's theory have rarely been pointed out. For instance, in Part IV (which we will be taking up shortly), Foucault brings up the 'failure' (aka success) of the prison in its reproduction of recidivists; but he gives no indication as to how this is to gel with the discipline formulated in Part III.

14. '[The prison] appeared so bound up and at such a deep level with the very functioning of society that it banished into oblivion all the other punishments that the eighteenth-century reformers had imagined ... But the self-evidence of the prison is also based on its role, supposed or demanded, as an apparatus for transforming individuals. How could the prison not be immediately accepted when, by locking up, retraining and rendering docile, it merely reproduces, with a little more emphasis, all the mechanisms that are to be found in the social body?' (Foucault 1979: 232–3/269).
15. 'Some sections of *Discipline and Punish* place delinquency on the side of the prison. But in fact there are two delinquencies, the "illegalism-delinquency" which refers to statements, and the "object-delinquency" which refers to the prison' (F, 117n22/69n20).
16. Translator's note: omitted in the English translation.
17. Deleuze writes as follows: 'it is *The Archaeology of Knowledge* which will draw out the methodological conclusions and present the generalised theory of the two elements of stratification: the articulable and the visible, the discursive formations and the non-discursive formations, the forms of expression and the forms of content. This book, however, seems to *grant the statement a radical primacy*. The bands of visibility are now designated only in a negative way, as "non-discursive formations" situated in a space which is complementary only to a field of statements' (F, 42–3/57; my emphasis). 'Between the two there is no isomorphism or conformity, in spite of a mutual presupposition and the primacy of the statement. *Even* The Archaeology of Knowledge, *which insists on [this] primacy . . .*' (F, 52/68; my emphasis).
18. According to Deleuze, in passing through *Discipline and Punish* it becomes retrospectively visible that even in his earlier works (*The History of Madness, The Birth of the Clinic . . .*) it had been the two formations which were at issue all along. In his review of *Discipline and Punish*, Deleuze writes: '[w]e begin to understand now why Foucault studies these two forms in his earlier books: the visible and the articulable, as he called them in *The Birth of the Clinic*; and, in *Madness and Civilization*, madness as seen in a general hospital and folly ... as it is described in medicine. What *The Archaeology* recognized but still

only designated negatively, as non-discursive environments, is given its positive form in *Discipline and Punish*' (F, 28/40).
19. Additional clarification is in order for these references. The first comes from the interlude between the first and second of the three newly composed essays, 'Strata or Historical Formations: the Visible and the Articulable (Knowledge)' and 'Strategies or the Non-stratified: the Thought of the Outside (Power)'. In the closing words of the former, Deleuze wonders what this 'third dimension' is which connects the two formations. 'What comprises this new dimension, this new axis?' The latter piece then begins with Deleuze asking 'what is power?' The second essay, amidst discussions of the relation between power and knowledge and the diagram of power, situates this 'third dimension' as power. That this 'third dimension' is understood as power is quite evident from reading this essay; but there are strong indications that Deleuze is avoiding having to assert anything declaratively.
20. 'Analysing the *lettres de cachet*, Foucault demonstrates that "the king's arbitrator" does not operate in a downward direction like an attribute of his transcendent power, but is solicited by the most humble, by the relatives, neighbours and colleagues of a nasty little troublemaker who want to have him locked up and who use the absolute monarchy like an immanent "public service" that can settle family or conjugal arguments, professional quarrels or disputes over byways' (F, 25/35).
21. As a grotesque example of how power comes from 'down below', we can point to the 'Anti-Leprosy Movement (*Muraiken-undou*)' in pre-war Japan. During the 1930s, a social movement broke out whereby patients of Hansen's disease were handed over to the authorities through anonymous informers and other means, to be forcibly confined to designated institutions, in an attempt to 'cleanse' each prefecture of this disease. While there was some governmental encouragement, it was precisely the people 'down below' who propelled this movement. Much of what I know about this movement I owe to Minori Takanashi's thesis, 'Power at Work in the Quarantine of Hansen's Disease Patients', Kokubun seminar, Takasaki University of Economics, 2013.
22. The development of Japanese law regarding *haken* labourers (temporary workers dispatched by staffing agencies) traces what Deleuze-Foucault have in mind in an almost obscene way. *Haken* labour was initially banned in the years following the Second World War; after all it is obvious that such labour is bound to promulgate social inequality. However, with the rise in demand for cheap, flexible labour-power, the law was changed to allow for *haken* labour in all its forms, in order to accommodate the appetite of 'big business'.
23. 'Perhaps, too, we should abandon a whole tradition that allows us to imagine that knowledge can exist only where the power relations are suspended and that knowledge can develop only outside its injunctions,

its demands and its interests. Perhaps we should abandon the belief that power makes mad and that, by the same token, the renunciation of power is one of the conditions of knowledge. We should admit rather that power produces knowledge . . .; that power and knowledge directly imply one another; that there is no power relation without the correlative constitution of a field of knowledge, nor any knowledge that does not presuppose and constitute at the same time power relations' (Foucault 1979: 27/36).

24. The phrase 'Foucault's pragmatism' is one coined by Deleuze himself (F, 44, 62/59, 81).
25. The term 'assemblage (*agencement*)' was introduced in *Kafka: Towards a Minor Literature* (1975), Deleuze-Guattari's second book following *Anti-Oedipus*. Basically, it is deployed to take the place of the concept of 'machine' which formed the core of the earlier work, and often appears in the compound form 'machinic assemblage'. Our hunch is that there remained in the concept of 'machine' an indissoluble ambiguity, and the two wanted to avoid having to plant themselves upon its bedrock again if at all possible (on this point, see above p. 106). Now, as we wrote in the main body of the text, there seems to be a strong sense of 'spontaneity' and 'autonomy' underlying this term '*agencement*', well-conveyed by the standard English translation of 'assemblage', which reminds us of a mechanical doll. I must thank here Gadai Suzuki, in private conversation with whom I gained valuable insight into the sense of 'spontaneity' inhering in the word '*agencement*'.
26. In the same place Deleuze also writes that 'the disciplines Foucault described are the history of what we are slowly ceasing to be, and our current apparatus is taking shape in attitudes of open and constant *control* that are very different from the recent closed disciplines' (original emphasis). However, Foucault's last word in *Discipline and Punish* is in fact on the shift from the violent exercise of power whereby the delinquent is made use of by the ruling classes, to a more serene modality of disciplinary power. It must be said that this remark of Deleuze's makes for some highly creative interpretation.
27. In French the term for passport immigration is '*contrôle des passeports*'.
28. When a railway company carries out occasional and unpredictable ticket checks in the carriage to screen out free-riders, this is disciplinary power. London's Oyster card system, by contrast, where the card is waved at various 'check-points' to have it deduct the appropriate sum of money based on the journey you have taken, and which will refuse you exit if your card has insufficient credit, would be an example of control power. Similar systems are in place for most urban public transport systems.
29. *A Thousand Plateaus* accords to archaeology an important place,

emphasising that philosophy must pay close attention to this field of research (TP, 429/535). As a matter of fact, in recent years the development of archaeology has shed new light upon philosophy, in particular research on ancient Greek philosophy (for instance, work on Plato is entering a new phase through the insights furnished by archaeology. Settegast 1986 would be a prime example). When one considers that the general currents in philosophy at the time had only just begun to make use of anthropology (via structural anthropology, among other things), this declaration of Deleuze-Guattari must be deemed exceptionally far-sighted.

Research Note V: The State and Archaeology

In their theorisation of the State, Deleuze-Guattari set off from the ancient autocracies (TP, 448/560), citing favourably (if only ultimately to criticise) the work of the anthropologist Pierre Clastres (1934–1977). Clastres tried to understand primitive societies as cabals, which oppose the State through warfare. War injects a constant dispersion into the collective, interrupting the concentration of power. As a consequence, according to Clastres, the Hobbesian proposition that '*the State opposes war*' must be reversed: '*war is against the State*, and makes it impossible' (TP, 357/442; original emphasis).

Now Deleuze-Guattari, by abstracting even further from these cabals, extract the concept of the 'war machine'. War machines work on a logic different from that of the State, as 'rhizomatic' collections of formless and disparate forces. In opposition is the 'tree' diagram of the State defined as an 'apparatus of capture', which exists in the interstices of primitive societies capturing their wealth, as empire. The State therefore exists in a state of tension with the primitive societies, and not as their extrapolation. If anything, the State bursts into being in the interstices of the primitive societies all at once. In other words, the State has always-already existed (TP, 359–60/444–5).

The problem with Clastres' account, however, is that in his zeal to highlight the anti-State nature of the primitive societies, he ends up conceiving them as self-sufficient entities with no relation to the society of the State (TP, 359/444). It is true that primitive societies have at their disposal a mechanism to ward off the State. Nevertheless, therein also exists an undeniable vector tending towards the State (TP, 431/537). What is more, primitive societies have always interacted with each other via the State.

> The self-sufficiency, autarky, independence, pre-existence of primitive communities, is an ethnological dream: not that these communities necessarily depend on States, but they coexist with them in a complex network. It is plausible that 'from the beginning' primitive societies have maintained distant ties to one another, not just short-range ones, and that these ties were channelled through States, even if States effected only a partial and local capture of them. (TP, 429–30/535–6)

Deleuze-Guattari point out that anthropologists (including Clastres) do not pay sufficient attention to the results of archaeology. The hypothesis of the '*Urstaat*', always-already existing since the dawn of human history, is in the process of being demonstrated conclusively by the excavations of archaeology

(TP, 360/445). Indeed it is the proto-city of Çatal Hüyük, whose ruins were exhumed in 1958 in the region of Anatolia, which serves as our model in theorising the ancient autocracies. It is thought that Çatal Hüyük exercised a zone of influence reaching 3,000 kilometres (TP, 429/535). While the archaeologist V. Gordon Childe (1892–1957) placed the origin of the State in the Neolithic Age (the so-called Neolithic Revolution), it may well have been a product of the earlier Palaeolithic Age. To fantasise primitive 'Stateless' societies in the Palaeolithic Age is but the shadow of the dream of disaffected researchers, who have despaired of the early modern period.

A theory of the State which settles its accounts with archaeology will surely renew our understanding of the economy as well. Citing historian-archaeologist Edouard Will (1920–1997), Deleuze-Guattari state that '[a]s a general rule, it is taxation that monetarises the economy; it is taxation that creates money' (TP, 443/553). The notion that money was created for the sake of exchange is deep-seated. However, '[e]xchange is only an appearance' (TP, 439/547). Instead, money is invented by the State *qua* apparatus of capture as the common denominator for taxation.

Our prevalent theories of the State and of money have been unable to cast off the garbs of idealism. For their part, Deleuze-Guattari take their cue from archaeology to furnish us effortlessly with a way to do just that. So surely we should pay more attention to this.

Afterword

Deleuze placed his hopes on the contingency of the encounter, by which thinking is forcibly drawn out. In fact, there is something irreducibly paradoxical about the encounter understood as contingency. Instinctively, the word 'necessity' brings with it an inexorable sense of universality, whereas the word 'contingency' basks in particularity. For this reason, a philosophy which privileges contingency would seem in the same stroke to be one which values the singular above all. After all, each contingent encounter can only take place in a singular and particular circumstance. And yet, the very conception itself, according to which the contingent encounter is what calls forth thinking, is one which can be applied anytime anywhere, irrespective of the specific circumstance. Whether this conception is universally valid or not, at the very least it is one which possesses a general sphere of applicability. And to that extent, it can be said to be abstract.

Through his collaboration with Guattari, Deleuze was to attain a theoretical perspective capable of analysing singular particulars via a critical interpretation of psychoanalysis. The fruit of this critical work was not a theory open to indiscriminate application without regard for circumstantial specifics, but rather a theory which enables us to shed light on these specifics themselves. No doubt such a perspective on its own is nothing especially remarkable. Nonetheless, what is remarkable is the fact that Deleuze-Guattari achieved such a perspective by choosing to focus on desire instead of power, and in doing so liberated psychoanalysis to cover the social field in its entirety. This theory founded on desire explains, with conviction, how it is that a certain form of rule comes to persist and endure. Setting out from the critical inheritance of psychoanalysis means that one cannot be satisfied with tracing out the broad orientations of the social, for it makes possible a gaze fine-tuned towards each of the singular components which come to constitute these very social orientations themselves – what in Deleuze-Guattari's lexicon would be termed the 'molecular'.

So long as we persist in overviewing these 'molecules' of the social as molar orientations, we cannot penetrate to the reality of society. In *A Thousand Plateaus* Deleuze-Guattari refuse collective representations of the social such as those put forward by Emile Durkheim (1858–1917), instead embracing the work of Gabriel Tarde (1843–1904), who conceived the social as built up from infinitesimally small particles. 'As Gabriel Tarde said, what one needs to know is which peasants, in which areas of the south of France, stopped greeting the local landowners' (TP, 238/264).

No social upheaval can do without these molecular points, the peasants of southern France who at a certain point stopped tipping their hats to the local landowners. It is this that 'one needs to know'. And then one must try to understand the assemblage of desire which brought about these changes at the molecular level. When and only when matters are grasped molecularly in their particularity, can one begin to see what is to be done in the circumstances. No longer a wait in the dark for a change forever to-come, no longer a forlorn anticipation of the 'failure' as harbinger of this change, but a torch capable of lighting the path towards real social transformation.

Deleuze-Guattari would term this 'path' the 'line of flight (*ligne de fuite*)'. The original French word '*fuite*' means, in addition to 'flight', a 'leakage'. Contrary to the Marxist doctrine, a society is not to be defined according to its determinate 'contradictions'. Rather, Deleuze-Guattari declare, a society must be defined according to its 'lines of flight', cracks from which water soundlessly leaks and pours (TP, 237/263). This means that society, though prone to be imagined as a monolithic system, is not in fact such a closed totality, but everywhere unable to contain its spills and leakages. In this sense we can say that the peasants of southern France who first refused to bow to their landowners were the 'lines of flight' of their time. 'There was oppression of the peasantry by the landed classes, against which the peasantry eventually rebelled . . .': such a molar, global explanation – or shall we say, an explanation which believes its job done as soon as it has 'discovered' the constitutive contradiction of the society – cannot make head or tail of these 'lines of flight', nor can it arrive at the assemblage of desire which made such leaks possible in the first instance. Only when we observe society molecularly from the perspective of the assemblage of desire, can such leakages which initiate social change be perceived for what they are.

In this way, it can be said that Deleuze-Guattari's 'monistic philosophy of desire', whose principle was established in *Anti-Oedipus* and whose applications were ticked off in *A Thousand Plateaus*, is one

Afterword

which blazes a new path in relation to the age-old problem of theory and praxis. Nevertheless, the present study has aimed only at laying the necessary groundwork which would enable us to read Deleuze. As such, we have not reached far enough to explicate the works of Deleuze-Guattari as a whole, in anything like the level of precision demanded by the task. Therefore, it is emphatically not the case that the problematic set forth in this book also finds itself exhausted herein. That problematic will be inherited by a future volume, *The Principles of Deleuzo-Guattarian Philosophy*: a comprehensive and detailed investigation of the collaborative works of Deleuze-Guattari must one day be written.

* * *

Thus we conclude this book, laying down the project which has been opened up by it. The overarching narrative the book has presented is that Deleuze overcame the deadlock in his theory by embarking upon a veritable experiment. There is, however, one last thing we must add. Namely that, following his collaboration with Guattari, Deleuze did not transform into a completely different philosopher. Quite the contrary, he did not change in the slightest. For it is only when he works hand in hand with Guattari that Deleuze brings up the assemblages of desire. And the moment he returns to his solitude, he reverts to being Gilles Deleuze the philosopher of transcendental empiricism.

We cannot help hearing what this remarkable steadfastness of the man himself whispers to us: that beneath Deleuze's self-comportment, his total self-deliverance to the contingency of the encounter, must lurk a veritable truth. This truth, such as it is, inasmuch as it indicates that 'encounter is possible', is one which urges hope. And yet, in one and the same stroke this spells the utter futility of hope, insofar as 'we are all subject to the necessities of contingency, and so in the end there is nothing we can do about anything'.

To live, then, such a truth, to live a world which admits of neither hope nor despair, what would this mean? A world without hope or despair: this is therefore a world which knows no possibility. For it is because men have placed their faith in possibility, that they leap up to hope or tumble into despair. Now it is precisely such a universe which Deleuze saw at work in the writings of Samuel Beckett. In a piece on Beckett entitled 'The Exhausted', he distinguishes what is 'exhausted' from what is merely 'tired': '[t]he tired has only exhausted realisation, while the exhausted exhausts all of the possible' (Deleuze

1995: 3/57). The tired, that is, still have faith in possibility, only they cannot realise it. But the exhausted have used up the modality of the possible itself. Nothing is even merely possible any more.

A world without hope or despair, a world which is neither hot nor cold: a world populated solely by events. Events that one may, at some point or other, come across, whence something or other may or may not come about . . . We imagine it is such a world that Deleuze was to call home for the duration of his life. Only now, it seems, after we have passed through the positively effervescent world of Deleuze-Guattari, can we catch a glimpse of this world which Deleuze himself lived.

* * *

Earlier versions of the chapters of this book were serialised in the journal *Shisou* (published by Iwanami Shoten) in five instalments (November 2011, May 2012, August 2012, January 2013 and May 2013). It was Mr Morio Tagai, the editor of this journal, who first suggested to me that I should undertake such a serialisation. The first time Mr Tagai and I worked together was on the Japanese translation of Jacques Derrida et al.'s *Marx & Sons*, published in 2004, and as such it has been more than fifteen years since he first graced me with his presence. And as it always seems to be with such happenstances, my encounter with Mr Tagai was one of utter contingency.

Already at that stage Mr Tagai was musing that he wanted me to do a piece on Deleuze one day. And this 'one day' was to come, without so much as a gentle knock. In all honesty, I did not have the confidence to put together an essay equal to the matter in question. And yet the deadlines impended remorselessly, and Mr Tagai laid down his ultimatum, that he would no longer have anything to do with me if these pieces on Deleuze were not interesting to read. So study I did.

Even after the serialisation began, I could still not imagine the final complete form my reading of Deleuze was going to take. That is how arduous the writing process was. Quite frankly the only reason I did not give up midway was that the pressures of serialisation forced the thinking out of me. In particular the challenges of composing Chapter 4, which Mr Tagai had said from the start would be by far the most difficult, were nigh on insurmountable. During the summer of 2012, my attention was devoted in its entirety to the writing of this chapter. My head became suffused with the signifier, and for a while I was incapable of doing anything else whatsoever. I shudder to

Afterword

think what a burden to his family a man whose head is replete with signifiers must have been. Which may well be why, when the end was in sight, and I was typing up the long quotation from *Anti-Oedipus* which closes the chapter, my eyes began to well up of their own accord.

For all intents and purposes this book was written *à deux* with Mr Tagai. It is impossible for me to express adequately the gratitude I owe to him. And finally, without the loving (and decidedly un-owed) support of my wife Ran and my daughter Hana, there is absolutely no way I could have completed this book. I wish to thank them here for their warm oceanic hearts.

Bibliography

Azuma, Hiroki (1998), *Ontological, Postal: On Jacques Derrida* (『存在論的、郵便的―ジャック・デリダについて』), Tokyo: Shinchosha.
Badiou, Alain (2000), *Deleuze: The Clamor of Being*, trans. Louise Burchill, Minneapolis: University of Minnesota Press.
Bennet, E. A. (1995), *What Jung Really Said*, New York: Schocken.
Bergson, Henri (1946), *The Creative Mind*, trans. Mabelle L. Andison, New York: Philosophical Library; *La pensée et le mouvant*, Paris: PUF, 1934 (2008).
Buchanan, Ian (2000), *Deleuzism: A Metacommentary*, Edinburgh: Edinburgh University Press.
Buchanan, Ian and Nicholas Thoburn (eds) (2008), *Deleuze and Politics*, Edinburgh: Edinburgh University Press.
Charbonnier, Sébastien (2009), *Deleuze pédagogue: la fonction transcendantale de l'apprentissage et du problème*, Paris: L'Harmattan.
Châtelet, François (dir.) (1972), *Histoire de la philosophie*, tome VIII: *le XXe siècle*, Paris: Hachette.
Deleuze, Gilles (1961), 'Lucrèce et le naturalisme', *Les Etudes Philosophiques*, 16(1): 19–29.
Deleuze, Gilles (1995), 'The Exhausted', trans. Anthony Uhlmann, *SubStance*, 24(3), Issue 78; 'L'épuisé', in Samuel Beckett, *Quad et autres pièces pour la télévision*, Paris: Minuit, 1992.
Derrida, Jacques (1987), *The Post Card: From Socrates to Freund and Beyond*, trans. Alan Bass, Chicago: University of Chicago Press; 'Spéculer: sur "Freud"', in *La carte postale: de Socrate à Freud et au-delà*, Paris: Flammarion, 1980.
Dosse, François (2011), *Gilles Deleuze and Félix Guattari: Intersecting Lives*, trans. Deborah Glassman, New York: Columbia University Press; *Gilles Deleuze et Félix Guattari: biographie croisée*, Paris: La découverte, 2007.
Egawa, Takao (2003), *Being and Difference: The Transcendental Empiricism of Deleuze* (『存在と差異―ドゥルーズの超越論的経験論』), Tokyo: Chisenshokan.
Foucault, Michel (1978), *The History of Sexuality, Volume I: An Introduction*, trans. Robert Hurley, New York: Pantheon Books; *Histoire de la sexualité*, I: *La volonté du savoir*, Paris: Gallimard, 1976.

Bibliography

Foucault, Michel (1978 [1994]), 'La scène de la philosophie', in *Dits et écrits, 1954–1988*, vol. 3, Paris: Gallimard.

Foucault, Michel (1979), *Discipline and Punish: The Birth of the Prison*, trans. Alan Sheridan, New York: Vintage Books; *Surveiller et punir: naissance de la prison*, Paris: Gallimard, 1975.

Foucault, Michel (1989), *The Archaeology of Knowledge*, trans. A. M. Sheridan Smith, Abingdon: Routledge; *L'archéologie du savoir*, Paris: Gallimard, 1969.

Foucault, Michel (2006), *History of Madness*, trans. Jonathan Murphy and Jean Khalfa, Abingdon: Routledge; *L'histoire de la folie à l'âge classique*, Paris: Gallimard, 1961 (1972).

Freud, Sigmund (1905 [1953]), 'Fragment of an Analysis of a Case of Hysteria', in *The Standard Edition of the Complete Psychological Works of Sigmund Freud*, vol. VII, London: Hogarth Press; 'Bruchstück einer Hysterie-Analyse', in *Gesammelte Werke*, Bd. V, Frankfurt am Main: Fischer, 1991.

Freud, Sigmund (1915 [1957]), 'Repression', in *The Standard Edition of the Complete Psychological Works of Sigmund Freud*, vol. XIV, London: Hogarth Press; 'Die Verdrängung', in *Gesammelte Werke*, Bd. X, Frankfurt am Main: Fischer, 1991.

Freud, Sigmund (1917 [1957]), 'Mourning and Melancholia', in *The Standard Edition of the Complete Psychological Works of Sigmund Freud*, vol. XIV, London: Hogarth Press; 'Trauer und Melancholie', in *Gesammelte Werke*, Bd. X, Frankfurt am Main: Fischer, 1991.

Freud, Sigmund (1920 [1955]), *Beyond the Pleasure Principle*, in *The Standard Edition of the Complete Psychological Works of Sigmund Freud*, vol. XVIII, London: Hogarth Press; *Jenseits des Lustprinzips*, in *Gesammelte Werke*, Bd. XIII, Frankfurt am Main: Fischer, 1999.

Freud, Sigmund (1923 [1961]), *The Ego and the Id*, in *The Standard Edition of the Complete Psychological Works of Sigmund Freud*, vol. XIX, London: Hogarth Press; *Das Ich und das Es*, in *Gesammelte Werke*, Bd. XIII, Frankfurt am Main: Fischer, 1999.

Freud, Sigmund (1926 [1959]), *Inhibitions, Symptoms and Anxiety*, in *The Standard Edition of the Complete Psychological Works of Sigmund Freud*, vol. XX, London: Hogarth Press; *Hemmung, Symptom und Angst*, in *Gesammelte Werke*, Bd. XIV, Frankfurt am Main: Fischer, 1991.

Fujita, Hiroshi (1990), *The Structure of Psychosis: Psychopathology of the Signifier* (『精神病の構造—シニフィアンの精神病理学』), Tokyo: Seidosha.

Gueroult, Martin (1930), *L'évolution et la structure de la doctrine de la science chez Fichte*, vol. I, Paris: Les Belles Lettres.

Hallward, Peter (2006), *Out of This World: Deleuze and the Philosophy of Creation*, London: Verso.

Hara, Kazuyuki (2002), *Lacan: The Exodus of Philosophic Space* (『ラカン―哲学空間のエクソダス』), Tokyo: Kodansha.
Hardt, Michael (1993), *Gilles Deleuze: An Apprenticeship in Philosophy*, Abingdon: Routledge.
Hardt, Michael and Antonio Negri (2000), *Empire*, Cambridge, MA: Harvard University Press.
Heidegger, Martin (1968), *What is Called Thinking?*, trans. Fred D. Wick and J. Glenn Gray, New York: Harper & Row; *Was heißt denken?* (1954), Tübingen: Max Niemeyer.
Hughes, Joe (2008), *Deleuze and the Genesis of Representation*, New York: Continuum.
Ishioka, Yoshiharu (2003), 'Michel Foucault and the Works "Outside Technique"' (「ミシェル・フーコーと「手法外」の作品」), *Gendai Shiso*, 'Feature on Foucault' (December 2003).
Jain, Dhruv (ed.) (2009), *Deleuze and Marx*, Edinburgh: Edinburgh University Press.
Kant, Immanuel (1998), *Critique of Pure Reason*, trans. Paul Guyer and Allen W. Wood, Cambridge: Cambridge University Press.
Kaufmann, Pierre (ed.) (2003), *L'apport freudien: Éléments pour une encyclopédie de la psychanalyse*, Paris: Bordas.
Kerslake, Christian (2009), *Immanence and the Vertigo of Philosophy*, Edinburgh: Edinburgh University Press.
Kokubun, Koichiro (2004), 'Singularity, Event, Compossibility: Leibniz and Deleuze' (「特異性、出来事、共可能性―ライプニッツとドゥルーズ」) (in 2 instalments), *Jyokyo: Period 3*, 5:7 (July 2004), 8 & 9 (August 2004).
Kokubun, Koichiro (2008), 'Translator's Afterword' (「訳者解説」) in Gilles Deleuze, *Kant's Critical Philosophy*, translated into Japanese by Koichiro Kokubun, Tokyo: Chikumashobo.
Lacan, Jacques (2006), *Écrits: The First Complete Edition in English*, trans. Bruce Fink in collaboration with Héloïse Fink and Russell Grigg, W. W. Norton & Company; *Ecrits*, Paris: Seuil, 1966.
Laplanche, J. and Pontalis, J.-B. (1973), *The Language of Psycho-Analysis*, with an introduction by Daniel Lagache, trans. Donald Nicholson-Smith, London: Hogarth Press.
Leach, Edmund (1989), *Claude Lévi-Strauss*, Chicago: University of Chicago Press.
Leibniz, Gottfried Wilhelm (1686 [1908]), *Discourse on Metaphysics*, in *Discourse on Metaphysics, Correspondence with Arnauld and Monadology*, trans. George R. Montgomery, La Salle: Open Court Publishing; *Discours de Métaphysique*, in *Discours de Métaphysique et correspondance avec Arnauld*, 5th edition, Paris: Vrin, 1988.
Leibniz, Gottfried Wilhelm (1714 [1908]), *Monadology*, in *Discourse on Metaphysics, Correspondence with Arnauld and Monadology*, trans. George R. Montgomery, La Salle: Open Court Publishing; *Monadologie*,

Bibliography

in *Principes de la nature et de la grâce fondés en raison / Principes de la philosophie ou Monadologie*, 3rd edition, Paris: PUF, 1986.

Leibniz, Gottfried Wilhelm (1967), *The Leibniz-Arnauld Correspondence*, trans. H. T. Mason, New York: Garland Publishing; *Correspondance avec Arnauld*, in *Discours de Métaphysique et correspondance avec Arnauld*, 5th edition, Paris: Vrin, 1988.

Lévi-Strauss, Claude (1963), *Structural Anthropology*, trans. Claire Jacobson and Brooke Grundfest Schoepf, New York: Basic Books; *Anthropologie structurale*, Paris: Plon, 1958.

Lundy, Craig and Daniela Voss (eds) (2015), *At the Edges of Thought: Deleuze and Post-Kantian Philosophy*, Edinburgh: Edinburgh University Press.

Matsumoto, Takuya (2012), 'Lacanian Studies of Psychosis: From the "Differentiated Diagnosis of Psychosis" to "Ordinary Psychosis"' (「ラカン派の精神病研究—「精神病の鑑別診断」から「普通精神病」へ」), *Shiso*, 1060 (August 2012).

Murakami, Yasuhiko (2008), *The Phenomenology of Autism* (『自閉症の現象学』), Tokyo: Keisoshobo.

Ogasawara, Shinya (1989), *The Books of Jacques Lacan: An Attempt at their Explanation* (『ジャック・ラカンの書—その説明のひとつの試み』), Tokyo: Kongo Shuppan.

Proust, Marcel (2001), *In Search of Lost Time*, trans. C. K. Scott Moncrieff and Terence Kilmartin, revised by D. J. Enright, vols 1–4, London: Everyman Publishers.

Read, Jason (2003), *The Micro-Politics of Capital: Marx and the Prehistory of the Present*, New York: State University of New York Press.

Schérer, René (1998), *Regards sur Deleuze*, Paris: Kimé.

Settegast, Mary (1986), *Plato Prehistorian: 10,000 to 5000 B. C. in Myth and Archeology*, Cambridge, MA: The Rotenberg Press.

Somers-Hall, Henry (2012), *Hegel, Deleuze, and the Critique of Representation: Dialectics of Negation and Difference*, New York: State University of New York Press.

Spinoza, Benedict de (1996), *Ethics*, trans. Edwin Curley, Harmondsworth: Penguin.

Thoburn, Nicholas (2003), *Deleuze, Marx, and Politics*, Abingdon: Routledge.

Uno, Kuniichi and Akira Asada (1997), 'Concerning Deleuze Again' (「再びドゥルーズをめぐって」), *Hihankukan*, II:15 (October 1997).

Voss, Daniela (2013), *Conditions of Thought: Deleuze and Transcendental Ideas*, Edinburgh: Edinburgh University Press.

Zaitsu, Osamu et al. (1996), 'Collective Debate: Deleuze and Philosophy' (「共同討議 ドゥルーズと哲学」), *Hihankukan*, II:9 (April 1996).

Žižek, Slavoj (1989), *The Sublime Object of Ideology*, London: Verso.

Žižek, Slavoj (2004), *Organs Without Bodies*, Abingdon: Routledge.

BIBLIOGRAPHY

Zourabichvili, François (1998), 'Deleuze et le possible (de l'involontarisme en politique)', in *Gilles Deleuze, une vie philosophique: rencontres internationales Rio de Janeiro-São Paulo, 10–14 juin 1996*, dir. d'Eric Alliez, Institut Synthélabo.

Index

Abel, Niels, 82
action
  dimensions of, 84
  movement-images, 84–6
  sensory-motor images, 85, 86
  and subjectivity, 90
  time-images, 85–6
actuality (*actualité*)
  actualisations of virtualities, 123
  of events, 47–8, 52
  of Virtual structure, 115
analytic method, 68–9
Anti-Oedipus
  analysis of capitalism and politics, 134–5
  concept of the machine, 105–6
  desiring-machines, 106
  dual writing of, 6, 102–4
  the multiplicity of desire, 110
  overview of, 131
  primal repression in, 131–2
  publication of, 1, 5
  schizoanalysis (*schizoanalyse*), 177
  Žižek's criticism of, 5
apprenticeship *see* education
archaeology, 187–8
assemblage (*agencement*)
  of desire, 172, 173–5
  as a political concept, 3
  term, 173
associationism
  Bergson's critique of, 15–17
  Kant's critique of, 31
  three principles of, 30, 43
autism, 63n

Badiou, Alain, 4, 9–10, 13–14, 18, 104
Barthes, Roland, 136n
Beccaria, Cesare, 153
Beckett, Samuel, 191
becoming
  becoming-molar, 47, 132, 189–90
  concept of, 4–5

Bergson, Henri
  critique of associationism, 15–17
  false problems, 78–82
  types of recognition, 86, 100
The Bicycle Thieves (De Sica), 85
biopolitics, 168, 169, 171

Canguilhem, Georges, 15
Cassirer, Ernst, 36
castration, 108, 123
Chaplin, Charlie, 85
cinema, 84–6
Cinema 1: The Movement-Image, 84
Cinema 2: The Time-Image, 84, 85, 86, 90
Clastres, Pierre, 187
Cogito
  concept of, 14, 19–20
  cracked Cogito, 22
  the image of thought and, 21
  Kant's critique of, 22
cognition
  in Kantian thought, 36–7
  a priori representations, 33
Coldness and Cruelty, 99
collective soul, 141–2
concepts
  of Cogito, 14, 18–19, 20, 22
  defined, 20
  formation of through problem critique, 21–3, 28, 76
  the image of thought and, 21
  within Leibniz's thought, 46
  philosophical formation of, 17, 18–21
  within the plane of immanence, 19, 20–1, 28
  as simultaneously relative and absolute, 21
Continental rationalism, 29
Courbet, Gustave, 141

De Sica, Vittorio, 85
death instinct, 53–4, 56–7, 58–9, 129
Defoe, Daniel, 39, 40

199

INDEX

Deleuze, Gilles
  as an apolitical figure, 3–5
  career of, 1
  collaboration with Guattari, 5–6, 92, 101, 131, 143–5, 189, 191
  Deleuze/Deleuze-Guattari relationship, 5, 6–7, 101–4
  philosophical method of, 5, 7–8, 9–10, 13–14, 76
  as a political figure, 2–3, 5, 6
  readership for, 1–2
  scholarship on, 2–3
  see also individual works
delinquency, term, 151, 155–7
delinquent, term, 151, 155–7
Descartes, René, 14, 18–19, 20, 68; *see also* Cogito
desert island (*île déserte*)
  concept of, 39–40, 42, 49
  in Deleuze's writing, 38–9
  Humean inspiration for, 43
  in relation to the Other, 40, 42–4, 49–50
  transcendental empiricism and, 38–9, 49–50, 71
Desert Islands and Other Texts, 38–9, 40, 43
desire
  assemblages of desire, 172, 173–5
  as the basic unit of political philosophy, 144, 145
  monistic philosophy of, 190–1
  power and, 170, 172–8
  repression of the desiring subject, 134, 177–8
  and the social, 134–5, 145, 177
desiring-machines, 6, 106
deterritorialisation, 6, 179–80
Difference and Repetition
  concept of repetition, 125
  Deleuze's philosophical method in, 5, 9, 35
  Deleuzian pedagogy, 100
  desert island concept, 38
  differenciation (*différenciation*), 48, 115
  differential relation (*rapport différentiel*), 48, 114
  genesis of thinking, 73
  on Kantian philosophy, 33
  the Lacanian Phallus, 122
  on Leibniz, 46
  minute perception, 115
  problem/question distinction, 81–2
  psychoanalysis, 50, 51, 57
  referenced in 'Machine and Structure' (Guattari), 105
  differenciation (*différenciation*), 48, 115
  differential (*différentiel*), 48, 114
  differential relation (*rapport différentiel*), 114
direct speech, 11, 12, 13
discourse analysis
  in *Discipline and Punish* (Foucault), 152–8, 159–60
  discursive formations, 149–50
  discursive/non-discursive relationship, 151–2, 154, 156–8, 159–60, 165–7
  non-discursive formations, 150
  power and the discursive/non-discursive relationships, 160, 163–5
Dosse, François, 101
dual writing (*écrire à deux*)
  of *Anti-Oedipus*, 102–4
  as free indirect discourse, 103–4
  practice of, 6
dualism, 165–6

education
  new subjectivity and, 90
  and the objectivity of the problem, 83
  power relations within, 163, 174
  role of thought, 77–8, 83–4, 100
Egawa, Takao, 73
ego
  defined, 122
  genesis of, 51–2, 122
  genesis of global egos from local egos, 122–3, 128, 132
  local egos, 52, 122, 130
  minute perception and local egos, 123, 128
  object-cathexis, 57–8
  in relation to the id, 51–2, 122, 128, 132
Empiricism and Subjectivity: An Essay on Hume's Theory of Human Nature, 15, 16, 29, 31, 35, 73
empiricist philosophy
  as conservatism, 29
  genesis of the subject, 30
  habit, concept of, 73–4
  Humean, 29–30
  in relation to transcendentalism, 31–2, 34, 35–6, 49, 59
  see also transcendental empiricism
empty squares (*la case vide*), 117–20, 126
Europe '51 (Rossellini), 86, 87–8

200

Index

events
  actualisation of, 47–8, 52
  concept of, 44–6
  contingent encounters, 73, 76–7, 189
  evental series, 45, 46
  as genetic principle, 46–7, 49–50
  minute perceptions, 48, 49–50
  one-off Events, 123–4
  the predicate as, 64n
  psychoanalysis as the science of events, 50
  of repetition and the machine, 105–6
  singularity-events, 44, 47–8, 49–50, 52
  thinking as an evental encounter, 76
  transcendental events, 44

false infinite, 26
Fichte, Johann Gottlieb, 69
The Fold, 46
foreclosure (*forclusion*), 111
Foucault, 10, 145, 149, 157–8, 165, 166–7, 169, 170, 179
Foucault, Michel
  The Archaeology of Knowledge, 146, 147, 149–51
  Birth of the Clinic, 150, 151
  Deleuze's reservations about, 170–1
  Discipline and Punish, 146, 151, 152–60, 165, 171, 174–5
  discourse analysis, 149–50
  discourse on sexuality, 167–8
  discursive formation, 149–50, 151
  dualism of, 165–7
  Foucault's links to Marxism, 156, 158–9, 160–1
  historical studies, 146–9
  The History of Sexuality, 146, 167, 168, 169
  on madness, 146, 147–8
  micro-analysis of power, 171–2
  as a neo-Kantian, 147, 164
  non-discursive formations, 150, 151
  theoretical methods of, 146–7
  theory of power, 145, 160–3, 167, 168–70
free indirect discourse
  concept of, 11–12, 103
  in dual writing (*écrire à deux*), 103–4
  problem of, 9–10, 13–14
  in relation to the image of thought, 19, 23, 28
  transmitter/transmitted relationship, 13, 23

Freud, Sigmund
  Beyond the Pleasure Principle, 53–4, 57
  death instinct, 53–4, 56–7, 58–9
  desexualisation of the libido, 58–9
  'Mourning and Melancholia', 57
  object-cathexis, 57–8
  Oedipus Complex, 51, 108–9, 123
  pleasure principle, 51, 53–4, 55, 56, 59
  primary topology, 51, 52
  the repetition compulsion, 54–5
  secondary topology, 51, 52
  speculation as transcendentalism, 55–6
  theory of the constitution of the subject, 50–3
  on the unconsciousness, 50
  see also psychoanalysis

genesis
  dynamic genesis, 47, 50
  of the ego, 51–2, 122
  the event as genetic principle, 46–7, 49–50
  of global egos from local egos, 122–3, 128, 132
  in Humean philosophy, 70
  in Kantian thought, 36
  lack of genesis of the subject in transcendentalism, 32, 34, 35, 36, 38, 49, 70
  Leibniz's theory of possible worlds, 44–7
  and the possibility of change, 35
  of the sign in Lacanian psychoanalysis, 109–10
  static genesis, 47, 50
  in structuralism, 106, 116
  of the subject, 30, 32
  theory of minute perception, 48–9
  theory of self and space-time, 42–3
  of thinking, 71–5
  in transcendental empiricism, 38, 42–4, 49, 76
  see also desert island (*île déserte*)
Giraudoux, Jean, 39
Guattari, Félix
  co-authored volumes, 1, 5
  collaboration with Deleuze, 5–6, 92, 101, 131, 143–5, 189, 191
  definition of structure, 106–7
  Deleuze/Deleuze-Guattari relationship, 5, 6–7, 101–4
  Lacanian psychoanalysis in, 107–8, 143

INDEX

Guattari, Félix (*cont.*)
　see also *Anti-Oedipus*; 'Machine and Structure' (Guattari)
Gueroult, Martial, 68–9

habit, concept of, 73–4, 105, 129
Hallward, Peter, 4
Hardt, Michael, 3, 7–8, 10, 18
Heidegger, Martin, 74–5, 77
history of philosophy
　concept formation and problem critiques, 21–3
　for the discovery of nature, 26–7
　philosophical debates within, 23
　role of, 14, 17–19, 28
　task of philosophy, 19–24
Hobbes, Thomas, 21, 162
'How Do We Recognise Structuralism?', 112–13, 120, 143
human nature, the problem of, 29–30
Hume, David
　associationism, 15–17
　concept of belief, 14
　empiricist philosophy, 29–30
　genesis in, 70
　Humean inspiration for the desert island, 43
　Kant's critique of, 31, 32, 34–5
　on social contract theory, 98
Husserl, Edmund, 34
Hyppolite, Jean, 15

id
　defined, 122
　desire to have the Phallus, 108–9
　id-egosuperego (secondary topology), 51
　local egos, 52, 122
　object-cathexis, 57–8
　the pleasure principle and, 51, 53, 58–9
　in relation to the ego, 51–2, 122, 128, 132
image of thought (*image de la pensée*)
　philosophical concepts and, 21
　thought, 18–19
　use of free indirect discourse for, 19, 23, 28
the Imaginary, 111, 132
the imagination, 36–7
'Immanence: A Life . . .', 36
In Search of Lost Time (Proust), 71–2, 77
indirect speech, 11, 12, 13

individual soul, 141–2
institution, theory of, 98–9

Jung, Carl Gustav, 69

Kafka: Toward a Minor Literature, 6
Kant, Immanuel
　on conscience, 51–2
　critique of associationism, 31
　critique of Hume, 31, 32, 34–5
　Critique of Judgement, 36
　critique of the Cartesian Cogito, 22
　on history, 37
　the Idea, 82, 83
　lack of genetic material in, 36
　permutations in the faculties, 36–7, 49
　a priori representations, 33
　question of right, 33
　relationship between nature and man, 37
　the schema, 164
　see also transcendentalism
Kant's Critical Philosophy, 33
kinship systems, 114
knowledge
　associationism, 15–17, 31
　of the philosopher's thought, 14–15

Lacan, Jacques, 107–10, 112, 117, 120
Lawrence, D. H., 141
Leibniz, Gottfried Wilhelm
　perception/apperception distinction, 48
　theory of the event/series, 44–6
　on the unconsciousness, 50
　see also minute perception
Lévi-Strauss, Claude, 114, 117, 120
libido, 57, 58–9
lines of flight, 190
linguistics
　floating signifiers, 120
　phoneme (*phonème*), 113–14
　the Symbolic, 109, 111
　see also signs
The Logic of Sense
　critique of Kant, 34, 35
　definition of structure, 106–7
　Deleuze's philosophical method in, 5
　desert island (*île déserte*), 38
　on Leibniz, 46
　psychoanalysis, 50
　the signifier and signified, 121
　structural transformation in, 120

Index

Lucretius, 26
'Lucretius and the Simulacrum', 26

'Machine and Structure' (Guattari)
  as anti-structuralist, 104–5
  detachment of the machine, 110–11
  Lacanian psychoanalysis and, 107
  the material machine, 106
  structure-generality/machine-repetition, 105
  the subject and the single signifier, 110
machines
  concept of, 105–6
  desiring-machines, 106
  detachment of, 107, 110–11
  events of repetition, 105–6
  history within the concept of, 106, 134
  paradoxical element, 106–7, 111
  temporality of, 105
Marx, Karl
  Foucault's links to Marxism, 156, 158–9, 160–1
  problematic of, 80–1, 83, 158
  psychoanalysis via the work of, 134
melancholia, mechanism of, 57–8
Melville, Herman, 141
'Michel Tournier and the World Without Others', 40, 43
minute perception
  the consciousness as, 48, 52
  differenciation (se différencier), 115
  as differential (différentiel), 123
  local egos and, 123, 128
  as model for genesis, 48–9
  partial objects as, 52
molar, 47, 132, 189–90
molecular/becoming-molar, 47, 132, 189–90
the multitude, 3
Murakami, Yasuhiko, 63n
Muyard, Jean-Pierre, 101–2
myth, 26

Nadaud, Stéphane, 102, 103
'Name-of-the-Father', 108, 113, 133
narcissism, 58, 108
naturalism, 26–7
Negri, Antonio, 3
neurosis (névrose), 132–3
Nietzsche, Friedrich, 71
Nietzsche and Philosophy, 71

objects
  melancholia as the loss of, 57–8
  object = x, 117–20, 121–2, 126
  object-cathexis, 57–8
  partial objects, 52
  recognition of, 86–9
  in relation to desertion, 39, 42
  in relation to the Other, 40–2
Oedipus Complex, 51, 108–9, 123
ordinary psychosis, 140n
the Other
  defined, 41
  and the desert island, 40, 42–4, 49–50
  effect of, 40–2
  in relation to the object, 40–2
  in relation to the Self, 41–2

passive synthesis, 74, 76
passivity, 5
the Phallus
  displacement of, 126–7, 131
  as eternal lack, 117, 119, 127–8
  the id's desire for, 108–9
  the Lacanian Phallus, 107, 120, 122
  as object = x, 131
  and primal repression, 111, 127, 131
  in psychoanalysis, 108, 117, 119, 120
  and the signifying chain, 127
phenomenology, 63n
phoneme (*phonème*), 113–14
plane of analysis, 31
plane of immanence (*plan d'immanence*), 19, 20–1, 28
pleasure principle
  within Freudian psychoanalysis, 53–4, 56
  the global ego and, 122–3
  and the id, 51, 53, 58–9
  and the repetition compulsion, 54, 55
  and the transcendental principle, 56, 59
Poe, Edgar Allen, 107
politics
  analysis of capitalism and politics, 134–5
  Deleuze as a political figure, 2–3, 5, 6, 145
  Deleuze as an apolitical figure, 3–5, 84, 144–5
  thought as a political practice, 84
  and the 'Virtual', 4
possibility (*possibilité*), 47
possible worlds theory, 44–7

power (*pouvoir*)
  biopolitics, 168, 169, 171
  desire and, 170, 172–8
  deterritorialisation, 6, 179–80
  the 'diagram (*diagramme*)' of, 163–5, 171–2, 179
  Discipline and Punish (Foucault), 152–60
  discourses on sexuality, 167–8
  and the discursive/non-discursive problem, 160, 163–5
  Foucauldian theory of power, 145, 160–3, 167, 168–70
  Marxist conception of, 158, 160–1
  micro-apparatuses of, 171–2
  power relations within education, 174
  power/knowledge relations, 163, 165–6, 174
  public executions, 152–3
  reterritorialisations, 6, 179–80
  and the rule of law, 162–3
  violence and, 161–2
primal repression
  in *Anti-Oedipus*, 131–2
  castration as, 123
  Deleuze's rejection of, 124–5, 143
  in Freudian thought, 124, 125
  the 'normal' human and, 133
  and the Phallus, 127, 131
  psychoanalysis, 116
  psychosis/neurosis distinction, 132–3
  schizoanalysis and, 133
  see also repression
problems
  conditions for the resolution of, 82–3
  Deleuzian thought and the problematic genealogy, 23–4
  false problems, 78–82
  identification of and concept formation, 21–3, 28, 76
  the Kantian 'Idea', 82, 83
  Marxist problematic, 80–1, 83, 158
  as a multiplicity, 83
  problem/question distinction, 81–2
  thought and the assessment of true/false problems, 78–80
Proust, Marcel, 71, 77
Proust and Signs, 71–2, 73, 74, 77
psychoanalysis
  Deleuze on Freud's unconscious, 50
  Lacanian psychoanalysis in Guattari, 107–8, 143
  Oedipus Complex, 51, 108–9, 123
  the phallus, 108, 117, 119, 120

primal repression, 111, 113, 116
primary and secondary topologies, 51, 52
psychosis/neurosis distinction, 132–3
signifying chains, 107, 109, 110, 119, 126
as transcendentalism, 50
unconsciousness in, 50, 51
see also Freud, Sigmund
psychosis (*psychose*), 132–3
pulsion (drive), 65n

Rancière, Jacques, 4
reading, 1–2
reality (*réalité*), 47
reality principle, 51, 53, 122–3
reason
  interest in nature, 37
  in Kantian thought, 36–7
  madness as unreason, 147–8
  in relation to the mind, 30
recognition
  attentive, 86, 87, 88–9, 100
  automatic/habitual, 86–7
repetition
  the death instinct and, 53–4, 56–7, 58–9, 129
  displacement of object = x as, 126
  of harnessing, 129–30
  machines and events of repetition, 105–6
  and repression, 124–5, 130, 131
repetition compulsion, 54–5, 124
repression
  in Deleuzian thought, 143
  a desiring subject's desire for its own repression, 134, 177–8
  disguise concept and, 125–6
  as repetition, 124–5, 130, 131
  see also primal repression
reterritorialisations, 6, 179–80
Rossellini, Roberto, 86
rule of law, 98–9, 121, 162–3

Sartre, Jean-Paul, 34
Schérer, René, 4
schizoanalysis (*schizoanalyse*), 131–2, 133–4, 143–4, 177
the self
  Freud's theory of, 50–3
  in the 'I think', 33–4
  in relation to the Other, 41–2
  temporality and, 22
  within transcendentalism, 34
  see also desert island (*île déserte*)

Index

sensibility, 36–7
sexuality
  discourses of, 167–8
  drives, 65–6
  the libido, 57, 58–9
Shakespeare, William, 79
signs
  and the apprenticeship to thinking, 77–8
  and the compulsion to thought, 72–3, 75, 76–7, 81, 100
  signifiers in Lacanian psychoanalysis, 107–8
  signifier-signified linguistic unit, 109
singularities (*singularité*), 44
singularity-events (*singularité-événement*), 44, 47–8, 49–50, 52
social contract theory, 98–9
Spinoza, Baruch, 68
the State, theory of, 187–8
structuralism
  criteria for, 113–19
  Deleuze's reservations about, 115–16, 118–19, 120, 143
  Deleuze's thought on, 104–5, 112–16
  differenciator/differenciation, 115
  the differential and the singular, 114–15
  the empty square, 117–20, 126
  object = x, 117–20, 121–2, 126
  problem of genesis, 106, 116
  the 'serial (*sériel*)', 116–17, 129
  the Symbolic, 113
  time in, 106, 116
  Virtual structures, 115
structure
  defined, 106–7
  the machine in relation to, 105
  paradoxical element, 106–7
subjectivity
  as failed attentive recognition, 89, 90–1, 100
  genesis of the subject in empiricism, 30
  redefinition of, 86, 88
  will and, 90
subjects
  and the concept of the predicate, 45–6
  in empiricism, 30, 32
  Freud's theory of, 50–3
  genesis of, 30, 32
  in rationalism, 30, 32
  in relation to desertion, 39, 42
  in relation to the mind, 29–30
  as represented by a single signifier, 109–10
superego, 51–2
the Symbolic (*le symbolique*)
  and the Imaginary, 111, 132
  the linguistic order of, 109
  series within, 117
  structural function of, 113
synthetic method, 68–9

Tarde, Gabriel, 190
'A Theory of the Other (Michel Tournier)', 40, 43
thought
  the apprenticeship to thinking, 77–8, 83–4, 100
  concepts in philosophical thought, 17, 18–21
  consciousness as minute perception, 48, 52
  in contrast to passive synthesis, 74, 76
  in Deleuzian thought, 71–3, 84
  as external to will, 74
  genesis of thinking, 71–5
  Heidegger's vision of thinking, 74–5, 77
  image of thought (*image de la pensée*), 18–19
  knowledge of the philosopher's thought, 14–18
  method for, 78–9
  and political practice, 84
  the sign as impetus for, 72–3, 75, 76–7, 81, 100
  and subjectivity, 90
  thinking as an evental encounter, 76
  violence in thought, 72–3
  will and, 90–1
A Thousand Plateaus, 6, 69, 173, 179–80, 190
time
  within Kantian thought, 22
  laws of transition, 41
  in structuralism, 106, 116
  temporality of the machine, 105–6
  time-images, 85–6
totemism, 117
Tournier, Michel, 40
tracing (*décalquer*), 49
transcendental empiricism
  in Deleuzian thought, 35–6, 49–50, 59–60, 70–1
  the desert island and, 38–9, 49–50, 71

transcendental empiricism (*cont.*)
  Leibniz's influence on, 48–9
  re-problematisation of genesis in, 38, 42–4, 49, 76
transcendentalism
  as founded in Humean empiricism, 31
  Freud's speculation as, 55–6
  genesis of the transcendental principle, 56–9
  lack of genesis of the subject in, 32, 34, 35, 36, 38, 49, 70
  overview of, 32–3
  a priori representations, 33
  psychoanalysis as, 50
  in relation to empiricism, 31–2, 34, 35–6, 49, 59
  in relation to the plane of immanence, 20–1
  transcendental events, 44
troubled spirits, 26–7
truth
  necessary/contingent truths, 64n
  as a philosophical aim, 23, 74
  thought and the assessment of true/false problems, 78–80
  through violence in thought, 72–3

unconsciousness, 50, 51

Vermeil, François-Michel, 153
violence, 161–2
virtuality (*virtualité*)
  concept of, 47, 49–50
  genesis of global egos from local egos, 123
  in structuralism, 115
  the Virtual, 4

war machine, 180, 187
What is Philosophy? 19, 22

Žižek, Slavoj, 3–4, 5, 84, 137n, 144, 145
Zourabichvili, François, 91

EU representative:
Easy Access System Europe
Mustamäe tee 50, 10621 Tallinn, Estonia
Gpsr.requests@easproject.com

www.ingramcontent.com/pod-product-compliance
Lightning Source LLC
Chambersburg PA
CBHW070354240426
43671CB00013BA/2492